Five Steel Stepping

Five Steel Stepping Stones

Growing up with mother

WILLIAM COOPER

© William Cooper, 2021

Published by G & R P Publishing

A CIP catalogue record for this book is available from the British Library.

ISBN 978-1-9989956-0-8

Book layout and cover design by Clare Brayshaw

Prepared and printed by:

York Publishing Services Ltd
64 Hallfield Road
Layerthorpe
York YO31 7ZQ

Tel: 01904 431213

Website: www.yps-publishing.co.uk

For Mary,
whose inspiration worked

Teesside

In April 2012, Sahaviriya Steel Industries (United Kingdom); SSI UK, re-opened the last remaining blast furnace on Teesside. Just four years later it closed, possibly forever. Iron and Steel making had begun less than two hundred years before and in that time Teesside had produced enough steel rails to circumnavigate the world at least once and to create some of the world's most iconic structures, for example, the Sidney Harbour Bridge. Today the area's traditional heavy industries have been replaced by high technology, chemical and service industries.

The hard physical labour needed to work the steel and stone; to produce Teesside's dramatic growth and transform its character, took its toll on the men who provided the labour, many of whom died young. Much of Teesside's strength has come from the women who held their families together beyond the short lives of the men. A single headstone in a Teesside graveyard lists the members of one family some of whom epitomise those women and is a testament to the resilience, determination and pride of the people of Teesside. This is their story.

William Cooper, Tees Valley, 2021.

Webster Family

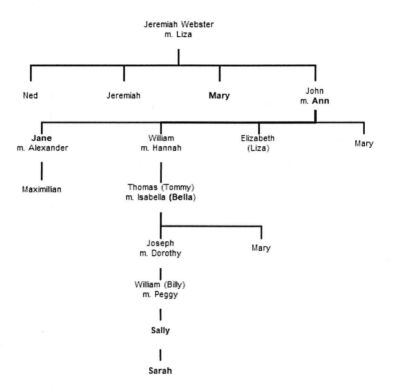

Jeremiah Webster
m. Liza

Ned

Jeremiah

Mary

John
m. **Ann**

Jane
m. Alexander

William
m. Hannah

Elizabeth
(Liza)

Mary

Maximillian

Thomas (Tommy)
m. Isabella **(Bella)**

Joseph
m. Dorothy

Mary

William (Billy)
m. Peggy

Sally

Sarah

Five Steps in Steel and Stone

Silent marshes, forgotten land
Tree clad hills on northern slopes
Rail bound coal meets tide bound ships
And waits the clamour of new found power

Out of the souls of iron bound stone
The furnace heat of blasted rock
Drilled and hammered and blown and mined
Boiled and puddled and poured to form

Heat to break the phosphorous ore
Limestone's pure white brick-lined womb
Smelt and roll, meld and mould
Forming metal, making Steel

Steam hammered plate
Cuts and shapes, builds and bends and stretches
Rails and ships, bridges and wire, mesh and girders
Circle the world with Teesside Steel

Worked out seams under silent hills
Nature's scarred blanket re-grown again
Men grown old and women left
Lives, loves, hopes, dreams, history holds

Five generations: farming, mining, iron and steel
A child of the future fresh eyed and bright
In a land made famous, left to sleep
By forgotten men working steel on stone

Eston – Spring 2014

Peggy stood at the entrance to her house looking down the street. It was just before half past eight in the morning. Her granddaughter Sarah should be coming round the corner at the end of the street soon. Peggy's left hand was clenched, with unconscious, but fierce emotion, round the rail that ran up the side of the three steps leading to the front door. There she was, what state was she in? Left to manage on her own, again. Peggy's daughter Sally no longer rang up to ask if Sarah could come and stay. It was left to the young girl herself now. It was most weeks and often for several days at a time. Peggy sighed and folded her arms under her chest, an instinctive, defensive action from when she herself had been learning what it meant to grow up. From down the street her granddaughter noticed and the misunderstanding continued. Unsure of what her Grandma would say Sarah thought back to her own confrontation with her mother:

'Mam, why can't I come with you ...' it was no good, not worth the effort. Her mother, Sally, was in a hurry. Disorganised as ever. Sarah could go to her grandparents couldn't she, didn't she like going there? They were always happy to have her weren't they? She always went there when there was a problem didn't she? Gone was the excitement of packing a bag, choosing what to take and the special preparations that Sarah's grandparents used to make for her visit. If their small one storey terraced cottage with its tiny old fashioned attic room had been bigger then Sarah might have had a room by now, but it didn't and anyway, Sarah did not want that. What Sarah wanted was a life with her Mam.

She had never had a permanent Dad. There had been a random succession of passing men in their lives, but none had stayed. The constant struggle to get by, to pay the steady procession of unwanted, unplanned and generally unexpected wolves, official or otherwise that beat on the door, arrived by post or left festering in unopened emails had made the two of them close, very close. Now that Sarah's hormones had boosted her resolve they could go from wordless love to strident hatred, and back, in seconds. The causes were as common as to be ordinary. A mistimed smile, an unthinking word, an unattainable promise, or like this time, a demand to be treated as an adult, denied by her mother, neither able to control the consequences of their chaotic life. Sarah's challenge was that she looked set to become the latest generation of misunderstood teenage rebels. Just as she was now battling with her mother, her mother had fought with hers. Sarah walked up the street certain that she and her grandma would disagree. She was right.

'She's messed up another day then,' said Peggy, realising as she said it that it was the wrong thing to say. That she was ruining any chance of the two of them having a meaningful conversation. Her shoulders sagged. This was not how she had wanted to greet her granddaughter. Where had the loving, close bond between them gone? She knew the answer. It had happened between her and Sally, Sarah's mother. When Sarah had been born Peggy had been determined not to let it happen again. Not to repeat the arguments she had had with her own mother, but just as then the angst of teenage hormones had intervened and taken over another generation.

'No, she just forgot. She's busy at the moment,' said Sarah, defending her mother with unthinking anger. She was the only one who could criticise her Mam. Why didn't her Grandma understand her anymore?

Society's unfair expectations blew flames onto the misunderstanding. It made no difference that Billy had never had to bear children, to juggle the family's money, clean the house, wash the clothes, nurse sick grandchildren, make them cakes, party dresses and sit on hard wooden school chairs. Grandda could do no wrong.

'Where's Grandda,' asked Sarah?

'Hiding in his shed,' replied Peggy, resigned to her loss, resenting the close bond between them, but smothering it with the unassailable love that drove her.

Sarah stepped past her Grandmother and walked through the parlour. As she did so she dropped her bag and coat on the sofa, went through into the tiny kitchen, out through the back door and across the yard. On the way across the yard her phone pinged twice. She willed herself not to look. It would be Mia. She should ignore her. Everyone said so, but that was them. Easy for them, not so easy for her. She heard her Grandda's voice through the open door of the shed, humming something. If she could just make it to the shed without looking at her phone.

* * *

Sarah Webster is thirteen. She is a slight, fair-haired girl with concerned blue-grey eyes and a deceptive frailty hiding a determination that has taken her through the first years of her life. That morning her mother, Sally, had forgotten that Sarah's school would be closed for a training day. Sarah's recent attempts to be grown up had let her down. She had begun with fierce determination, no she would not stay at home on her own, she hated the untidy house, but in the end, less skilled in the relentless, unthinking lies of survival, she had cried bitterly at her Mam. Sarah had been left to ring her grandparents and Grandda had agreed to spend the day with her. Grandma was going on the bingo club trip to Meadowhall in Sheffield. As she had left she had remarked that it would be more like Sarah looking after Grandda. Not that he minded, he was much taken by his only granddaughter and it was not as if it was an unusual event.

With Grandma gone, they had made dinner, Sarah had smiled as she helped with the old fashioned food that her Grandda still liked and assumed she would too; doorstep meat sarnies, cheese slices, apples, crisps, and cartons of blackcurrant, all packed into Grandda's faded khaki backpack. Dinner prepared they had set off to climb the bank, through the housing estate, over the parkway and up the steep-slippery-rotten wood steps through the trees. They had paused to let Grandda catch his breath and peer down the old drift entrance at the top of what had been 'New Bank' incline.

As he rested Billy Webster had been aware, in one corner of his restless mind that his granddaughter was quiet. This was a rare event when the two of them were on one of their adventures as Billy liked to call them. Sarah's continuing silence had interrupted a steady flow of ideas and words racing around in Billy's head. He had been keen to get up to the Nab so that he could sit and let the words travel down his arm, across his wrist and out through his pencil onto a page of the latest of a steadily growing shelf of notebooks he kept in the parlour. He had been about to ask Sarah what was causing her prolonged silence when she had spoken first:

'Grandda?'

Billy had stopped thinking of poems. The tone of the single word suggested that Sarah had been chewing on something for a while. He had guessed it might not be a simple question.

'Now then young Sarah,' he said after a long pause. He paused again and smiled. Once more he reminded himself, not for the first time, that he should make an effort to stop calling his granddaughter 'young Sarah'. She was growing up and beginning to question the careless rose-tinted imagination that had filled her childhood up until now. In a moment of clarity he had realised that, this time, she wanted to be treated as an adult. Goodness where had their lives gone to? So he had waited for her question, sure that it would be serious, but not quite ready for what she asked.

'Grandda, will I grow up like Mam?'

It was Sarah's first adult question to her Grandda and she needed an adult answer. Knowing that he would take a while to answer she had sat down on the remnants of the mine-entrance wall and waited for his reply. She was right she did have to wait a while. While she waited she had watched a beetle trying to climb up a squashed beer can as it searched for whatever beetles go looking for. The beetle had several attempts at the shining red surface of the can: it took Sarah off into her imagination.

Instinctively Billy had known that his answer would stay with his granddaughter for the rest of her life – so he had wanted it to be genuine, unlike the mistakes he had made in the past, especially with his daughter Sally.

* * *

Sally Webster has managed to avoid the most damaging consequences of her lifestyle. She has not succumbed to uncontrollable dependence on alcohol or drugs, drawing on an inbuilt ability and subconscious determination to resist addiction to both. She enjoys them, but is not dependent on either, at least not yet. The frustration with Sally is her inability, or unwillingness, depending on her friends' and family's point of view, to channel her determination into controlling or improving the way she lives.

She cannot hold down a job; routine and discipline are beyond her. She cannot manage money; it comes and goes with scarcely enough time to be spent, let alone be put to sensible use. Sally is intelligent; clever even, but only when she puts her mind to being so. She is great fun, in a haphazard, unpredictable way that her irresponsible friends love and her family despair of and she is full of good intentions, but devoid of any planning, organisation, or the dependability needed to bring them to fruition. Despite this her parents have to admit that she is not a completely useless or completely irresponsible parent; she is fiercely protective of her only child, Sarah.

* * *

Sally is late for work, nothing unusual, but later than normal. It is about 9.00 am and it's a Tuesday, so she is stuck in traffic between Eston and South Bank. On a warm spring morning Sally has the window of her small car wide open and the radio tuned to a local station. The traffic is queuing behind her, probably all the way back to the cemetery. On Sunday; Sally, her Da, and Sarah had been to the family grave to leave flowers for Sally's Grandparents. The visit had been planned, a rare concession to Sally's determination to never think beyond the moment. Sally's Grandda and Grandma were hit by a runaway van whilst standing at the bus stop in Eston village centre. They were waiting to catch a bus to go and visit Grandma's best friend Dorothy Williamson in the North Riding Infirmary. Although they got to the Infirmary they never got to visit Dorothy, they had both died before they arrived at the hospital.

The radio interrupted Sally's musing:

'I don't know what's up today. It's Tuesday, busiest and noisiest day of the week I know, but there are traffic delays everywhere. We think the worst place is the Asda roundabout near South Bank. We've got Sandra on the line to tell us what's happening.'

Sally knew what was happening and was day dreaming, wondering how she would be able to manage another evening out. It made her think about her daughter and her Da, Sarah's Grandda – all Webster Grandfathers were called Grandda, a family tradition. Her Da was obsessed with the family's history, it seemed daft to Sally, but her Da had always been interested in his ancestors. Sally thought about their visit to the family gravestone on Sunday; where all the Websters back to someone born in eighteen twenty something were buried. For a few seconds she wondered what life might have been like then, but as perhaps the scattiest of the Websters she lost the memory and recalled the top she wanted to go into town and change on Saturday. Would she get away with asking her Da – no point asking her Mam – to let Sarah stay over again? She decided to ask straight away, Sally had no sense of timing or tact; she did and said the first thing that came into her head. She reached across to her bag for her mobile and pressed the icon for Sarah's number:

'Hi Sar, everything alright, is Grandda asleep yet, where are you? It was always three questions at a time with Sally. Sarah waited until she had stopped.

'We're climbing up onto Eston Nab Mam, Grandda's brought the telescope. We're talking about our ancestors, it's really interesting,' Sarah said.

'That sounds fun,' interrupted her Mam, 'can you put your Grandda on please?'

'Grandda says he can't hear through these new-fangled phones. He wants to know what you want?' replied Sarah.

'Ask him if you can go round and stay on Saturday?' said Sally.

Sarah sighed and her anger returned. Her Mam only rang if she wanted something. Despite her best efforts and determination Sarah struggled to contain the confusion, increasingly the hurt and recently the anger that came over her when her Mam went off on a day or an evening out and spent the next day off recovering, without Sarah. Sarah felt she wanted to spend more time with her Mam; to talk to her about growing up. She did not mind staying with her Grandma and Grandda, in fact she quite liked it, but time without her mother did not feel right. Her awakening emotions were making her resent her Mam's frequent, selfish decisions to go out and leave Sarah alone or with her Grandparents. She hunched her shoulders and turned to her Grandda, her voice tight and flat:

'Mam says can I come and stay on Saturday?'

Billy Webster sighed as well. His daughter was a source of unending frustration to him. He and his wife Peggy did not mind at all having Sarah to stay but they knew that she had begun to resent her mother's behaviour and this time he could see the pain and anger in her face. It was getting worse and no amount of excuses or stories could hide it. The standards and values that he and his wife had learnt the hard way seemed even farther away from the latest generation than they had been from the thoughtless young people they remembered so clearly themselves. He smiled:

'That's no problem lass, you tell your mother we'll be fine the three of us. Maybe we can find out some more about the Webster family,' he heard himself saying.

Sally ended the call and dropped her mobile into her lap. She waited for the traffic to move. Her latest job was in the superstore by the roundabout at the end of Normanby Road; she was nearly there now. It had taken three weeks sticking to the boring, repetitive job before her bank card had stopped saying 'insufficient funds' to let her get at any money. Even then the thirty pounds she had left, after all the deductions for things she couldn't avoid having to pay, had only lasted the weekend. On Saturday she had talked Jimmy over the road into jump starting her car and she'd gone to the supermarket for petrol. That was how on this Tuesday morning she was driving to work, three miles, an easy bus ride. A lift from Marnie at the end of the street would have been even cheaper but that would have meant planning and time keeping. The clock on the dashboard, five minutes late, told her she was already twenty minutes late for work. She'd had one warning already, but warnings had the same importance as planning and time keeping in Sally's life. Fifteen pounds had gone on Saturday night. Now she held the last of the money between the index and middle fingers of her right hand.

As she day dreamed it slowly burnt away in a trail of smoke across the car and out of the window; the last cigarette in the packet. Sally wondered if she would get away with another visit to the corner newsagents in South Bank and try the supermarket voucher for more cigarettes again. Oh sorry I thought it was a fiver, here's a twenty – hand them a tenner, no change I'm afraid. Fumble in her bag while they served someone else and then, I gave you a twenty, I saw you put it in the till. Probably not, the girl at the till had been new. She'd catch on or have been told. She'd have to smile at Lenny again and let him drool over her tits. Sally knew how to handle him. Not like the guy in the club that she'd got a lift home with on Saturday night. She'd nearly woken Sarah, first getting his hand out of her jeans and then getting him out of the door. Woody – named after some footballer and left by a previous boyfriend, a half-starved and savage-as-a-result dog had done the rest. No, that guy's eyes had gone right through her clothes and nearly up to her fanny, but she'd managed to get a lift with him and got rid of him from the house without waking Sarah, she was sure.

The traffic moved in blocks of green light down the road, across the roundabout and ten minutes after she should have started her shift, into the superstore car park. Sally parked across two spaces in the 'wrong' place, customers could walk couldn't they, and went into work.

'Sarah, my daughter, she's had to go to the doctor's this morning. I'm a bit worried about her really (no point in being too worried, they might send her home) so I had to take her on the way in. I'll make up the time. It's not easy being a single Mum or a parent, you'll find out soon enough. Nice man like you'll have kids before long; then you'll understand.'

Bryan, a trainee manager, on his way up, nodded a sympathetic smile on his lips.

'Yes, Mrs Webster (the wedding ring had helped her get the job), I understand, but you must try and keep to your proper hours. Please make sure it doesn't happen again. I'm sure I can rely on you.'

Stroke of luck that, Annie Thomas, the regular supervisor would have been straight through her and she'd be on her first written warning. This way she could forget it.

'Yes Bryan, very understanding of you, I'd better start work hadn't I.' Sally smiled, with her only daughter please be nice to me smile. It worked. She left the manager's office, saw Lenny going for his first smoking break and followed him out. Sally sat down at her checkout half an hour after she was supposed to and began to put her float into the till, slowly. Her first customer was through just in time for her own first break.

She made her first £2.00 of the day from a distracted office manager type. He had waited impatiently behind Mrs Brown for 5 minutes. Mrs Brown was a regular. Every Tuesday, same time, same list, same conversation. As she left Sally waited just long enough for the man to get really agitated and hopping up and down, probably needed a piss, should have gone before he shopped. Sally turned away and undid the top buttons on her overall. She smiled as she turned back and put his packet of sandwiches, crisps, energy drink and mars bar through the till. Good £5.85, Sally had always been good at numbers. She could work out the darts for her Da from about ten onwards. She took the ten pound note, picked out the change and bent forward to give it to the man. His eyes left the proffered hand and looked down at the edge of her black bra as she sighed. She banged her hand on the edge of the till and swore:

'Oh! So sorry Sir, I've dropped your change.' She bent over; the line of her bra kept the man's eyes busy as she tucked £2 under her thigh and straightened up. The man took the crumpled receipt and handful of change, dropped it into his pocket, grabbed his lunch and hurried towards the toilet just before the exit.

A harassed Grandma, an absent pensioner and another ogler, all strangers, made her enough for drinks at the club that night. The job was boring but it did give her some spending money. She would stick at it for now, but if she was going to go out that night she should try and get Sarah to stay at her Mam and Dad's overnight. For a moment she wondered about Sarah's reaction. Last week, for the first time that Sally could remember Sarah had raised her voice in protest; she had threatened to leave home if she was left alone in the house overnight again; not that she would leave of course.

When Sally went out for another smoke with Lenny she reached into her bag for her mobile and called Sarah's number, she had already forgotten about Saturday:

'Hi Sar, everything alright, are you at Grandma's, are you having a good day?' Three questions as usual. Sarah, scowled, why couldn't her Mam remember anything, but Sarah knew she wouldn't. She waited until her Mam had stopped, half guessing what was to come.

'We're up on Eston Nab Mam, I already told you,' she replied, her voice flat; Billy stopped his writing and paused to listen.

'Oh! That's nice hon, what have you been doing?' said Sally, her enquiry about her daughter's day a sure sign that she wanted something. She didn't wait for a reply, but went straight on with her request. 'Can you ask your Grandda if you can stay for the night, I've got to go out, something's come up that I need to sort out?'

Sarah became hot and angry. She wasn't sure how to deal with it. She felt a lump in her throat. It was the deception in her mother's words which she had started to recognise recently. Her mother didn't care about her day she just wanted to go out that evening, Sarah was sure of it. She wanted to share the excitement of her day with someone and it would have been nice if it could be with her Mam.

'What is it love?' asked Billy, his voice careful, trying not to break into his granddaughter's conversation.

'It's Mam; she wants to know if I can stay for the night,' she paused, trying to hide the pain in her voice. She stumbled over the untruth, but repeated it anyway. 'She says that something has come up that she needs to do.' Her voice tailed off.

'Tell her it would be …' Billy stopped. There was no sense in sharing the pain and frustration with his granddaughter, it would not help Sarah. 'Yes, love, tell her that's OK.'

Sarah gulped and held back an angry tear. Why did she have to cry so much? She hunched her shoulders with childish adolescence and put the phone back to her ear: 'Grandda says that it's OK Mam.' She paused again, fighting the bitterness in her voice, 'hopefully, we'll see you later,' and switched off her phone.

Sally missed the reference to hopefully. She put her phone in her bag and grinned. She was already thinking about what she might wear that night.

Step one – Bella

Faded memories
Of glass and brass refound
War, death, redemption

Sarah, Eston Nab – Spring 2014

Billy Webster struggles to explain his thoughts out loud. He is much happier writing things down and finds it easier to explain what he thinks with stories. He has often dealt with difficult decisions and situations through his life by referring to the stories that his grandma, Bella, shared with him when he was young. Sitting in the parlour at Prospect View he had listened intently as Bella had brought life to the people, especially the women whose names were etched on the family gravestone that they had visited just this last Sunday. The hard physical labour of iron and steel making had taken its toll on the men, many of whom paid for their efforts with early death, recorded with cold stony simplicity on the headstone; leaving the women to provide the longevity and the strength to shape the way the family had developed. Could any of their lives and experiences help Sarah to understand her life and how she might grow up? He had sat down next to Sarah and wondered how best to answer her question. Sarah was busy watching something, he was entranced by the way her imagination showed her the world. While she dreamed he had time to think about the women that Bella had described.

Mary was the first of the Webster family to be touched by the coming of iron and steel making to Teesside. She had lived all her life on a farm whose traces could still be found in Eston if you knew where to look. Although Bella had edited her account for the ears of an impressionable young boy, Mary's life had been marked by tragedy. If only half of what Bella had told him about Mary was true her life was not the sort that he would want Sarah to emulate.

Mary's brother John had married Ann, perhaps the most mysterious of their ancestors. Billy recalled Bella's careful explanation of Ann and her upbringing and recalled that he had always meant to find out more about where Ann had come from and how she had met John. If Mary's life had tragedy, Ann's early life had sounded traumatic and remained shrouded in hushed rumours glossed over by Bella's account – another life perhaps best not shared with Sarah.

Ann and her husband John had clearly devoted their lives to their only child, Jane. Jane Webster, or Mistress Jane Beaumont as she had insisted on being called, appeared to have had none of the life-changing experiences that her Mother and Aunt had endured, but was she a good role model for Sarah? Given Bella's description and opinions perhaps not.

Which had led Billy back to the source of Sarah's question – his daughter Sally. Billy had recalled he and Peggy's struggles with Sally's rebellious childhood, particularly after the death of Sally's grandparents. The memory had made him think of his own grandmother, Grandma Bella. He had smiled to himself. He could do with a pound for every time his errant daughter had made him think of Bella. He often wished that she had still been alive through the trauma of Sally's adolescence, but she hadn't been. Perhaps Bella would be the best person for Sarah to relate to. He was sure Bella would have had some good advice, but before committing himself he had decided to try and find some reason for the question.

'Well Sarah, that's a big question. Where's that come from?'

Sarah had come back from the magical land of beetles and forests of tin cans and hidden caves. She had looked down at her feet that didn't quite reach the ground and swung them backwards and forwards as she thought. A whole flock of thoughts had been churning round in her head since her mother had dropped her off near Prospect View that morning. She loved coming to see her Grandda and Grandma. She loved the smell of cooking on her Grandma's pinny when she snuggled into it in the cake-scented kitchen. She smiled. She no longer fitted under Grandma's snuggly chest. She wondered if her own growing breasts would grow as much as her Grandma's, hopefully not. She loved the quiet of the parlour where the Webster family clock had ticked for over a hundred years. She had no reason not to want to visit them and yet this morning as she had walked up the street there had been a bigger than normal ache of loneliness and frightened foreboding deep in her stomach and she still didn't know why.

She loved Grandda's stories and his funny poems, the way he answered her questions with them. Sarah knew that she should tell him that she was no longer a small child; that she was starting to have older interests, some of which he might find difficult to understand, but she had not had the courage or opportunity to do so yet. Besides which she did enjoy her time with him; his stories took her mind off the struggle she was having to grow up.

She knew what it was that prompted her question. This term at school, she has been learning about genes and inherited traits; the things that help to determine the way people develop as they grow up. She understands that a part of her character will be determined by her genes; part will be learnt; part shaped by her environment, and part by her family, in particular her Mam.

Sarah loves her Mam, but does not understand her. Her Mam has always been the same and, unaware of any other way of living, Sarah has, until now, accepted it, and, confused by the admission, knows that her Mam will never change. At thirteen years old Sarah has begun to think about her life; thoughts that are raising questions and some unexplained doubts in her mind. She has been struggling with her question and it will not settle in her normally ordered mind. This morning, prompted by her Mam's behaviour, it had resurfaced, sharper and more focussed than ever: would she grow up like her Mam; a Mam that she loved without question; a Mam whose frenetic lifestyle reached into Sarah's awakening adult life and had, just that morning, accelerated the process of growing up beyond the events of today and next week and had asked questions about her future. Like many children trying to come to terms with adult life what seems at one minute to be obvious and easy to explain the next minute seems impossible to put into words. Suddenly Sarah felt disloyal to her Mam and embarrassed by her question. She didn't know how to reply to her Grandda, so she had shrugged and said:

'Oh, I don't know Grandda it just came into my head – I don't know why.'

Billy, much more in tune with his Granddaughter than he had ever been with his daughter, recognised her dilemma. Sarah needed more time to understand what she wanted to know, anything he said now could confuse her and do more harm than good. Recalling his handling of his own daughter's questions and his wish to do better second time around, he had compromised:

'Tell you what; let's get to the top first. Maybe by then you'll be able to tell me why you want to know and why you asked.'

'OK Grandda, I'll try.' Sarah had jumped down off the wall and set off along the path through the trees towards Eston Nab. She wasn't sure that she would ever be able to explain her question, but she was sure that to ease the knot in her stomach she wanted an answer, any answer and she could think of nobody else to turn to except her Grandda. Following behind her Billy knew that he owed her an answer that would avoid his experiences with his daughter, an outcome that he hoped fervently was not going to repeat itself. He too had a lot of thinking to do. As he had followed his granddaughter, he had his Grandma Bella in his head; what would she have said?

They had threaded their way along the pitted tracks and abandoned mine workings before heading up through the gorse and bracken to the cliffs on Eston Nab. At the top they had found a sheltered spot between two mauve grey slabs of rock and settled themselves down. Sarah had laid down on the sun warmed grass and looked up at the sky. She was soon lost in her thoughts so her Grandda left her to her dreams. Billy had got out his notebook and pencil – he could think clearer when he was writing.

* * *

Billy Webster is a small white-haired man with piercing crow's feet blue eyes, high cheekbones, determined jaw, and a thin mouth curled up at the corners. He is perched against a slab of rock, knees bent, notebook balanced on his thigh, pencil held delicately in big calloused hands, bare arms still showing the muscles built through fifty years of steel making on the southern banks of the river Tees; he is scribbling away. He retired from the steelworks eight years ago. His retirement dinner had coincided with the visit of a delegation from Tata Steel, Jamshedpur, India (he often smiled at the paradox of faded empire giving way to emerging global power). Never short on being direct, Billy had got into conversation with a visitor from the steelwork's Indian owners. Sahaj – he never found out what Sahaj did – was a student of Matsuo Bashō, a seventeenth century Japanese writer who wrote poetic stories that ended in short three line poems with a strange name; a name that Sarah had never managed to get her head round – hikers, or something like that. Her Grandda has been attempting to write in the same style, or his own interpretation of it, ever since. Today his words were focussed, perhaps even more than usual in his life, on his daughter:

Sally

Spring, selfish daydreams
Fumes, queues, text, noise, shops, youth, choice
Material things

Sarah got up and climbed onto one of the rocks. She opened her pink backpack and took out the family heirloom. When she first saw it mounted on a wooden stand on the bureau in Grandma and Grandda's parlour in Prospect View she asked what it was, misunderstood what was said and struggled to pronounce the name. Since then it has always been called a scalarope. The old telescope has been in the family since 1829 when it was given to Mary Webster by an old sailor called William Snow.

Years of moderate care have left the optics in poor condition. The brass-work is scratched and there is a pronounced dent in the side half way along the outside case. It does still have a sliding lens protector on the eyepiece, although the removable lens cover has disappeared. It measures 22.5 inches extended and 8.25 inches closed. Sarah couldn't understand inches but that is what Grandda said – he also said it weighed about half a pound – she couldn't understand that either; but she had agreed in the hope that he would continue to let her use it sometimes – now was such an occasion and Sarah was making the most of it.

Holding the telescope and with her earlier question consigned to the back of her mind Sarah asks another:

'Grandda, how come you got to have the telescope?'

'My Grandma, Bella left it to me in her will,' he replied.

'How did she come to have it?' asked Sarah.

'Oh she wanted it for Tommy,' he said.

'Tommy, you haven't mentioned him before. Who was he?' asked Sarah.

'He was my Grandda, Bella's husband. I never knew him, he died when I was very young. Apparently Bella went to a great deal of trouble to get the telescope for Tommy,' said Billy.

'They must have been very much in love, how did they meet?' said Sarah.

'Yes, they were,' said Billy, 'no one seems too sure how they got together, but once they were they were never apart again.'

'That sounds very romantic,' said Sarah, 'will you tell me about Grandma Bella?'

Billy shivered, this was scary. He had come to the conclusion during their climb up the bank that if any of their descendants would be a good role model for Sarah then it would be Bella. Recalling his determination not to ignore Sarah's questions as he had his own daughters he seized the opportunity.

'Yes pet, I can do that,' he paused and took his courage in his words, 'and maybe Bella's life can help you to answer your question about how you'll grow up.'

'Oh, yes,' replied Sarah, surprised and a little concerned that her Grandda had remembered her question, 'maybe it will.'

Bella Macaulay, California – 1897

Isabella Mary Macaulay was eight when she and her family moved to the Ironstone mines on the north escarpment of the Eston Hills in North Yorkshire. It was a move that was the making of Bella. The family's life in a busy mill town in South Yorkshire was hard on them all. The tiny particles of cotton and other textiles that hung in the air over the town whenever the wind dropped got into everyone's lungs and led to respiratory diseases. The comparatively clear air of the Eston Hills, even in the eighteen nineties was to be a refreshing and healthy change. Bella was tiny, even when she was fully grown she never did reach five feet tall – she could not remember having stockings; in later life they still felt odd when she put them on – tight and restricting for her feet. Her tiny wiry body had no spare flesh, anywhere. The Macaulay's did not starve, but neither did they eat well, like many of the urban families of the Victorian industrial dream they lived, neither starving nor free of the occasional poverty that characterised the rise and fall of new industries in the late-nineteenth century in Britain. Industries that were started by unskilled entrepreneurs attracted by the outward riches of a few clever men – women had no place or at least very rarely any chance in Victorian business.

Bella's father had heard of booming mining and steel making industries up on Teesside at the town's reading society that he went to on a Saturday night. They had invited a travelling speaker, who was touring the North, to visit their weekly gathering. Patrick Macaulay was determined to take advantage of the stories of opportunities on Teesside and in eighteen ninety seven when a brief downturn in production at the mill he worked in – the end of another war, this one in Matabeleland – saw him jobless, he decided that the family should move north. He used their meagre savings to buy a mule from a tinker and loaded it with the family's few belongings, or as much as the scraggy beast would carry – precious little as it turned out – and they set off for the Eston Iron and Steel works on the banks of the River Tees.

They did not get that far. The mule died when they got to Stokesley where a man was recruiting for men to work on the Cleveland railway and the Macaulay family moved into a barn near Pinchinthorpe. They lived there for a year until Patrick had a piece of luck. Through his interest in reading he got to know a supervisor at the ironstone mines on the other side of the Eston hills. The family moved north again. This time the family were housed in a two-roomed cottage with a space to sleep in the windowless attic that the children got to by climbing up a wooden ladder with two rungs missing – they had a home.

By eighteen ninety eight California was a settled well established community, no longer the shifting sometimes lawless place of the early days of mining in the hills. So the family, although viewed with suspicion with their bright red hair and strange accents, were helped by all their neighbours. A family called Webster mended the ladder for them and the wife, called Liza took Bella's mother to visit the company shop where everyone lived on credit, spending their earnings for the next year. It made for a loyal unchanging workforce who could not afford to pay off their debts and move on. For all that, it was a happy place and the tiny bright red haired young girl fitted in well and before long everyone in the small community knew the Macaulay family and especially Bella. Her infectious laugh and readiness to fight lost causes made her liked or grudgingly respected by everyone, including Tommy Webster, Liza's nephew. Tommy was so quiet that the boys called him the ghost, but the girls liked him and took pity on him; they chased the boys away when they followed Tommy up the lane and howled after him like the new horror character Dracula that had just appeared in the papers.

With a stable job and the increasing availability of free education Bella's parents were able to let her go to school in Eston. Her first day set the scene for her entire stay. She clashed with her teacher, the daughter of the local parson. This young woman was appointed through her parents influence and not for any academic skill. She was known by all the children and in the villages as Miss Dither. Bella had not meant to start off so badly, the opportunity to go to school regularly and not just when her parents could afford it, was exciting. She was keen to learn and willing to help if she could. The morning she started school one of the boys was passing out slates to everyone for the writing lesson; when he reached Bella she ignored the teacher's uncertain command – more of an anxious request than an order – to sit still and wait. Instead impetuous Bella jumped up to help. She knocked the slates out of the monitor's hands. Bella spent the rest of the lesson outside the door and her parents were sent a bill for five new slates. The street all helped and the bill was paid, but Bella received a belting from her Dad that left her sore for several days. It would be good to know that Bella had learnt her lesson, but that was not her character, she continued to battle with her teacher until one day she came to school to learn from the headmaster, who had spoken to them all in the school hall that they would be sorry to hear that

Miss Dither had moved to Darlington. The Governors and the head teacher took this to be a testament to the good work and reputation of the school, the rest of the village breathed a sigh of relief. Bella flourished with the new teacher and her name began to appear on the various lists of pupils who did well – someone who brought honour to the schools name, as the headmaster put it. It was during a ceremony to hand her a certificate for reading that Bella first came across the name of Jane Webster. Bella asked Tommy if Jane was a relation of his. He replied that she had been but was not anymore; she had moved away and nobody had heard from her since. Bella's further inquiries were met with excuses and some anger by the Webster family, none of whom had anything good to say about Jane. She gave up asking in the end.

Bella & Tommy, Eston – 1919

Tommy Webster's efforts to get close to Bella were fraught with problems and set-backs. It was not as if he had not tried everything he could think of. From the very first day he had come to school and seen Bella, they were both eight at the time; he had wanted her as his girl. Some of the set-backs were of his own making. His shy diffident way made him invisible amongst the boisterous gang of youngsters that seemed to gather around Bella wherever she was. If that was not enough he stammered. On the few occasions when Bella stood still long enough to let him speak to her he took so long to get his head and mouth around what he wanted to say that she had been taken away by someone else. The result was that all through their childhood the closest Tommy got to Bella was three rows back at school and four cottages down on Prospect View. That was until the Great War came.

As war with Germany became more likely the young men and boys in the village were swept up in the wave of patriotism that gripped the country and they were all determined to be a part of it. Naturally they all wanted to join the cavalry or fire the giant guns that were pictured in the papers; papers that an increasing number of the population could now read for themselves. Tommy's size, indifferent health and his stammer did not help his efforts to enlist in the army at first. He watched as the girls idolised the new soldiers in their smart new uniforms and shiny boots. At first every young man and boy wanted to sign up and go off to fight, but then the telegrams and letters from wounded men began to arrive home. There were many more of them than there were returning soldiers. Those that did return, mostly invalided out of the army, said very little about what it was really like and even then they talked in secret, but despite the stories the young men of Britain continued to sign up, the fear and stigma of cowardice was overriding. Finally in nineteen seventeen Tommy Webster got his wish. By then there were a lot fewer volunteers so that even protected jobs like miners were being called up. He left the mine where his father and grandfather had both worked and joined up. His thin, wiry body finally made it through the increasingly lax medical checks and along with another fifty men, or by now boys – Tommy was amongst the oldest volunteers – they marched off to the railway station for the long journey to death or disease.

Tommy was never quite sure if he was lucky or not. On bad nights as he lay in bed on a hot summer evening struggling to breathe with two scarred and damaged lungs he wasn't sure, but then his wife would appear at the bedside with a jug of steaming camphor smelling water and an old towel and the feel of her gentle hands and soft caring voice would help sooth him off to sleep. He would leave the house the next morning as wages clerk at the steel works more than grateful that he had come home from the Great War and its Western Front Line. He never tired of remembering how he came to win Bella.

* * *

Bella was on her way to work when they bumped into each other. As usual Bella was in a hurry, she got to the station as the train from Eston Junction was pulling into the pit head station. She needed a ticket so she hurried into the ticket office, paid for her weekly ticket and ran back onto the platform to catch the train before it left. A last straggling incoming passenger had struggled to get off the train after everyone else had disappeared from the station so he had to wait until the new passengers had climbed into his carriage. Finally, he was able to climb down off the train just as Bella, who was not expecting anyone to be getting off the train, crashed into him. They both fell to their knees. Getting to their feet each thought they recognised the other.

'Tommy Webster?' said Bella.

'Bella Macaulay?' the man replied, his voice barely audible as he rasped, the words coming through an only partly healed throat and mouth still scarred by gas burns. Bella stopped and stared at the gaunt pain-drawn man struggling to his feet in front of her and her caring nature took over. She helped him to his feet across the platform and sat him down on a luggage trolley.

'Look Tommy, it is Tommy isn't it, I've got to go. I'll come and see you tonight,' she said quickly. She squeezed his hand and ran back to the train just as it was starting to leave. Two men whistled out of the nearest carriage window, opened the door and dragged her up into the carriage.

'Come on Bella we'll look after you,' said one of them.

By the time she had dealt with them and turned round to look out of the coach the train had left the station and she could no longer see the man sitting on the trolley.

If she had she would have seen just the ghost of a smile on the ravaged face; smiling was still very painful for Tommy. After all this time he had had his wish, Bella Macaulay had spoken to him, but she was in too much of a hurry to wait and hear his reply and he was too ill to make the most of his opportunity. His only consolation was her retort to one of the men as they pulled her into the carriage:

'You can keep your hands to yourself Jimmy Thompson or you'll get the sharp end of my elbow in your ribs.'

The train had gone and the platform was empty except for one small relic of the world's greatest human conflict. A pale shadow of the keen, sparkling young soldier who just twelve weeks before had stood proudly on the same platform waiting to change the world. Now the world had changed him for ever.

Tommy sat in the parlour of the Webster family home in Prospect View. On the mantelpiece was the empty stand where the family heirloom, a telescope had once been – a constant reminder of the split in the family. To the left of the hearth stood the clock, brought from the farm when the horses were taken off to the war three years ago; as a result the family had been unable to keep the farm going and it too had been sold. All the Websters now worked in the mine.

In the silence of the early evening Tommy's breathing could be heard. He had learned to breathe with his mouth open and that was about all the help and advice he had received from a grateful nation. Dead heroes were good for recruiting, cheap to compensate and easy to forget. Wounded heroes were dangerous; they had an annoying habit of telling the truth, of spreading realism, of reducing the role of proud Tommy. He nearly laughed at the irony of his own name, but laughing disturbed his chest and throat and caused him to choke and put back the slowly healing tissue by weeks if it was too bad, so Tommy had taught himself not to laugh and to smile carefully. It was a habit he was to carry with him for the rest of his life and would make all but his closest friends misunderstand what a friendly easy going man he was.

Tommy was dozing, wondering what he might do now that he had achieved his first goal since crawling back across no man's land and dropping into the bottom of a stinking trench face down to wait and pray that he would be found alive before he drowned or was buried in shell -scattered soil from the battlefield – he had made it home. The kindly-spoken doctors with wound-numbed empty eyes had given him a hopeful send off. People had recovered from worse burns than his. It just took time, but not their time, not the army's time and definitely not his country's time. Tommy wondered who would have time for him now, a shell of a man. The mine he had left just three months ago needed men ready for hard physical labour; men who could breathe deeply to survive the heavy aired atmosphere below the ground. Men with strong chests who could drill and load and push the ironstone filled tubs to the mine head. There was no way back to that work for Tommy Webster. He sighed carefully and looked out of the window. It was peaceful and the late evening sun cast a shadow across the room. A pink-edged cloud appeared in the corner of the window as the clock ticked away and he dozed again.

* * *

He was woken by a voice that he had not expected to see again and definitely not so soon – Bella's. She had come hurrying in through the kitchen – exchanging minimal greetings with Tommy's family who were discussing his future in whispers and very little hope or idea of what to do for him – and strode into the parlour, no knocking or asking, Tommy tried not to smile too broadly, same old Bella.

'Oh Tommy Webster, what have they done to you? Stupid, cruel war; what for? Just men's misplaced pride? What happened to you? Was it gas? Did they say how long to recover? How are you? What can I do to help?' Bella stopped.

Tommy looked at her. Why had this tiny dynamo of a woman, everyone's friend, why had she come to see him – pity probably? He unravelled her dozen questions and wondered which one to answer first. He could see her itching to, to do something, to take charge, to organise him, the village the war, the world, everything – she had not changed. He could feel a laugh – fighting to come through – he knew what to say. He smiled his careful care-worn smile and said in his slow rasping voice.

'You could try and not make me laugh, that would be really kind.'

Bella stopped, her world stopped. She had spent the day planning and organising how single handed, amongst all her other causes and commitments she would be able to help Tommy Webster and she had failed to even consider what would be the best and only way she could really help him, and when she realised, she fell in love. It was not there and then like the piano accompanied bolt of love in the silent film they all went to watch in the new cinema. No it was a dull relentless ache in her heart and soul that was fuelled by Tommy's careful smile; by his stoical patient acceptance and then by his steely fight to recover.

It was through the year that it took for the scars to knit together into new skin and his lungs to heal enough to breathe enduring life through his body. It was through his steadfast refusal to blame anyone for what had happened to him as she railed against all the agencies who had conspired to drift gas across a mangled field of mud to dash the hopes of whole villages of men and leave their families to mourn through four generations until old age and neglect would dull the wounds of the most pointless conflict that man had unleashed on himself. And lastly, it was through his sense of hope. Despite all he had been through Tommy Webster was hopeful and it was that hope-filled outlook on life that Bella finally fell openly in love with.

* * *

They proposed to each other. Bella could not allow such an important event in her life to go past without being equally involved. Tommy had said jokingly to her one day, soon after she had started to come and visit him, that one day he would take her up to Eston Nab and when he did he would ask her to marry him.

As it turned out, they took each other and sitting watching the smoke and dust of the industrial might of Britain that stretched out ahead of them across the Tees valley they both spoke together.

'Tommy?'

'Can I ask you something first Bella?'

'Depends on what it is because I want to ask you something as well'

'Well I was going to ask you to marry me.'

'So was I, shall we both say yes together.'

And that's what they did.

Tommy pulled a small knotted handkerchief out of his pocket and undid it with shaking hands.

'I was given this by a lad I met in France,' he said to Bella. 'He said I was to give it to a really special person because that was what he had been going to do with it. Will you wear it for me Bella?' He handed Bella a small narrow gold banded ring with a single stone set into it.

Bella held it in the palm of her hand and quite suddenly she did something that she hadn't done for many years, she started to cry. She suspected that the ring had not been given up easily or handed over until its owner had seen no hope of delivering it to its original recipient; it gave her a lump in her throat as she pushed it onto her ring finger.

She was right. Like most of the unknown heroes of the conflict Tommy had not told anyone how driven on by adrenalin he had carried his pitifully young lieutenant, three quarters of the way back across the muddy no man's land before he had had the knotted handkerchief pushed into his hand with orders to honour his officer's last request and keep it; he had watched the man die in the water-filled crater. Some did receive medals and commendations for such acts but not Tommy Webster. He had failed to save the man's life, and anyway, the knotted handkerchief, when he undid it was more than reward enough from the young man that he had followed into the drifting death that had come towards them.

'Aye lass it looks well on your finger. Don't suppose you'll do much obeying but I'd be glad if you would be prepared to love and honour me by being my wife,' said Tommy.

'Tommy Webster! I'd be proud to be your wife,' Bella paused, 'and honoured to bear your children if God sees fit to let us have any.'

Tommy laughed for once, it did not hurt so much now but it still made him choke. The spasm passed and he wiped his mouth.

'Perhaps I ought to kiss you,' he said with a twinkle in his eye that Bella hadn't seen before.

'I thought you'd never ask Tommy Webster.'

'So did I,' replied Tommy and leaned over to kiss his new fiancée. They were married two months later.

* * *

The wedding was a great success. Bella knew everyone and the idea of the wounded war hero marrying his childhood sweetheart caught the imagination of the two villages and they all turned out to see them. Bella organised everything, she even interrupted the vicar at one point in the service to put him right on something. Most of the congregation laughed. The men nudged each other and said they hoped there were two pairs of trousers amongst the wedding presents – one for each of the grooms. The women were captivated by Bella so tiny yet so overwhelming with her long red hair left loose for the day hanging down to her waist. In stunning contrast to the creamy white of her dress cut down by Tommy's mother from Bella's mother's own dress that she had carried all the way from South Yorkshire; carried in the prayed for but often despairing hope that her domineering, loving, caring and sometimes scatty daughter might one day find a man strong enough to deal with her. Tommy Webster must have hidden depths was the consensus among all the women who had been convinced that no man would be brave enough or tolerant enough to take her on.

The couple spent their two nights honeymoon at Saltburn – courtesy of a friend of Bella – and were back at work on Monday morning. God must have smiled on them because their first child was born just nine months later, final proof to the doubters in the villages that Tommy Webster had not lost everything in France and that Bella must have stopped talking just long enough to have been a dutiful wife. Neither opinion was correct, the couple, once they had stopped to recognise their love practiced it wholeheartedly and without any of the hang ups that their often troubled characters could have put in the way. Not that it put Bella off her many causes, missions and pursuits. In fact it led to the one in particular that would test her resolve to the limit. One night as they lay in bed listening to the Webster clock ticking away Tommy said to Bella:

'There's always one thing I would have liked pet.'

Bella leaned over and kissed his nose. She peered into his open, honest brown eyes and asked:

'What's that Mister Webster?'

Tommy smiled, he liked the way she called him Mister Webster; he felt that he belonged to someone special. He said, 'I often wonder if Aunt Jane still has the old telescope and if she still wants it. Grandda often spoke about it and told us some of the stories about the old sailor it came from. Still I don't suppose she'll have kept it; much too old and battered for the high society in Darlington that Jane moved to I should think.' Tommy squeezed his wife and rolled over. Soon the rasping sound of his now settled breathing filled the room and he slept. Bella lay awake for a long time that night – off on another mission. She was planning how she would satisfy the wish of a man who asked for nothing much and gave everything he had in return.

Bella & Tommy, Eston – Summer 1942

In nineteen thirty nine Britain went to war again and Tommy Webster signed up to help his country – this time he became a fire warden. For nearly three years he spotted fires, helped move people from shelters and back, sat and drank tea and read the papers. While he was doing this he sometimes compared his work to his experience in the first Great War. He smiled at the incomparable nature of it and yet he also thought that the war of his youth had touched him much less than this one was doing. For Tommy the end would come at some time and he was able to sit patiently and wait for it to happen.

Unlike her husband Bella was never able to accept his outlook on what the world brought – she needed to interfere, to put it right; this madness, this second power struggle between men who could not bring themselves to agree to live together. Throughout this Second World War she worked tirelessly for anyone and everyone who needed help whether they knew it or not.

* * *

Half way through the war, one night in late summer Tommy was manoeuvred into working Jack Brown's late shift. As usual Bella railed against the scheming man – why didn't Tommy stand up to him. Despite her frustration at her husband for his ability to live in harmony with anyone around him, before she went out to work that afternoon she packed up his flask and bait tin and left him with his paper in the parlour.

'I'll see you in the morning pet,' he said as she went out of the door.

* * *

Somewhere above northern Britain a German aircraft was lost. It hadn't been lost when it had crossed the coast earlier that night heading for industrial targets in the North East of England. Then, as the aircraft, a bomber, had crossed the North Sea, in comparative safety before they came into the range of the British radar, its three crew members, ordinary young men, had been discussing Helmut's impending wedding. Helmut was the youngest of the three – a serious, bespectacled boy-turned-man. This was Helmut's first flight – into danger over the enemy's territory, their commanding officer's description at that mornings briefing. Helmut had been a diligent pupil at the Luftwaffe's navigation school. In the calm of the classroom he had performed well and as a result was now on his first mission. He was being teased by his more experienced crew mates, Adler and Erhardt, but Helmut who had very few friends and was shy of most people was pleased to be a part of the banter – he felt that they had accepted him. They were talking about his fiancée, Rupetta, the daughter of the local grocer, a formidable man whose presence was only overshadowed by that of the man's wife. Helmut and Rupetta were to be married in two weeks.

'You do realise that you will have two wives when you marry Rupetta don't you Helmut,' said Adler

'Three more likely.' said Erhardt, 'The mother-in-law and round Rupetta.'

'That'll make four,' said Adler, 'her mother is as big as she is.'

Helmut did not care what they said about Rupetta, she was the first person who had spoken to him and taken any interest in him at all in his short life. He was in love as only a shy, nineteen year old only child from a tiny village in nowhere could be – he did not care.

'Everything will be fine, we will be really happy,' he said.

'Just as long as you get us to our target and back home,' said Erhardt.

The cramped navigation seat that Helmut had been shown when he had climbed into the aeroplane, knees shaking and heart beating, was nothing like the training room table that he had used for all his navigation until now. There he had been able to set out his charts, pencils and slide rule in the repetitive order that made his life bearable – a life style that Rupetta was happy to share. Now the incessant noise and the lack of space on a tiny metal map table that vibrated through his body and set his nerves on edge were playing games with his hitherto competent navigation skills. He had coped with it until they crossed the coast of England and an enemy fighter had found them. A series of neck-aching, stomach-turning, knee-scraping disorienting moves from Adler at the controls of the aircraft had found them the safety of some thick cloud in the not quite dark night of late summer over northern Britain. They were lost and at that moment Helmut had no idea where they were.

'Adler, thank you for getting us away from the Hurricane, we are indebted to you as always. However, we have used too much fuel to be able to complete our mission so I recommend that we return home immediately,' shouted Erhardt above the noise.

'Ever the optimist,' shouted Adler over his shoulder. 'Helmut, give me a bearing to get back to Germany.

Erhardt tells me that we have to return home now or we will run out of fuel,'

The moment that Helmut had been dreading since the aircraft had returned to a relatively stable, horizontal position had arrived. He had recovered his charts and other equipment from the corners and cracks that it had fallen into. What he had not recovered was any control over his ability to complete the steps necessary to work out where they were or how to work out what course they should set to get home.

'Helmut, now would be a good time to give me a bearing,' said Adler, 'This aircraft will be difficult to park while we wait for you to work it out.'

There was no response from the panic stricken young navigator – his brain had stopped working.

'Erhardt, see what he is doing back there, we need a course now,' shouted Adler.

Erhardt made his way to the navigator's position. He and his pilot Adler had survived this far into the war much longer than the closely guarded statistics would say they should have done. They had done so as much as anything by not panicking and treating their missions as a job. They planned each one; they did not drink themselves to a state of readiness as some of their compatriots did. They had had a number of navigators, this one, young Helmut, had like the last one frozen when the true reality of what they had to do caught up with him. Unlike Adler though, Erhardt was a reasonable man and quite liked the shy young man.

'Now then Helmut, let's get this course mapped out shall we. Where's the chart?' he began.

Helmut couldn't think. He had no idea where they were, and then for some reason, he remembered some advice from a fellow navigator one evening a few weeks before.

'If you don't know where you are just steer one hundred degrees – it'll get you to Germany. If you're still flying and still alive after an hour you should be over Germany somewhere; it will be light by then and you can work out where you are.'

'We should fly on a bearing of 100 degrees ,' he said this with a confidence he did not feel, but it seemed to satisfy Erhardt who went off to give the instruction to Adler who banked the aircraft to starboard and they began their flight home.

Erhardt had checked their fuel tanks as he had made his way forward and had said to Adler at the same time:

'We should get rid of the bombs. That way we'll save fuel and have more chance of making it home.'

They argued for several minutes about this until Adler was convinced by Erhardt that it was their best option.

'We should not waste the bombs,' said Adler. 'Helmut, are there any big towns or industrial targets near here? Check your charts and let me know.'

Helmut, who had no idea where they were, recalled the geography of the North East of England. He was reasonably sure, well hopeful really, that they would fly over the coast of North East England when they had changed course

'There are three large rivers in the area, each one of them has large industrial targets where they reach the coast. Can you see the sea yet in front of you?'

Adler put the nose of the plane down slightly and banked the aircraft to port. As he did so a gap in the clouds about them parted and he saw a pale strip of water below them. There's a river below us on the port side,'

'There will be industrial targets along the banks of the river,' said Helmut.

'Good,' said Adler, 'Erhardt, prepare to release the bombs.'

* * *

Tommy set off for his shift in early evening of the 3rd August. He reached the wardens shelter and settled down for a quiet undisturbed night. It wasn't that they never had anything to do. Fires still broke out and German bombers did come over, but they were not common. Tommy heard the intermittent noise from the vibrating engines as the stray German bomber came towards Teesside, flying along the river, making its way to the sea before heading back to Germany. Tommy got up and walked out of the shelter to check that there was no one about – as he did so he saw a thin shaft of light half way along the street. A blackout curtain had been caught in a window as it was opened on the warm summer evening. The light was visible for two minutes at the most. Tommy assumed there were people in the house and hurried down the street towards it.

'I thought I saw a gleam of light – there straight ahead of us;' shouted Adler, 'Prepare to release the bombs.'

'The bombs have gone,' reported Erhardt – unnecessary given the perceptible lift in the aircraft's flight as the weight of the bombs left it.

'Excellent,' said Adler, 'Let's go home.'

In his tiny compartment Helmut felt a sense of relief. He had managed to get them to the coast and heading in the right direction for home. He would have a real story to tell Rupetta tomorrow. Already bursting with pride for her fiancé she would be over-joyed to see him.

For the second time in his life Tommy had to cross no-man's land to safety. This time he had no-one to carry, the house had been empty. He had switched off the light. He set off back to the shelter. His wounds from his last journey across no-man's land had left him short of breath and unable to run at anything more than a slow trot. Tommy Webster was in the middle of the street fifty yards from the house when the bomb went through the roof of the house – Erhardt would have been proud of his accuracy.

The aircraft was crossing the coast. At the last coastal defence gun placement the anti-aircraft gun crew let off a last defiant burst of fire into the air at the departing aircraft. The bullets were at their farthest range when they reached the aeroplane. Only four penetrated the fuselage and the undamaged plane flew on.

Erhardt peered around the corner at the young man, head in his arms on the map table.

'Leave him to sleep,' said Adler, surprisingly considerate after Helmut's efforts before. The two men had flown back from Britain into the dawn across Germany enough times to be able to pick their way back to their airfield and leave their navigator in peace. Adler taxied the aircraft to its place by the runway and he and Erhardt were in a hurry to get home. They both had young families and the uncertainty of the war made them anxious to spend at much time as they could with them.

As they climbed out of the aircraft Erhardt shouted to Helmut:

'Come on Helmut, Lili Marleen will be waiting for you.'

'And her keeper the rund schwägerin,' added Adler over his shoulder.

One of the ground crew found Helmut an hour later – one of the four bullets had found a lethal target. Helmut had died somewhere over the North Sea when a blood vessel, caught by the bullet that had knocked him unconscious in his tiny seat, had burst. The following Wednesday there were two funerals. Both were attended by heart-broken women – victims of a war that neither understood nor wanted.

* * *

After Tommy's funeral one of the people who came to the wake – there were a lot of people there – reminded Bella of the telescope she had retrieved from Jane and then hidden from the means testers; she retrieved it from behind the toilet cistern to sit once more in the parlour. It didn't bring Tommy back, but it was a comforting reminder.

Sarah, Prospect View – Spring 2014

Sarah felt drawn to her Grandda's Grandma Bella. She was sad when he had told her about Tommy dying in the Second World War. She thought her great, great, she counted on her fingers, yes that was right, great, great, Grandma would have been really sad and wanted to know more about her. She helped her Grandda to pack his shabby old backpack and they set off down the bank back to his house in Prospect View.

When they reached the front door Sarah stopped and asked:

'Grandda, what happened to your Grandma Bella? Did you know her well? How did she die?'

Billy laughed:

'Just like your mother in some things, lass. Always three questions at once. Why don't we get through the door first?'

They went into the parlour, stopping off in the kitchen to get a drink and a hug from Grandma and to hear about her trip to Meadowhall. They sat down in the two timeless big chairs that faced each other across the parlour.

Billy thought for a minute or two as he sat drinking his tea; he was trying to decide what to say:

'No lass, I don't think I did know Grandma Bella well. I often went to see her, the whole family did. Everyone had a story about Bella; she touched all our lives in one way or another. She was the one everyone went to see if they had a problem. Everybody shared their troubles with her. We all relied on her in one way or another.' he said eventually.

'So did she touch your life?' Sarah felt sure that there was more to what Grandda said and, for some reason she could not work out, she felt that if she could persuade him to tell her what happened it would help her to understand her own life a bit better. 'When was the last time you spoke to her?'

Billy sighed; typical of the lass, always knew how to get right to the point. 'I last saw Grandma the day she died, and now that I've said that I suppose I better tell you what happened or you'll never give me any peace until I do,' he added ruefully.

'Oh yes please Grandda, what year was that?' Sarah asked sitting up in the big old chair.

'1964, 12th December, a Saturday, I don't suppose I'll ever forget it,' he said.

Bella and Billy, Middlesbrough – Winter 1964

It was a still cold winter's morning, the second Saturday in December and Billy Webster was waiting to go to Middlesbrough, to the match with his mates. He was on the back door step arguing with his mother.

'If you're going to the Boro' you can call in and see your Grandma, it's only round the corner. If you get the earlier bus you'll have time,' she said.

'Ah! Mam, we're going to the pub first, I'll not have time to see Grandma as well. I'll go another day; promise. Now can I have a lend of a quid, I'll pay you back next Thursday?' pleaded Billy.

'You can have a quid if you promise to visit you Grandma,' his Mam countered.

'Yeah, of course Mam, I'll go tomorrow' – anything to get away, he thought.

'Go on then,' his mother laughed. Dotty Webster was a soft touch, everyone knew it, even she did, but she loved her son. She went to the biscuit tin on the mantelpiece over the stove and opened it. She picked out a pound note, it left her short for the rent but she could find that somewhere else and handed it to her son. He gave her a quick hug and a kiss on the cheek and ran out before she changed her mind.

Billy ran down the back lane turned right, out of sight of the cottage and slowed down. He paused to light a woodbine, cupped it in his right hand against the cold breeze, pushed his other hand into his pocket, hunched his shoulders and walked along the street to the bus stop. He sang as he walked, thinking about his girlfriend Peggy as he did so, his thoughts brought the words of a song to his head:

'When I look in your eyes I get a surprise.'

Billy had decided that this was the girl, at last. He thought of the others, briefly, but no, Peggy was the real thing. They just felt right together.

'Because there's nothing but happiness there.'

Last Saturday outside her door, before her Dad had chased him off to the last bus she had whispered in his ear that he was the only boy she had ever really loved. That was twice in the same day.

'It's the sound of your voice, it's the light in your smile.'

He had repeated her words to himself over and over on the way home, sitting upstairs on the bus in the smoke filled, sweaty, damp atmosphere along with another twenty drunk, or lovesick, or heavy eyed, or lonely young people. Old people never seemed to go anywhere, they just sat at home and moaned about the weather, or the country, or kids, or standards, or anything.

'As you sing all my trials away.'

Billy felt that now was his time to do whatever he wanted. After all, if the Russians could send men into space why couldn't Britain, Billy wanted to go up into space, but before that he was going to see Peggy. She had asked him to get the early bus so that they could go into Middlesbrough and buy the latest Beatles record. He caught the bus and carried on singing to himself all the way to Linthorpe Road where Peggy lived. Her Mam opened the door and Billy groaned when she said:

'She's not here son. She's had to go and babysit her sister's kids as Janie's gone to the doctors on account of her stomach which is really painful. I was only saying to Beryl the other evening at the club that I thought as Janie looked a bit pale and she said aye she does that. We thought then as she should go to the doctors but she wouldn't have it so I said to Beryl, Beryl I said you mark my words she'll be at the doctors before the weeks out...'

Billy stopped listening, which was a mistake because at that moment Mrs Ryan said:

'Get yourself in lad and have a cuppa, the kettles on and it'll just take a minute to boil.'

Billy tried to think of a way out of spending the hour before the match, that he had been going to spend with Peggy, with Mrs Ryan. She had already decided he was a part of the family and kept making hints about weddings. Inspiration came from his mother's last words – you can have a quid if you promise to visit you Grandma:

'That's really nice of you Mrs Ryan but I promised me Mam that I would visit me Grandma before I went to the match, so I'll have to go.' As he said this he retreated into the street and turned and walked away quickly in case Mrs Ryan thought of a way of keeping him at the house. She was still talking as he crossed the street and set off the half mile down the street to the Infirmary.

Grandma Bella Webster lay in a hospital bed. The doctor whom she had seen earlier that week had told her that there was little they could do for her cancer. At seventy four Bella was unperturbed by the news. She insisted that they told none of her relatives or friends – there were many of both that came to visit – Bella was a popular and well-known figure on Teesside. She never did get to become a

51

member of parliament like her hero Lady Astor, but she had been a councillor, activist, feminist and supporter of all manner of social causes through the whole of her life. Bella had supported lots of people through their last days so she now accepted that the same thing was happening to her. Death was a natural part of life, so she was ready.

She found it difficult to concentrate for very long now. The clock on the wall at the end of the ward would move several hours at a time between the times that she closed her eyes to collect her thoughts or to take a breath. Bella was drifting into death down a gentle slope shrouded in mist and lined with faded memories of her life. Ever since she had nursed Tommy, when the gas in his chest had brought them together, and had felt the pain in his voice she had learned to accept it without complaint. The morphine helped, turning the sharp twisting throbbing in her chest and stomach into a dull ache. It was difficult to remember now what day or time it was. Whenever a visitor arrived it was a surprise.

So when she saw Billy come through the doors she smiled and waved an unsteady hand at him. Billy smiled back, a tentative scared-of-where-I-am smile. He came up to the bed and stood at the end, not sure of what to say. He looked at his Grandma and suddenly realised how old and ill she looked. Her face was lined and sunk into her cheeks; the skin on her face and hands was a pinky-grey colour with tinges of yellow around her thin pale lips. The eyes that had been bright greeny-blue and had always twinkled when he was small were cloudy now and the thick white hair that he remembered had fallen away into straggles across her head, but there was still an edge to her voice.

'Well young Billy, have you finished staring at me?' she demanded.

'Yes Grandma, I mean, I didn't mean to stare, it's just you look...' he faltered and stopped.

'I look so old. Yes, I do, but I can still hear so fetch a chair and come and talk to me for a while.'

Billy found a chair and sat beside his Grandma. There was silence.

Bella had never found it hard to talk to young people so she started to get Billy to tell her about what he was doing. She began slowly, no sense putting him off, or frightening him away.

'Have you come in to see the match?'

'Yes, that's right Grandma', Billy replied.

Bella sighed, this might take a while, she thought back to when she last went to a match; it must have been with Tommy, before the war. 'Do they still wear red shirts, white shorts and stripes on their socks,' she tried.

'Oh no Grandma, there's new kit this season they've got big white yoke collars on their shirts and just the one stripe on their socks. The yokes look a bit daft, like girls' blouses Joe says,' Billy stopped, embarrassed.

Bella was unperturbed, 'will you be going to the pictures after that? What films have you seen this year, which was the best one?' She thought that three questions might just start Billy off on a conversation; it did, but not perhaps a conversation that she had expected.

'No, not tonight, but we went the other week, me and Jacky went to see Zulu. It was great, all about the Zulu wars in Africa in the last century. We won of course – the battle scenes were great.' He carried on telling Bella about the final battle scene with spears and bayonets. Bella closed her eyes and remembered Tommy finally telling her about the horror of the Great War in France and sighed as she thought about how short people's memories were. It was only nineteen years since the Second World War had sent home another generation of men who never wanted to fight again, including Tommy, and yet here was her grandson revelling in the idea of killing people. She opened her eyes as Billy's voice stopped and she saw him looking at her anxiously:

'Are you all right Grandma? Do you want me to get someone for you?'

'No son I'm fine. I was just remembering your Grandda and his time in France in the 1914-18 war.'

'Oh I'm sorry Grandma; I didn't mean to go on.' Billy said.

'It's fine Billy. I sometimes wonder what will happen when the countries we ruled for all those years begin to be more powerful than Britain,' she mused.

'That won't happen Grandma, now the country's growing again we'll be just as strong as we were before. Did you read about the Forth Road Bridge, it's the largest suspension bridge in Europe, the fourth largest in the World? We made the steel for it here on Teesside as well. Me and Joe have finished our apprenticeships Grandma. No worries about a job now. The world still wants Teesside steel; we're set up for life now. Don't you worry about us Grandma we'll be fine.'

'That's what your Grandda Tommy said son, when he came back from the war in 1918. We were just married. Tommy said there would be work for everyone – the government had promised them all,' she drifted off to sleep for a few minutes and Billy groaned to himself. He'd heard from his Da about Grandma Bella's thoughts on the Great Depression. He glanced at the clock and wondered if he could slip out while she was asleep, but he found he couldn't bring himself to move. Bella stirred again and carried on her thought:

'It was only the war in the 1940's that saved Teesside. You've heard of the Sydney Harbour Bridge I suppose?' she asked.

'Oh yes Grandma, there's a picture of it in the main offices at the works, we built that as well.' Billy said proudly.

'Did you know it was made at a great loss and that Dorman Longs nearly closed, partly because of it?' she asked.

'No Grandma, that can't be right surely,' he said.

'I'm afraid it is son. I was on the council by then and knew some of the union men at the works. All the young ones who were unemployed, who hadn't been through the first war, were hoping that the next war would come for the extra work. It did and gave us another thirty years of work, and now here we are struggling for work again and uncertain of the future.' She paused again out of breath.

'Surely not Grandma, British Steel is famous all over the world we'll always have places to sell to, what with the Commonwealth and that,' Billy said.

'I'm not so sure son, do you know what I think, I think that one day Teesside will stop making steel altogether and the works will close. See what's happening to the railways and the iron ore mines. Now that North Skelton has closed all steel-making on Teesside depends on importing iron ore from abroad. You mark my words Young Billy (he hated being called Young Billy), steel making will finish on Teesside, maybe not in my lifetime, but most likely in yours.'

'That's rubbish Grandma, Dorman Long is a giant company, it'll never go under, I'll have a job for life. You do have the daftest ideas. Next thing you'll be saying it will be owned by foreigners. How about India Grandma; that would be good wouldn't it,' Billy laughed. Then he stopped. His Grandma was serious. 'Grandma there's been steel-making on Teesside ever since anyone can remember.'

'Ah well Billy that's not quite true, you see your great, great Grandda, John, was born in 1829 and when he was born there was no steelworks, no mines, no Middlesbrough and no railways, so you see it doesn't take long for things to change does it.'

Billy was silent for a while. 'No, not when you put it like that Grandma.'

Bella dozed for a few moments and then another memory came to her; she opened her eyes and said to Billy:

'John's sister Mary knew a man who fought in the Napoleonic wars in the eighteenth century, William he was called, just like you. He left Mary a telescope that he got while he was a sailor. He left it to Mary when he died. It's still in the family, it's in the old bureau at home, would you like to see it,' she asked.

'Yes, that would be great Grandma, as soon as you get home you can show it to me,' said Billy, careful not to remind his Grandma how she always mentioned the telescope when he came to see her. 'Now if it's alright I need to get off to the match, it's been good to talk to you, I'll come again, take care of yourself Grandma.' Billy got up and leant over and kissed his Grandma on the forehead and smiled at her, 'see you soon.'

'Oh yes son, you get on now, don't miss the match, and take care of yourself, and that young Peggy you're so smitten with, take care of her as well.'

Billy left without looking back and never saw his Grandma again.

Bella smiled to herself, exhausted by the conversation with her Grandson but happy that she had a last chance to see him and knowing that the telescope would have a good home. She died later that evening in her sleep.

Step two – Jane

High summer morals
No ironstone mole lives here
Dreams, ambition, hope

Sarah, Prospect View – Summer 2014

The bus broke down outside the Fountain Hotel on Ladgate Lane; so naturally the girls told the driver they would wait for the replacement inside. It was quiz night. Iqbal Masurkar was in the lounge with his friends, studying the environment and the people in it. He had come straight to the pub from his grandparents' home and he had in his pocket his grandmother's term time bribe. Iqbal had come to 'research' the social history of Britain for his University course. Until recently he had never been into a pub, but the friends he was with had and they had decided to take his research into hand. This was, they said, the fourth sort of pub to visit, one that provided hotel accommodation as well a place to drink.

Iqbal's research had caused a fractious and heated argument with his grandmother which had only reinforced his determination to finish his project. Tonight's challenge was to talk to some 'locals'. Recalling the dire consequences that his grandmother had spelt out, Iqbal went up to the bar. He arrived just as Sally and her friends came through the door to wait for the bus to be fixed or for a replacement to appear. To Sally the tall, narrow hipped, darkly handsome young man was just who she needed to keep her in drinks while she waited for the bus. Her friends told her that he probably would not drink, well not properly, and would not speak to her. Sally could not resist the challenge; she walked up to the bar. The quiz was well under way.

'When did the first horse drawn carriage appear in Mumbai?' the man by the bar asked.

'I bet you'll know that one, where you come from,' said Sally.

'Pardon?' said Iqbal.

'That one, that question, about the carriage,' she said.

Iqbal smiled, politely, the wrong message, Sally was sure she was in, and for some strange reason she was. Iqbal never quite understood what happened in those few moments between them. As for Sally, without her knowing, the broken down bus was to give her a life line. All she had to do was not to let go or break it. Being Sally she would do so several times but that was in the future. For now she needed a drink and a challenge. She was sure she could get the young man to provide both.

'As it happens, I do know,' said Iqbal.

'Hey, you sound just like Jimmy.' Sally sounded surprised.

'Who's Jimmy?' asked Iqbal.

'Oh, he lives just across the road, fixes my car. He's lived on Teesside all his life.'

'So have I.'

'You're kidding; I thought you was' – Sally paused – even she had heard of racism. 'Well, you know, you being, well,' she stopped.

'Well what?' Iqbal began to realise her hesitation.

'Well, like, Indian and that,' said Sally.

Iqbal considered his options. He could walk away and leave this, hmmm, late thirties, perhaps early forties, badly dressed, cheaply made up woman at the bar. On the other hand, he paused, he needed someone like her for his social history research. He sighed, quietly, and made up his mind to take the chance.

'1874,' he said.

'What?' said Sally?

'1874, the date when the first horse drawn carriage appeared in Mumbai,' he explained.

'There I knew you'd know.' She turned to her friends, smiled, winked and then turned back.

'You gonna buy me a drink?' she asked.

Iqbal thought of his grandmother's reaction and smiled to himself. He waited to see if this woman who appeared to have no manners and no scruples would say anything else, please perhaps. No, she didn't. It was 10.00 pm and Sally had already had six vodka splits before they caught the bus and her smile wasn't quite as in control as she thought – it ran across her face in a slightly, leery, silly way. Only someone else who was the wrong side of sober would have been taken in. Certainly her eyes looked past the young Teesside University student researcher with only one marginally thought out purpose. Sally wanted to enjoy herself.

'Yes, why not, what would you like,' said the student.

'I thought you'd never ask, vodka split, handsome. I'm sitting over there with me friends. We're waiting for the bus to be fixed. Thought we'd pop in here for a drink. What you doing here?' said the woman.

'We've come for the quiz,' said Iqbal pointing over to his friends who had stopped listening to the quiz and were busy speculating what their sometimes erratic friend might end up doing this time. 'May I take you over and introduce you?' he added.

Sally giggled and wobbled at the same time. This combination unsettled her flimsy top so that even Iqbal had to notice her breasts as they struggled to stay out of sight. Turning away quickly he ordered the vodka split, tentatively as it was the first time he had ever done so and just a little suspicious that she might be winding him up. There was no reaction from the man behind the bar so he also ordered another of the family of nondescript 'fresh' orange juices that the pub trade provided as its answer to the painfully, slowly and only minimally improving, responsible drink-driver community that visited pubs. It was all there was to satisfy drivers who didn't want to fart all night on lime and lemon or coke. Iqbal handed the bottle to Sally.

'Do you want a glass?' he asked. Straight away from her reaction he knew it wasn't the right thing to say.

'No darlin', I feel safer with a bottle, strange men can't put things in it so easily.' Sally was sure he wouldn't, but she put her thumb over the top anyway, habit as much as anything. They went over to the table where Iqbal's friends were sitting. He began to introduce them. Dave, Leon and Joe. Sally leaned over obligingly and shook the proffered hands. Leon was across the table and as she reached over she sensed the glue in their eyes as they took in her body. Kids she thought.

'Oh, I'm Iqbal by the way and I'm sorry but I don't know your name.'

'I'm Sally. Thanks for the drink. I think I'll get back to me friends, don't want to miss me bus do I.'

Iqbal took his chance. 'Would you consider helping me with research for my University project?' he asked. Dave nearly swallowed his glass and Joe spat peanuts over the table, inevitably one found its way down Sally's top and began to itch almost immediately.

'Your what?' for once she was thrown by a man's chat up line. What sort of a question was that?

'My project, I'm doing a project on the social history of Teesside and I need to speak to different sorts of people. I wondered if you would help?' He paused. 'I hope you don't mind me asking?'

* * *

Sally didn't go home on the bus. Iqbal gave her a lift home. She asked him in and he saw, or rather he heard the dog as soon as he got through the door. Iqbal was scared. He didn't do dogs at the best of times and this one was savage. Sally was astride the dog. It was the only way she could hold onto it. Balanced on her high heels with her legs wide apart, Iqbal, crouched down in the corner by the front door could see clearly that Sally had matching red and black underwear. For a few seconds he was absorbed by the red silken material with black edging on both panties and bra at the end of her legs and under her top, which was now really askew. Sally backed slowly and awkwardly along the corridor, dragging the dog with her. She reached the door, managed to get it open and somehow got the dog outside. Muffled swearing and the rattle of a chain came through the now closed door. Iqbal began to straighten up, from his knees bent, arm protecting crouch and started to leave. Sally returned through the door, without the dog.

'Hey don't go; it'll be fine now, come into the front room. I'll introduce you to...' Sally stopped, 'shit' she said, 'I've forgotten the bairn.' Go on in I just need to ring me Dad, Sarah's round there.' She took Iqbal by the arm, and to his surprise managed to guide him un-protesting through the hallway door into the jumbled front room where he was sat down between the magazines, clothes and odd pieces of discarded food containers.

* * *

It was almost midnight; even by Sally's standards she was late. Sarah could hear her Grandparents talking about it in the kitchen.

'The bairn needs to get home to bed, she's school tomorrow,' she heard her Grandma say.

'Aye I know Peg, you don't need to keep on so,' replied her Grandda.

'You've got to say something to her, you're the only one she'll take any notice of Bill,' said her Grandma.

'I've tried. God knows I've tried, but you know as well as I do that Sally's agreeing and Sally's doing are altogether different things.'

'Huh! There's nothing in her head except herself.'

'Hush Peg, the bairn'll hear. Where did we go wrong with ...' Grandda's voice was cut off by the closing of the kitchen door so Sarah never got to hear what the 'with' was, but she knew really, they'd had this conversation before. Her Mam was never able to do what she said or planned. Sarah sighed and snuggled back into the big chair. It was three months since she had asked her Grandda if he thought she might grow up like her Mam. She had thought about it once or twice since then and because she could think of no answer that she liked had decided to try and accept the way they lived, after all, it was the only way she had ever lived. It was not as if her Mam had ever been any different. It looked likely that she would be staying the night again.

She looked across at the telescope on its rack and wondered if she could persuade her Grandda to tell her some more about her family. She had been captivated by Bella and for a long while afterwards had thought it would be good to be like her, but at the same time she was fascinated by Aunt Jane. She sounded very clever – maybe she would be like Jane – that wouldn't be too bad would it? In the kitchen Billy and Peggy were repeating a conversation they had had before and would have again and were unlikely to come to any conclusion or agreement on.

As soon as her Grandda came back into the parlour Sarah asked him her question:

'Grandda, you remember when you told me about Grandma Bella and how she planned to get the telescope back from Aunt Jane?' she began.

'What's that love?' replied Billy, distracted by his argument with Peggy and his concern about how late it was and Sally's non-appearance. They would have to make up the fold away bed again so Sarah could stay the night. It wasn't the first time and despite his protestations to his wife, deep down Billy knew it would not be the last.

'Aunt Jane, how did she end up in Darlington, didn't you say that's where she went to live? Did she get married and have any children? How did Grandma Bella find her and persuade her to give back the telescope?'

Billy swore under his breath, frustration getting the better of him. How could his daughter pay so little attention to this bright, inquisitive girl who wanted to know about the whole World and how it got there? He spoke with a lump in his throat:

'Sarah lass I think you're going to have to stay over tonight, there's no sign of your Mam. I'm going to make up the fold away bed. You can sleep in one of your Grandma's old nighties,' he said.

'Oh! That'll be a laugh,' said his granddaughter and stood up from the old chair. 'Then you can tell me about Jane so I can lie in bed and dream about what happened?'

Billy, sighed, he wished the innocence of youth had stayed in his life. That way perhaps he would be able to accept how Sally lived in the same easy manner that Sarah seemed to. He hesitated over his next thought. Maybe Sarah was more like her Mam than he wanted to admit. They made the bed up together. Sarah went into the kitchen, made her Grandma laugh and came back with some biscuits and hot chocolate. Billy smiled, for such a scary lady his wife could be a real softie sometimes. Perhaps Sarah had the right idea, life would do as it liked despite everyone else's plans – best let it get on with itself. He sat down in his chair, now jammed against the end of the bed and reached for one of his notebooks. He turned to the back where he wrote down the family's ancestry in each notebook whenever he started a new one.

Peggy Webster paused at the bedroom door to sneak a look in and to listen to the conversation. For once she had much the same thought as her husband. The lass was happy so what did it matter what her home life was like. All the while they could help they would. Then she shook her head, the two of them were off into the Webster family history again; she went back to the kitchen, there was some ironing to do. She still had some of Sarah's school clothes from last week; she may as well get them ready for the morning.

In the parlour Billy was recounting what his Grandma Bella had told him about Jane.

'Jane was always determined to move away from Eston. When Grandma Bella found out about her she discovered that Jane had done everything she could to avoid being associated with us Websters. Apparently she managed to get introduced to a well to do Darlington family and married the eldest son,' – Billy consulted his book:

'Alexander, they were married in eighteen eighty three. I think that was after she started to teach at the girls' school in Eston when it opened in eighteen seventy four.' Billy consulted his notebook again. 'Jane and Alexander Beaumont had just one child, Maximillian Albert Alexander Beaumont, that sounds grand doesn't it; I wonder what he was like? Grandma Bella never met him, but she heard that he went off to Canada,' Billy chuckled as he remembered his Grandma's account, 'probably to escape his mother. There, that should be enough to get you dreaming and off to sleep. Good night pet, sleep well.' Billy stood up to leave the parlour; he went to the top of the bed and leant over to kiss his granddaughter on the forehead before leaving the room.

'Grandda,' said a sleepy voice.

'Yes lass,' he said.

'I don't want to leave me Mam, she's the only Mam I've got and she needs looking after,'

Billy coughed and left the room, the lump back in his throat.

Sarah snuggled down into the big double duvet that covered the small fold away bed entirely and went off to sleep in Victorian Eston where, unlike Sarah, her ancient relation Aunt Jane had dedicated her life to escaping from her family.

Jane, Eston – 1857

Jane Webster was always going to be spoilt. Her parents were both determined for different reasons to ensure that her life should be everything that theirs had never been. Her father was determined that she should have the love and care of the parents that he never had; her mother that she should never in her life have to endure the trauma that blighted her youth. So in the critical formative years up to her fourth birthday she had the unrestricted, unchallenged attention of five adults showered onto her in an unremitting period of indulgence. When Jane sat down at the head of the table in the Webster's farmhouse kitchen for her own unshared fourth birthday tea party, an event unknown for the majority of other four year olds in either Eston or California, her character was already set.

In eighteen fifty seven the two villages were full of growth and opportunity. The new settlement of California had several streets of single-storey mine cottages. One of the streets Prospect View was where the youngest branch of the Webster family had made their home. Ann Webster, the mother of the household, would never recover from her experiences in Middlesbrough, but the fear and loathing with which she had come to view her life had subsided and she now channelled the fierce steel centre of her otherwise frail body into her small family. Ann sacrificed everything she had for John and Jane. Mary her sister-in-law, with whom she had a close but not emotional relationship, had tried to get her involved in the village life of Eston –

with no success. She had also tried, with the help of the parson's wife, to get Ann to talk about her troubled life. She would to a point; she would talk animatedly about her childhood in a lead-mining community high up in Weardale where she had grown up. About Sundays with her father and learning to read and write at the chapel with the minister, but when they tried to find out what had happened to her family and how she had ended up in a Middlesbrough brothel she would withdraw in on herself and all conversation would stop.

The only real benefit from their visits to the parson's wife was an offer to educate Jane. Jane had inherited her father's inquisitive, questioning nature and her mother's steely determination and the combination proved an excellent foil for the bumbling efforts of the parson's wife – Jane absorbed everything that she was taught and over the next ten years she began to realise a dream that she developed at an early age – a wish to get away from the simple, hard-working largely contented farming and mining communities that she grew up in. She was determined to make something of herself, as John put it. To do so she would need money and she soon learned how to manipulate her parents into a very efficient money saving team. Ann spent her life economising on everything they lived on in order to give Jane what she wanted. John applied his thin wiry body to his new job at the Venture mine obsessively and as a result of her parents' efforts and her own determination to learn Jane, gradually outgrew her humble upbringing and became a demanding, driven young woman who was increasingly alienated from her Webster family and through her contact with the parson's wife began to develop a circle of acquaintances – it was unlikely that Jane ever had friends, another inheritance from her mother – away from Prospect View. Jane grew to hate her life there.

* * *

In so far as it was possible to become an educated and accomplished woman in the eighteen sixties, Jane Webster – even her name caused her to wince – had a number of very clear goals in her life. The first was to become a teacher. She had decided, in conversation with the Parson's wife, that being a teacher was one of the only ways a Victorian woman could become independent.

Jane's second goal was to get married. She had observed the relationship between her parents and between the Parson and his wife and had decided that the two men's subservient manner was the proper order of things so that was what was needed. Jane was a naturally domineering young woman and was determined not to be controlled by any man. It was ironic given the circumstances of her mother's experience of men; it was just what her mother might have advised her had they ever been close enough to discuss anything so personal. The two of them never did, Jane treated her mother as a servant, a role that Ann accepted, much as she had accepted everything in her life after her escape from Commercial Street. Jane needed a safe, pliable, middle-class Victorian man and it was whilst visiting the Parson's wife that she identified the perfect candidate, Alexander Beaumont. Mistress Jane Beaumont had the necessary ring about it to satisfy her aspirations and when she thought about it, it would be the perfect solution to her other objective as well. Once she had found herself a position as a teacher she would turn her attention to the entrapment of Alexander, she would refuse to call him Alexey as his other friends appeared to do.

Jane's final objective, based on her conversations and her occasional expeditions with the Parson's wife, was to live in Darlington; with its increasingly modern transport networks, including a link to London, the capital of the world. London: a place you could get to from Darlington in a day despite the enormous distance – nearly three hundred miles, four to six weeks walk for her father and uncles. Darlington was to Jane the civilised centre of the North and certainly the only place to live in the Tees Valley. That was where she was going to live.

Her plans did not come to fruition overnight. To get a working-class girl from the mining and farming communities of Eston and California to be a successful middle-class and influential woman in Victorian Britain was going to take some doing, but if anyone could do it, it would be Jane. Her plan began to have some chance of progress when the two villages started to talk about having their own schools. The remote nature of the area and the increasingly harsh, heavily polluted environment, brought about by heavy industry (albeit recently placed on the map of the civilised world courtesy of a visit by the prime minister) would make it difficult to attract teachers. Jane realised this would help her in her efforts to have herself considered for the role of teacher. By courting the patronage and contacts of the Parson's wife and in turn their influence on Alexander's parents she would eventually get the opportunity to apply for the position of teacher at one of the new schools. Before that, and to be able to get into a position where she could apply, she needed money; for that Jane put more pressure on her parents to help. They were embarrassingly proud of their daughter's aspirations and resolutely ignored the incredulous comments from their friends and family. To pay for the clothes and materials she would need, John took on a second job as a Night-watchman.

With her plan in place Jane was ready to take the first steps in her ambition to leave her roots behind. It was about this time that she decided that she should have the family heirloom, the old sailor's telescope. It sat in dusty neglect on the mantelpiece of the rarely used front parlour in the Webster farmhouse parlour. Jane told her father that it would make a suitable twenty-first birthday present and being Jane assumed that was that; the telescope would arrive when she expected it.

Jane, Eston – 1867

Jane's escape from Eston was helped as much by the Victorians' increasing resolve and understanding of the need to educate the working classes as it was by her privileged status in the Webster family.

For the latter there were five adults to raise income from the farm and two jobs that John struggled with; combined they managed to afford to pay for schooling, so Jane attended school regularly from the age of six. Additional private tuition from the Parson's wife helped to give Jane a much wider education than she would have received from the narrow curriculum of the voluntary school she first went to. That, plus Jane's regular attendance at school helped her to be chosen as a monitor, a position that gave her the opportunity to teach others. It also enabled her in eighteen sixty seven, at the age of thirteen, to take up a position helping a teacher acquaintance of the Parson's wife. Jane's determination and opportunity allowed her to sit and pass the Queen's Scholarship examination so that two years after the new girls' school opened in Eston Miss Jane Webster was appointed as a teacher, a noteworthy and rare event.

Although when in conversation with her acquaintances Jane averred that her success was almost exclusively down to her own efforts, there was a necessary acknowledgement of the part played by the Parson's wife. Jane had to admit, at least to herself, that without that lady's help and patronage she would never have been able to get where she wanted to be.

Along with this personal support, Jane was helped immeasurably by the development of education in Victorian Britain. Two particular milestones in this development were key to Jane's success. The first was the Science and Art Departments' examination introduced in eighteen sixty six which Jane passed successfully in eighteen seventy four; the second was the Education Act of eighteen seventy which led indirectly to the building of two new schools in Eston, one of which, a school for girls, had given Jane the opportunity to get her first teaching position.

Jane quickly established herself as an excellent teacher in the eyes of the people she wanted to impress, the governors and sponsors of education in the Tees valley. She was able to keep discipline in her class and in her eyes, as a consequence, achieved excellent results amongst the girls she taught. She had little patience or inclination to teach boys, they were much better employed working anyway.

What was of most importance to Jane though, even in the success of her new position, in what was a very male-dominated society, was the opportunity her new status gave her. The most practical consequence was that her new role paid her money. With money Jane could afford to dress to conform to the level of society that she aspired to join. The fact that she had to wait until she was twenty five to make independent use of her money was not a major impediment, her grip on the affections of her father meant the money was relatively easy to get hold of.

Despite her new found ability and means to look the part in Victorian society, Jane knew that her only real avenue into the level of Darlington society that she wanted to be a part of was through marriage and that was Jane's next challenge. Jane set about ensnaring Alexander Beaumont.

Sarah, Prospect View – Summer 2014

A month later and Sarah was on her way from school to her grandparents' house. Today they had been talking about exams and jobs so they could think about subject options. Maybe Sarah should become a teacher like her great, great, however many times it was, Aunt Jane. It was the same day that her Mam had been contacted by the Housing Association office to make an appointment to visit the head office in Middlesbrough. Sally had rung during her dinner break:

'Nothing to worry about,' she had told Sarah. She had rung from Iqbal's car, 'It'll be the usual shit, just forms to fill in I expect. Can you ring your Grandma and tell her I'll pick you up from there tonight, catch you later.'

Sarah had never got used to her Mam swearing, but it was what she did. Her Mam was often going to offices to fill in forms for something. She agreed with her Mam; their life must be on more pieces of paper than anyone else in the world. Sarah had switched off her phone. Her Grandma didn't like phones so it was best not to ring, especially on a Monday.

When she arrived at Prospect View she smiled her Grandma into toast and peanut butter, horrible stuff her Grandma said, and went into the parlour to ask her Grandda about great Aunt Jane and what a Victorian school was like, but then she remembered, when she thought about it – her Grandda would be out, up at his allotment feeding his pigeons. There was no point in asking Grandma, she had no interest in family history, especially not on a Monday.

* * *

'It's up to you Mrs Webster,' the woman in the Housing Association office had said.

Sally had picked up the papers on the desk and folded them into her bag. It was a nice bag, leather, well cheap lookalike leather – she'd got it that Saturday. She'd wanted to get the shoes as well but she needed the money for drinks that weekend. If she didn't buy a round or two soon the girls would stop inviting her – so the shoes had to wait, just this once. Sally had replied to the woman at the desk in front of her.

'It's very kind of you to try and help us Mrs Ling.' Sally had paused to remember her story line. 'I'll be sure to get these filled in as soon as I can. I can bring the bills in with me too.' She had remembered to shake hands and smile before she left the office. Stupid Cow, what did she know? It was always the same. How did people like that get that job?

Hai Ling had got up from her seat and gone to the toilet. She had a few minutes before her next client arrived so she might be able to get a cup of tea as well. She had sighed as she sat in the cubicle, a moment of quiet in the often emotionally charged housing enquiry office where she worked. She had tried to imagine a culture that allowed its citizens to go through life with no effort to do anything except... She had paused in her thoughts, got up from the seat and remembered to put the paper into the pan and flush it all away – another change from her childhood upbringing. What sort of parents could bring up children to be like Sally Webster?

Sally had walked along the street towards the car park where Iqbal was waiting.

'Why shouldn't I come?' he had asked, 'wouldn't it help if you could say you were in a regular relationship?'

'No pet, you just wait here, trust me, I need to go on me own,' Sally had replied.

As she walked back to the car she stopped at a couple of shops and despite their agreement dipped into the final twenty pound note, almost without realising what she was doing, but the top was a bargain, only four ninety nine. By the time she got back she had the rest of the day and the evening sorted in her mind.

'How did you get on?' Iqbal had asked. He hadn't minded the wait he had used the time to read a business planning book. It was dry stuff, but he found it interesting.

'I fancy going to the pictures tonight, there's a new movie about a couple who meet on a bus. Do you fancy coming too?' Sally had asked as she climbed into the car, ignoring Iqbal's question.

'What happened? At the Housing office, you did go in didn't you? 'Iqbal had repeated.

'Oh that, yes, of course I went in, I said I would didn't I. It was the same old shit, just forms to fill in. There must be more forms with my name on in the world, than anyone else you can think of,' Sally had replied.

'So when are you going to fill them in?' Iqbal had repeated, unsure how anyone could be given a responsibility and not deal with it at once.

'Don't you start, you sound like that woman in the office or my mother. I'm getting enough aggravation from them without you joining in.'

'I'm trying to help. You said you wanted to get your life sorted out. You said you wanted my help. Last night, don't you remember?'

'Yes, probably.'

'Well then, when are you going to fill the forms in?' Iqbal had begun to get frustrated and his voice began to match his mood.

'Look Iqqy, I promise I'll fill them in, just not now, not today. I'm stressed out and I need to relax, to have some fun.'

They had driven out of the town back towards Eston. Neither of them had spoken again. Sally had desperately wanted a cigarette, but it wasn't her car and even she could see that Iqbal was in a bad mood. What was up with him? They were only forms. She'd get round to them sometime.

Iqbal was remembering his mother's advice. No, not advice stern warning, he had a lot of thinking to do. What sort of woman was this he had got into a relationship with? Maybe he should stop visiting this erratic woman and do his research another way? Sally surprised him again and drew him further into a relationship he had little control over.

'Come on Iqqy, (why didn't he say he hated being called Iqqy?) Tell you what, you said you wanted to find out about my life. Well it's the leek club quiz tomorrow night. You're good at quizzes, why don't you come, it'll be a laugh? I'll bet you'll get on great with old Freddie – he'll tell you all about leek growing.'

* * *

Sarah had to wait another two weeks to learn any more about the sort of Victorian school that great Aunt Jane might have taught in and by a bizarre stroke of luck it would be her Mam who, without doing anything in a planned way, helped her to do so. Sally was never able to say no to a good cause and equally she was never able to remember whose cause she had last supported so when she was handed the second prize in the leek club's raffle – she had no recollection of buying a ticket. Probably because it had been bought by Iqbal, who against all his better judgements had gone to the quiz night and had unaccountably enjoyed himself. Sally had hoped the envelope would contain money. No such luck, it contained two tickets to Beamish Museum – no use to Sally, but for some reason, just for once, she did not throw them away. So when Sarah asked her, more in hope than likelihood, if she could go and visit Beamish museum Sally was able to help.

'Mam, I don't supposed you've got any money for me to go to Beamish museum with Grandda have you?'

Sally grinned with the triumph of unplanned success:

'I can do better than that. I won some tickets for Beamish at the leek club. Just need to remember where I put them.'

Sally did manage to remember where she had put the tickets, behind the clock in the kitchen. Sarah had never expected her Mam to take her to the Museum; she knew her Mam had no interest in her Grandda's hunt for the Webster family. No, what was important to Sarah was that her Mam had remembered she had the tickets and much more impressively that she had delayed her Saturday shopping trip for half an hour while she looked for them. Sarah knew how much shopping meant to her Mam so she really appreciated the gesture. It was left to Grandda to work out how they would get to Beamish.

* * *

So on the first Wednesday of the summer holiday at quarter to nine in the morning Sarah and her Grandda were standing at the bus stop outside Eston Church Lane clinic waiting for the number 455 bus run by Leven Valley

Coaches. They travelled along Ladgate Lane and on into Middlesbrough via Linthorpe Road arriving at the bus station just after nine o'clock. From there they caught the X1 Arriva bus to Chester-Le-Street. Sarah had never been so far on a bus before and could not wait to tell her Grandma that they had seen some buffaloes on their way to Durham. They had enough time at Chester-Le-Street to have a drink before getting their last bus, a Go North East number 28 to Beamish. They got to the Museum at twenty past eleven.

Once they got through the entrance and into the Museum they stopped and looked at the map they had been given. Grandda asked Sarah what she wanted to do first. Sarah remembered her unasked question about Great Aunt Jane's school.

'Can we go on the tram, and look inside the school?' said Sarah, looking at the advert in the entrance foyer.

'Aye lass, then we can walk along to the old town,' Grandda replied.

They got off the tram at the top of the bank and walked down to the old school. So thanks to her Mam and her Grandda Sarah got her wish to visit the sort of school that Jane would have recognised, a school not that different from the school she had taught in a hundred and thirty years before. They walked along the street, turned in through the school entrance and along the corridor to the main classroom. Sitting in the desks, his knees bunched up under his chin – he would suffer when he got up again – Grandda talked about his own childhood at school. As usual he got carried away with his memories and Sarah drifted off into her own thoughts.

She got up and looked at the old maps and diagrams on the wall of the classroom. One of them was a map of Great Britain and Sarah tried to imagine Jane teaching her class geography – lists of rivers around the country: Swale, Ure, Nidd, Wharfe, Aire, Colne and Calder: lists of the world's oceans: Pacific, Atlantic, Indian, Antarctic – all ruled by the Royal Navy when Jane was teaching. Remembering the telescope Sarah turned back to her Grandda with another question:

'Grandda?' She asked.

'Eh, what's that pet,' he replied, interrupted from his day dream?

'Do you think that Jane took the telescope to school to show her pupils?'

'She might have done,' he said, 'what do you think?'

'I think she took it to school to show the children and when she did she managed to impress Alexander and that's how she got to marry him,' said Sarah.

'Very romantic,' said Grandda, unaware of how close to the truth his granddaughter had got.

Jane & Alexander, Eston – 1883

It took Jane another nine years after she started to teach at Eston girls' school before she managed to ensnare her man. It was not that Alexander was particularly difficult to ensnare. It was not that his parents, aware of his limited appeal to most of the eligible young girls that would make a fitting wife for their youngest son, were unprepared to consider any possible match for their son. No it was the enormous gap in social standing that was the main impediment. However, with the help of Jane's tenacious efforts to improve herself and the unstinting support of the Parson's wife the barriers were eventually broken down. The final step was achieved with the help of a visit to the school of a notable scientific dignitary from Darlington and his agreement to introduce Jane to Darlington society that gave her the introduction she needed; oh yes, and the telescope.

In truth Jane had forgotten all about the telescope. She had not needed it at all for her new position; she had just wanted to prove that she could get it. After Aunt Mary's death in eighteen seventy nine it sat in Jane's room in Prospect View and gathered dust. Then in eighteen eighty two an inspector from the Science and Art Department was scheduled to visit the school and it was agreed that he would observe one of Jane's lessons. Jane was determined to make a good impression as she had heard that the inspector lived in Darlington and she had never given up on her ultimate ambition to live in what to her was the only place to live in the Tees Valley. She prepared her lesson with great care.

'What are you going to teach the children Jane?' asked her father as he stood in the entrance to Jane's room in the cottage.

'I shall be teaching them some music and history,' Jane replied, 'I have read in the London papers,' – Jane still received second hand copies of The Chronicle from one of her acquaintances in Stockton, several weeks old, but socially acceptable nonetheless, – 'that a new symphony has been composed by Tchaikovsky called the 1812 overture. It was written to commemorate the retreat of the French Grande Armée from Russia in the winter of 1812. I shall instruct the children on the dates and events of that time.'

'Why don't you show them the old telescope,' suggested her father. He was the only person in the Webster family that Jane had any time for, mostly due to her need for money to help her keep up her position and continue her quest to move up in society. Even so Jane treated the suggestion with the condescending affection that she had developed towards her father.

'Hmmn, I have not settled on a definite plan yet so I might consider that idea, however, what you might help with Papa is some money towards a new outfit that I shall definitely require for the event. I plan to go to Stockton-On-Tees this weekend to have a fitting.'

'Aye, pet, I think I can do that,' replied her father – he loved to see her all dressed up, it made him very proud.

Jane winced at his term of endearment; she was not some sort of animal to be called a pet, it reinforced her wish to be elsewhere than the rough working class community she was forced to live in by the accident of her birth, but she did need the money.

'That would be most kind of you Papa, how much might I expect?' she added.

'I suppose I could give you a sovereign,' he said slowly. He had been saving carefully; John was an inveterate saver by both habit and need. His plan to build a new bed would have to wait. Ann and he would have to continue to sleep in the rickety bed they had now had for nearly thirty years.

'That would be most satisfactory Papa; I am most indebted to you,' replied Jane.

John smiled; his pride in what his strange daughter had turned herself into, and his wife's slavish efforts to protect her at all costs, concealed the way she treated them; her two sisters and brother had never managed to compete with her in either attention or care. He knew when he thought about it that he and his wife had helped to make Jane the spoilt, demanding woman that she was and that in doing so they had done nothing to make her want to stay with them. He accepted that eventually she would leave, but he still hoped that she would stay in touch with them.

Jane, in her own time, decided that the telescope would be a useful aid to her teaching and so it was taken down from its rack above the mantelpiece, cleaned and polished – by Ann of course – and studied by Jane. Whatever her faults might be, planning and preparation were not amongst them, so by the time the inspector's visit came around Jane was as well prepared as any of the teachers. It was no surprise that she was picked out for special praise in his remarks to the governors as he was leaving the school. Amongst the various visitors and their friends were Mister and Mistress Beaumont and their son Alexander. It was a while since Jane had seen Alexander. She recalled the ill-fated excursion to Harrogate with her then friend Emily, Alexander's cousin. Jane brushed aside the embarrassing events of that day, now eight years ago, when her lack of money had caused her to be treated with pity by Emily – their friendship had waned from that date, mostly because of Jane's refusal to accept any sort of charity from anyone.

Mister and Mistress Beaumont, as Governors of the school had come to witness the inspector's visit and their son Alexander had accompanied them. Along with the other dignitaries they had sat at the back of the class to view Jane's lesson on the history of the French retreat from Moscow in 1812 – the girls had behaved very well, reciting the various dates and events that Jane had drilled into them with no prompting and no mistakes, but it had been Jane's knowledge and reference to the telescope – somewhat far from its true origins it must be said – that had captured Alexander's imagination.

As a result of the inspector's visit and his glowing testimonial to Jane, shared with several of the Beaumont's acquaintances in Darlington, she managed to secure a position as a private tutor to a series of influential families in the Town and some small but acceptable lodgings with a respectable widow on the edge of the right part of the Town. Jane had her fingers into the corner of her lifelong ambition, to move away from Eston. Once away from Eston, she worked with determination and some guile – there was not much romance it must be said – to manoeuvre Alexander and his family into accepting her as an acceptable wife and daughter in law. It was generally accepted in their part of Darlington society that the parents were more enamoured by the union than was Alexander.

No Websters went to the wedding. It took endless patience from Alexander and a rare and lucky over indulgence in wine by his wife to consummate the marriage one late snowy evening in March of eighteen eighty four and so it was that Jane had to suffer the messy, unfulfilling and tiresome event of childbirth. Her disgust in the whole business of sex had a strange parallel to the experiences of her mother – the two of them had never exchanged a word about the carnal nature of marriage so like her mother Jane was totally unprepared for what she had subsequently informed Alexander would be the only time she would be caught out again. Maximillian, their son, grew up believing that parents always had separate rooms. It took some time for Jane to realise that having a son had some kudos in the society she was adopting, by which time he had been handed over to first wet nurse and then a series of nannies and governesses. Relieved of the onerous and very tiresome duties of parenthood Jane was free to indulge in the last part of her childhood ambition to become a leading figure in Darlington Society. Jane Beaumont, neé Webster had arrived. She never looked back.

Jane & Maximillian, Darlington – Winter 1896

In December of eighteen ninety six on a cold foggy morning the postman delivered two packages to the Beaumont house in Woodland Terrace. The two items had been posted from unconnected sources. It was not until they arrived on the Beaumont's drawing room table that they began to work together to influence the lives of Jane and her son Maximillian, through a series of events that would dictate the outcome of their lives and the telescope that was now housed in a glass case in the same drawing room.

Jane no longer needed to rely on an acquaintance's second hand copy of the London Chronicle to impress her visitors with. The latest news from the capital and around the world was delivered direct to her house. Next to the rolled up newspaper in its brown-paper wrapping, on the polished mahogany table that Jane had just purchased, was a large package from Suffolk, from a school run by the Religious Society of Friends, Quakers.

The newspaper was the same one that had helped Jane to impress Alexander with her knowledge of history and music at Eston girls' school. This time though it wasn't Jane that would draw inspiration from its pages it was to be her son. In eighteen ninety six Maximillian, now twelve, had inherited his father's shyness and was a source of frustration to his mother. Jane wanted him to have the same determination and drive as she did, to have a clear idea of what he wanted to be and to pursue it with the steely intensity that she had inherited from her mother, but he didn't.

Maximillian had no idea what he wanted to do or become, he showed no sign of ambition at all. As a result his mother was faced with a dilemma. Most of her plans for the further progression of her family and therefore of her own, still much inhibited by being a woman, were going to depend on the successful advancement of her son. As a result Jane, never a close loving parent had come to the conclusion that a spell away from the family home might do him good. She was concerned that his close relationship with his father, who encouraged his softness, was in danger of making the boy a mollycoddle. A pampered effeminate son was not anywhere in Jane's plans.

When she had arrived in Darlington she had come to appreciate the impact of the 'Quakers' on the town and its society, particularly its middle-class educated society, the society that Jane aspired to and the society that she had married into. Recently she had brought into her circle of close acquaintances a member of the group with whom Jane had had an interesting discussion about alternate methods of education and had been told about Quaker Schools and in particular one in Saffron Walden, in Suffolk, that her new acquaintance had recently sent her two children to. Jane had decided to find out more about it. The package was from the school.

Maximillian had inherited one attribute from his mother, he was a compulsive reader and he had recently discovered that the London newspaper his mother displayed in her drawing room for the benefit of visitors was a source of interesting information. The copy that arrived that December morning was no exception; it contained an article that caused him to retreat to his attic room, to sit in the window, knees pulled up under his chin, allowing his imagination to put himself into a position of strength and determination well above his age. He lay awake most of that night planning his new life. Next morning it was a pleasant surprise for Jane when he approached her with a request.

'Mama?' he began.

'Yes Maximillian,' Jane always used his full name, unlike Alexander who called his son Max when she was out of earshot.

'I've been thinking.' He said.

'Good that's encouraging, and have your thoughts borne any fruits of action or ambition?' Jane asked.

'Yes, Mama they have. I have a request,' he replied.

'Maybe I should sit down,' said his mother. She had that ability to undermine whatever attempt he made to speak to his mother positively, but this time he was sure he had found a way out of his depressing life. He thought again about the article in the London newspaper. Gold had been discovered again. This time in the Canadian provinces in the Yukon, wherever that might be, and people were leaving from Europe in their hundreds to make their way to a place called Dawson City to make their fortunes. Maximillian had decided that this would be the answer to his miserable existence. In one move he would be away from the misery of his life at home; constantly either berated by or ignored by his mother; doted on with overwhelming and suffocating affection by his father. Not only that his school life was an equally constant trial of bullying and attention. He was clever, which bought him to the attention of the teachers prompted by his mother to push him on, and the resulting resentful animosity of his fellow pupils who had neither the capability or the wish to be so 'damned clever' as 'matchstick' was.

'Is the old telescope going to be mine?' asked Maximillian.

Jane had forgotten all about the telescope in its glass case in the drawing room. When she had first set up home with Alexander she had little of her own to make an impression with so she had persuaded him to let her have it mounted in a case so she could point it out to visitors. Jane had outgrown it soon enough and whilst it remained in the drawing room it seemed to shrink into the background to be forgotten by everyone except the maid whose job it was to dust and polish it once a week. The telescope was farthest from Jane's mind that morning. While her son had been swept away to the Canadian mountains in search of freedom and gold Jane had been planning out his education and future political career. She answered without considering the question.

'Yes, it will, why do you ask?' she replied. To her amazement Maximillian, didn't reply straight away, but asked another question. She began to focus on his request and consider what might lie behind it.

'Do you think it is worth very much?' asked her son.

Jane paused before answering; why would he ask that she wondered. Did he have some silly scheme to sell it, but why would he want money. She thought back through the few occasions when she had spoken to her son recently to see if she could recall anything he might want. No, nothing came to mind, she would have to go along with his questions for the moment.

'Well it might be worth something, it's a genuine relic from the Great War. There are people who are collectors of Napoleonic memorabilia. It would have to be valued to get a proper opinion.' she replied.

Maximillian was surprised; he had expected an outright refusal to discuss the telescope. He was never able to understand his mother; there was no point in trying now so he might as well continue with his plan.

'Who would be able to value it?' he asked trying to sound non-committal.

Ah, thought his mother he does want to sell it, but why?

'Well the best person would be a specialist maritime antique dealer. Most likely in Newcastle upon Tyne,' she said, interested to see her son's reaction to this complication.

Maximillian tried to avoid the flicker in his heart beat. His plan needed to get him to a port to find out about passages to Canada and he had been unsure how he would be able to without arousing suspicion. Here was an opportunity given to him by his mother, how could he make the most of it. Incredibly she provided the answer to that as well.

Jane needed to test his resolve for whatever plan he had in mind. Normally Maximillian was easily put off most of his plans when decisions had to be made or decisive actions taken.

'I shall enquire as to the best establishment to approach and then as you are of an age where an expedition might be of benefit to your education I think we might consider allowing you to travel to Newcastle upon Tyne yourself to find out the value of the telescope. Do you think that would be an acceptable plan?' She added the last question in as off-hand manner as she could to see if there would be any clue from her son as to the true purpose of his request, she was disappointed Maximillian for once played her at her own game.

'That would be most acceptable Mama, I am grateful for your interest, how might I be able to travel to Newcastle?' he said, still not sure he was getting the agreement of his mother to his plan.

'Oh I think you should go on the railway. Mrs Brown can accompany you to the train station.' she replied.

So it was that a week later, following Jane's enquiries and subsequent correspondence with a Ships' Chandlers in Newcastle upon Tyne, that Maximillian found himself on a train leaving Darlington station heading north. He pushed himself back into the corner seat trying to make himself invisible to the world. There were two other people in the carriage. In the opposite corner a man, at least Maximillian assumed it was a man, sat behind a newspaper that had not been lowered or folded; in fact had hardly moved since the housekeeper had left him in the carriage at Darlington. Two large, black, slightly scuffed boots stuck out from a pair of black trousers which disappeared up under the foot of the newspaper.

Opposite Maximillian sat a woman with a stained mob cap and a long black dress that reached the floor. She was looking out of the window so that only the right side of her face showed. A red, tear-stained eye on a weathered, blotchy, tired face. Neither had spoken to Maximillian.

Next to him on the stained green leather seat was a package. It was about two feet long and cylindrical. The woman, peering at it through the reflection in the window tried to imagine what it could be. A tube, but a tube of what? It had looked quite heavy when the large, round, friendly woman who had accompanied the boy into the carriage had set it down next to him. It could be valuable, or at least precious; the boy kept checking it was there. Food? No food would only be valuable to someone who was poor and the boy did not look poor at all. Well fed, well dressed, well cared for. Papers? Legal stuff? Possibly? The train passed out of the cutting and the reflection disappeared. The woman lost interest and peered, half-heartedly across the overgrown shrubs and brambles towards a small meandering river beyond. She had no idea what was in the parcel.

Maximillian's journey to Newcastle upon Tyne was an immense disappointment to him. He wasn't sure if it was his visit to the Shipping Agents office of Shaw Savill & Co where he was advised that he should tell his parents or guardian that the fare required to board an emigration steamer would be forty eight pounds of which fifteen pounds would be required as a deposit beforehand, or his subsequent visit to the Ship's Chandlers where he was advised that the telescope was not an uncommon object and more importantly it was unlikely to be worth anything like the amount he needed for the passage to Canada, always assuming he could get to Liverpool anyway. Maximillian returned home deflated and ready to accede to his mother's far better thought out and funded plan.

At the age of thirteen Maximillian left home for the Saffron Waldron Friends School where he spent the next five years. Jane's plan, hatched to assist her continuing quest for prestige in the community she had married into, was the making of her son; he flourished at the school. From there he went onto Cambridge University where his knowledge of and deep interest in science enabled him to graduate in the summer of nineteen hundred and five. Maximillian returned home to Darlington that summer determined this time to fulfil his still-held dream of leaving the overpowering influence of his mother and the continuing cloying affection of his father. This time though he had the skills and the knowledge of how to achieve his objective; without knowing it Jane had enabled Maximillian to achieve his objective and to frustrate her own plans; all Maximillian needed was the money to put his plan into operation. His father provided that. Two weeks after returning home Alexander Beaumont, long suffering husband of Jane Webster and frustrated father of Maximillian suffered a seizure and died in his bed; Maximillian now had to wait only until his birthday in December to assume the family fortune, however much it might be, to be able to fulfil his dream and escape to Canada.

Jane & Maximillian, Darlington – Spring 1905

Maximillian achieved financial independence from his mother by reaching his twenty-first Birthday. Despite Jane's best efforts this was still very much a male dominated society – so just six months after his father's death he was in a position to fulfil his dream and get away from his Mother's almost overpowering domination. His first step was to demonstrate to her his independence. He chose to do so by repeating his plan of nine years before, to go to Newcastle upon Tyne on the train and have the telescope valued. This time the value would not matter, it was the fact that he could sell it that would give Maximillian the most pleasure. He had confronted his mother soon after his father's death with his decision to emigrate to Canada. They had argued bitterly about it; all of Maximillian's pent up frustration with his mother mixed into the row which lasted off and on for a week and was never fully resolved – they would part without reconciliation.

'I have worked hard this last nine years to ensure that you are properly qualified to assume a seat in the Houses of Parliament,' she said at one point.

'And you never once asked me if that was what I wanted to do,' he replied.

'Most men would give anything for such a position and such an honour,' she retorted.

'The honour would be yours mother,' – he had discovered that she hated to be called mother so he did so whenever possible.

'But your father would have been so proud of you. All of his money has been used to get you the best education and the best opportunity. I am sure he would have wanted you to enter parliament. Can you not at least honour his memory, how can you be so ungrateful and selfish?' she cried.

'Mother, this plan is yours, to suit your grand design, to demonstrate your position in Society. It has nothing to do with anything that father or I ever wanted. My mind is made up entirely. Now that I am twenty one I can decide my own destiny, and (he paused) use my inheritance for my own wishes. I intend to emigrate to Canada. Naturally, I will ensure that you are well provided for, but please be sure to understand that I am going whatever you might do or say.' He left the room before his mother could respond.

After he left Jane smiled to herself. She had dealt with a few of her son's misguided attempts to be himself before and was sure she would prevail. She was not concerned, he would come round to her way of thinking; her son's determination was a tenuous thing without real conviction unlike her own strong will and clarity of thought. She went into the hallway to prepare to leave for her next appointment, she would use the time it took for him to come to his senses to progress her latest personal crusade; she had become obsessed with a plan to become the first elected councillor for Darlington. As she left the house she put her son's minor rebellion to the back of her mind.

Maximillian on the other hand decided to prove to his mother that he could and would do what he wanted, whatever she might think. So two weeks after his twenty-first Birthday he once again boarded the train for Newcastle upon Tyne with what was to him the most symbolic part of his inheritance, the old family telescope. He wasn't too hopeful about its worth. The letter back from the Antique Dealer in North Shields, with a specialism in maritime memorabilia had not sounded encouraging. Artefacts from the Napoleonic wars were not uncommon and as it was the anniversary of the Battle of Trafalgar quite a few such relics were being taken to dealers to see if they would be worth any money.

Just as he had done nine years before Maximillian settled back into his seat and peered out of the window. He realised after a few minutes that life in the country had never appealed to him. He also realised that he had never really looked through the telescope very much; in fact it had sat in its glass case for most of the years that he could remember untouched. He studied the other passengers surreptitiously. He had a flashback to his last visit to Newcastle; there had been two passengers in the carriage then as well. The woman in the opposite corner seemed harmless enough; she was looking out of the window too. The other passenger, a man in the corner by the compartment door, was as on his last trip hidden behind a newspaper and as before judging by the speed at which the pages were turning he would continue to be hidden all the way to Newcastle. Maximillian decided it would do no harm to have possibly his last look through the old glass. He picked it up and took it out of the wrapping – an old piece of bed sheet. His mother had said very little about it other than that it had been given to her by a grateful relative, her being a suitable person to entrust it to. Up until that morning it had been in its usual place, in the case on the drawing room sideboard, not in pride of place but not hidden either. It was quite heavy, brass by the look and smell of it – he sniffed it to confirm the familiar metal odour that he normally associated with the instruments in the laboratory at University. This one had that combination of brass and polish that was common in early twentieth century Britain. Yes it was brass. The eye piece had been made as a separate part as had a curious extendable sleeve at the other end. He wondered what it was for. On closer inspection he found that it slid backwards and forwards to shield the main lens for some purpose. Perhaps to stop the sun hitting the glass and blinding the viewer he mused. He tried to pull the sleeve right out. As he did so he noticed a dent on one part of it almost as if it had been hit by something hard, or even, Maximillian rather liked the thought, had been used to hit something, or even more excitingly to hit somebody. A pirate, a French boarder, who knew, but the idea caught his imagination and he day-dreamed of swashbuckling pirates until well after Durham station. As the train left the station over the high ground he couldn't resist the temptation to look through the lens down across the countryside. Despite the dirty coach window and the scratched glass of the lens and eye piece it was clear that it had been and indeed still was a strong powerful, yes that was the word, a powerful instrument.

Maximillian began to pick out and focus on different things to look at. He became engrossed in what he was doing and so he nearly dropped the glass when a woman's voice interrupted him:

'That's a canny glass you've got there son, it reminds me of one my family used to have when I was a bairn.'

It was the woman in the opposite corner of the compartment. She was looking across, not at Maximillian, but at the telescope. She laughed.

'I don't suppose it's got a dint on the lens shield has it?' she asked.

Maximillian was startled by her comment. He glanced involuntarily at the shield and at the dent that he had noticed before. She must have seen it as she looked across he thought and yet it was not immediately obvious and was, when he thought about it, on the opposite part of the telescope to where the woman would be looking. This was a startling coincidence and set him thinking. His natural curiosity, inherited from the Webster side of the family – the side his family never spoke of, was piqued. For some reason he decided he needed to know more about the woman and her question about the telescope. After all the marine chandlers had stressed that there were quite a few such pieces around at the moment. He decided to test the woman's interest; he tried to make his question sound neutral:

'There are a lot of these instruments around I'm told, a relic from the last century,' he said.

'Ours, and I would guess that one too, is from the century before that. If it's like ours was, it'll have the makers name just under where your right hand is, now then let's see if I can remember, Broad and someone else, maybe Clark or some name like it I think I recall. Oh yes, and it would have a number there too, ours was one four seven, funny how you remember things. We always thought it was its number, you know like the number that was made by the maker. Has yours got a number on it?' she asked.

Maximillian hesitated, instinctively he was reluctant to lift his hand and look, but his curiosity was really aroused now and he had a strange premonition about what he might find. He struggled to set a flat unconcerned look onto his face and with as much nonchalance as he could he moved his hand so that he could see without the woman being able to as well. He prepared his response in his head. Dealing with his mother stood him in good stead at this point, he was often forced to adopt this strategy with her to avoid harsh admonishment when only one answer was correct and it was not the answer he was able to give truthfully.

'Well bless my soul, it is the same maker. The instrument must be older than I thought. I'm much obliged to you madam. I'll take better care of it now,' he said and began to wrap it up again in the piece of old sheet, careful to conceal both the dent and the engraved writing as he did so. He was conscious as he did so of the woman's piercing, expectant look and concentrated on his task to try and settle his fast beating heart and racing thoughts.

'Oh yes,' he said at length, 'the serial number' – he paused – 'it's different to yours I'm afraid.' He raised the wrapping once more and looked again at the number that was firmly etched both in the metal and on his mind. He did a quick simple sum in his head involving his age and said to the woman: 'One hundred and twenty six, somewhat earlier than yours I think. I must say you have given me pause to think more about this glass and my plan to sell it.' He had found in dealing with un-truths and his mother that as much of the real truth as possible should be employed in any subterfuge as it left far less opportunity for discovery and consequently for less dire consequences later. He suspected that this situation could be of a similar nature and acted accordingly.

The woman subsided back into her seat and appeared to be satisfied. She thanked him for sharing the information about the glass with her and wished him well in his quest with the telescope. It was only as they were leaving the train at Newcastle's central station that she nearly succeeded in catching him out. She spoke to him over her shoulder as she climbed down from the carriage ahead of him and the man with the newspaper who had come out of his literary reverie and hastily gathered together his belongings to leave the train at the same time.

'Good day to you young man. I've enjoyed talking to you. My name is Liza Webster by the way. I am pleased to have made your acquaintance,' she walked briskly along the platform without looking back and disappeared into the crowd.

To be certain of not bumping into her again Maximillian allowed the newspaper reader to get off before he did and walked slowly along the platform behind him. Maximillian was a young man in a quandary now, with more questions in his head than answers and unbeknown to him he had not convinced the woman at all. Jane's sister had found what the family had been looking for, some idea of the fate of the telescope. She hoped that she had unsettled the young man, presumably Jane's son – what a turn up, none of them had believed that Jane would ever have any children – sufficiently to make him think twice about selling the glass.

The more Maximillian thought about it the more uncomfortable he felt. He had never been close to his mother, he wondered if anyone ever had been, but he had thought that she had an honourable character, her values always appeared to make her an inherently honest person in his eyes. The Beaumont family lived by her values. There were only three of them; there had never been much more than slightly distant, quite formal contact with his father's people. They were treated with tolerance by his mother and rarely came to the house. Maximillian was by necessity a lonely young man. He knew nothing of his mother's family. His early childhood enquiries had been met with frosty silence from his mother so he had gradually stopped asking and over time he had let them drift to the back of his mind. His encounter on the train had reawakened his curiosity.

* * *

Maximillian was on his way home from the Marine Antiques dealers in Newcastle upon Tyne. He had walked along Grey Street, turned into Dean Street and caught his train back to Darlington without giving much thought to his surroundings. Normally he would have been keen to look around him as it had been many years since he had last visited the city, but he had a lot of other things to consider and two things in particular. Firstly, his discussion with and subsequent offer from the man he had met at the dealers. The other thing was the memory of his conversation with the woman on the train that morning on his way up to Newcastle. He needed to think and this time Maximillian, who had until now always made important personal decisions on his own, needed someone to talk to, something he had never done before; he had no knowledge or experience of how to go about doing so. He approached the task as the mathematician and scientist he had become – logical thought inherited from his mother. For the moment he set aside the Antique dealer's offer and the consequent fate of the telescope. He focussed his mind on the woman on the train, Liza Webster, he recalled her name. For some reason the name seemed to trigger a thread of memory, but the thread was so thin and tenuous that it made no sense to him and soon blurred into the other things milling about in his head. He couldn't think how to make the memory clearer, which raised in his head the question – did he really want to make it clearer and follow it to a conclusion, and yet what possible reason could there be for holding on to the woman's words, finding out more about them and in consequence more about her.

As the train swayed and rattled across the points crossing onto the entrance to the High Level Bridge Maximillian resolved to do something he had become good at over the years. If he wanted something from his mother he had found out that he needed a plan and a strategy to get his mother to agree to. His father, compliant, friendly, long suffering, and unfortunately at this point dead, would agree to anything, but his mother needed reasons, facts, justification, commitment; so Maximillian had worked out a way to test out the effectiveness of any idea or request that he had. He put the woman and her revelations to the back of his mind, a strange idea; as if minds had separate compartments that did different things – academic nonsense his father would have called it when his wife was not about.

He looked out of the window, sat back in the seat, closed his eyes and waited for the woman to either disappear or remain in his mind, in whatever form that might be. By the time the train reached the high viaduct in Chester-Le-Street Maximillian was convinced the woman was not going away. He needed to find out who she was and what connection she had with the telescope. Starved of company by his shyness, except for his parents and a series of tutors, governesses and the few Cambridge dons who he felt able to approach and exchange a few words with he had become an avid reader. Reading provided him with conversation and a source of imagination and entertainment for himself. At the moment he was quite absorbed by Sherlock Holmes. Maximillian was a bit frightened and in awe of Sherlock Holmes himself, but his solid dependable friend Doctor Watson was an appealing character for the young man and he decided that he would consult the Doctor in his investigation. What would the Doctor do first? Assemble the facts, and then Maximillian had a moment of inspiration, he didn't recognise it as such, perhaps as Doctor Watson might not, but it happened, he was reminded of another person in his life, Mrs Jamieson, his nurse and governess for the first eight years of his life. She lived in Darlington; she would know lots of people, well a lot more than he did anyway. He just needed to find her.

Mrs Jamieson, he had always called her that, had once taken him to visit the part of Darlington where she lived. They had fed the ducks on the small river – the Skerne – near where she lived. River was a generous term for the wet odious flow of polluted black liquid that flowed north to south through the town. So where was that – the maid would know, he would ask her. He would accept the usual sharp-tongued ridicule that she appeared to save just for him. His mind set, plan in place he settled back and dozed the final part of the journey home.

It took him a lot longer than he had anticipated to find out anything more. The delay meant that his ambition to escape the controlling and well-established plans of his mother were put back as well. Jane was sure he would come around to her way of thinking. She interpreted the delay in his 'leaving' for the colonies to be permanent and that he was just holding on to his stubborn refusal to admit that she was right. Jane regaled her inner circle of tea friends, picked personally for their potential and actual influence, with her plan for the advancement of her son and so by default the advancement of Jane herself.

The real reason for the delay was nothing to do with any indecision on Maximillian's part, it was much more to do with his lack of experience in talking to anyone outside the Darlington society that his mother had kept him a part of and even then it was just the friends that his mother allowed him to have contact with. He bungled his first attempt and if it had not been for the fortunate intervention of his mother's real love, her Pekinese dog, Magenta, he would have never got another chance.

His planning, another skill he got from his mother was impeccable. He got the maid's name from her pay envelope, which with the death of her husband Jane was required to get Maximillian involved with, just for appearances and legal necessity, there was no way Jane had ever trusted either of the men in her house with money. This was a detail not shared with her inner circle.

The maid's schedule was easy to understand, he just had to watch. It was the watching that caused his undoing. On Thursday mornings, Magenta was entrusted to the maid for a short walk in the park, weather permitting. The park was close to the house. Maximillian decided that as this event coincided with his mother's regular morning appointment with her coiffeur – Jane had never lost her enchantment with the French language – then it would be a good chance to interview the maid. So two Thursdays after he had returned from Newcastle he was waiting behind some trees – later he was not sure why he had felt the need to hide, but he had. When he stepped out in front of the maid she screamed and slapped his face before realising who it was. She had worked hard to get this job and she was determined to keep it. Her immediate reaction, designed to protect her job proved a disaster for both of them.

'Oh my God, it's you,' she said, 'you gave me such a turn. What do you want?'

Maximillian had little experience of talking to women and none at all of beginning a conversation with an unaccompanied young girl:

'I have been endeavouring to get you on your own for a week now,' he began.

'What do you mean?' the maid interrupted him, 'You've been following me, waiting 'til I'm on me own, I've heard about men like you.'

'Oh no,' replied Maximillian, horrified at her reaction, 'I meant no harm to you I merely wanted to talk to you.'

Instinctively, and wrongly, he put out his hand to touch her arm.

The maid was wearing a new petticoat that morning. Well it wasn't new, it was cut down from one of her Mam's, but she hadn't worn it before so it felt like new. She had pestered her Mam all the previous evening to finish it. Her Mam had stayed up late to finish sewing the new hem along the bottom and with about three inches left had run out of cotton yarn. She had hung the petticoat over the chair and gone up to tell her daughter it wasn't ready, she needed some more yarn. She could get some from the covered market the next day and finish it then, but her daughter was asleep. The excited young girl had got up before her mother that morning, seen the petticoat on the back of the chair and holding it up to her body had assumed it was ready. She put it on and went off to work without seeing her mother. As she worked around the house first thing the unfinished end of the hem began to unravel. It continued to do so when she took the yapping dog into the park and by the time she reached the tree that Maximilian was hiding behind there was a loop of material hanging down at the back of her petticoat. As Maximillian put his hand out the frightened maid turned and backed away from him. As she did so her petticoat caught on the buckle of his shoe and she fell sideways. Maximillian went to catch her, but with his foot trapped in her underskirt he lost his balance and the two of them ended up in a tangled heap on the grass. Lying on the floor with the maid next to him Maximillian caught his breath and began to realise the compromising position that he was in. He began to untangle himself from the maid but as he did so he also realised that his right hand had ended up underneath her clothes right at the top of her thigh. The female body had always been a mystery to Maximillian. At University he had studied science but had never had any interest in biology. He had never seen, let alone touched, any part of the female form except for face, hands and the occasional foot. His hand felt hairs and then, surprisingly, an opening in the top of the girl's thighs. The analytical part of his mind was fascinated and for a second or two he moved his fingers. The maid screamed and pushed him away.

'I know your game,' she cried out loudly. 'You're after my body. You posh people, you're all the same. Just 'cos your father is dead you think you can take advantage of me. You've been watching me these last two weeks I've seen you, no use pretending. You think you can do what you want with me, well you're wrong, I'll show you. You'd better keep away from me or I'll tell your Mam. She won't stand any nonsense from you. She'll sort you out, just wait till I tell her.' She picked herself up and after catching the tiny dog – Mistress Jane was a scary woman at the best of times, who knows what she would do if the maid went back without the dog, whatever the circumstances – and ran away across the park towards the entrance by the house.

Maximillian stood shaking, his plan in ruins, how would he be able to find out anything about the Websters now, but there was worse in store for him, his efforts to stop and interview the maid had been witnessed.

Jane reacted swiftly and consistently. In front of the housekeeper and Jane the maid wilted, lost all her indignation and was brow beaten into silence – she was dismissed. Despite some initial misgivings, Mrs Brown's advice was sound, the chance of a hysterical young girl causing any sort of embarrassment was non-existent and no more was heard from the maid about the incident.

Maximillian though was another matter. The witness to the incident – the park keeper's wife who had been taking her husband's dinner to him in his small shed at the top corner of the park – could not be ignored so easily and so action was required and her son dealt with. She recalled his hair-brained scheme to go to the colonies, Canada she seemed to recall. Maybe the experience would do him good. He was still only twenty one, six months away would allow the incident to be forgotten and when he came back her plans to get him elected as a member of parliament would have progressed and in the meantime she could pursue her own career. After all if that Lucas woman could become a councillor any one could.

Jane confronted Maximillian when he returned – he had taken refuge in the library for the afternoon, none of his schemes to extract himself from the horror of his efforts in the park had stood up to close scrutiny. He still had no idea what to do when he walked through the front door that evening to meet his mother waiting in the hall. Help was to come from the most surprising source.

'Maximillian, I have heard about your encounter with the maid and I have dealt with her. It seems I must do everything for you even now that you have come of age and are the head of the household,' the last bit she delivered with more than her usual level of sarcasm.

'Mama, I am quite capable of looking after my own affairs thank you. Why must you constantly interfere,' Maximillian was in despair. He had put his plan to go to Canada on hold until he sorted out what to do about the telescope and now that too was in disarray. He knew though that this was the only opportunity he would ever get to assert some sort of authority over his own affairs. If he was unable to do it now then he would spend the rest of his life under the wing of his mother. Her next statement – when they talked about anything she only ever made statements – caught him totally by surprise and by the time he had recovered he had lost all chance of standing up to his mother.

'I've been considering your ambition to travel to the colonies, Canada I think you said. Well I am persuaded that the scheme might have some merit so I am prepared to support you with it,' said his mother. She moved past him to the window of the drawing room and stood looking across at the entrance to the park where the incident had taken place. This was the only possible solution; surely her son would see that and accept her offer.

Maximillian said nothing for a few minutes. Of all the things he thought his mother might do, this was never one of them; what had caused her to change her mind. He considered the options. He knew her ambitions for him. She had tried for many years to persuade and manipulate Alexander into politics and now she wanted to transfer that ambition to him. There would be no sense in letting him go off to Canada though, he might never come back. He thought about that, would he come back, he did not know, certainly there was nothing to keep him here now. He now realised who it was that he wanted, the one person he had ever been able to talk to – he missed his father. The one person who had been interested in him rather than the benefit his education and knowledge could bring to the family. The more he thought about it the less reason he could see for coming back now that he had the opportunity and his mother's blessing to go. He thought about thanking her and then he wondered if he was too effusive in his thanks then she might suspect that he would not return and change her mind. No, better a passive acceptance, let her believe that she had won again, play to her ego. Maybe she just wanted him out of the way until the incident in the park settled down. It could not be that important could it? He had been away from home at school and then University a long time so he had forgotten the struggle his mother had to maintain her position in the narrow social society of Darlington especially given the hazy understanding of her origins. This reminded him of the telescope and the woman he had met on the train. Was she connected to the family? Should he try and find out more? What did he want most? He made his decision and turned towards his mother.

'That is most magnanimous of you mother. As you say I have had the notion to travel for a long while and now that Papa has gone I believe it might be good for me to take some time away to gather my thoughts before pursuing a career.' He stopped at that point. He knew that his mother was very clear that he should have a career and not just drift through life like so many of the people he had met at University. He had also been careful to say nothing about how long he might stay away and on reflection he decided to keep his curiosity about the telescope and the Webster woman to himself – he could take up that quest when he returned from Canada.

'Excellent,' said his mother, 'Your father's death has left our fortunes uncertain so I am afraid there will not be a great deal of money available for your expedition. However, I am sure we can equip you for the journey and provide some small allowance while you are away. We can visit the bank tomorrow to make the arrangements if that is acceptable.'

Maximillian could not resist a smile. He had already visited the bank and found out exactly what the family could and could not manage to do. His mother's careful stewardship of the Beaumont family affairs – fronted by his father but very definitely controlled by his mother meant that they were able to survive Alexander's death. The family book business was in good hands and would continue to provide them all with a comfortable existence.

'That will be acceptable mother. Now I am going out this evening so I shall bid you good night,' he said and left the room.

'Hmmmn,' said his mother, content with the result of the exchange, but still exasperated by her son.

A month later Maximillian Beaumont bid his mother goodbye and left home, first for Liverpool and then on an emigration ship headed for Canada. He never returned. He forgot all about the telescope and his doubts about who it really belonged to, but his encounters with Liza Webster and the maid would be sufficient to give Bella the clues she needed to find it fourteen years later.

Sarah, Beamish Museum, Summer – 2014

Sarah and Billy caught their buses home from Beamish. After a long day both of them slept between Chester-Le-Street and Middlesbrough. It was only when they had boarded the last one, the sixty three for the final part of their journey that Sarah started to think more about her family.

Sarah felt a tear in the corner of her eye at the thought of selfish Jane leaving them all behind to move to Darlington. Billy stopped looking out of the window as they passed the crematorium and looked across at his Granddaughter. He saw the tear on her cheek and reached into his pocket for his handkerchief. Crumpled, stale and a bit grey, it had escaped the attentions of Grandma, but it did what was required and the two of them sat for a while in silence looking out of the window as the bus turned into Ladgate lane. Sarah was the first to speak:

'So how did Grandma Bella get the telescope back to us Grandda? Great Aunt Jane sounds like a very scary lady'

'Yes, by all accounts she was,' replied Billy, 'but she met her match in Grandma Bella,' he chuckled, 'just like we all did at some time or other.'

'What even you Grandda? How did that happen?'

'Oh yes, Grandma Bella even sorted me out, but I expect you want to know how she got hold of the telescope first don't you?'

'Yes please,' she replied quickly and added, 'so what year did Bella get it back?'

'Nineteen nineteen,' Grandda replied.

'Oh we haven't been there yet, wasn't that just after the First World War?' said Sarah.

'Yes,' said Billy, 'Now if you've run out of questions I'll tell you a bit about how Grandma Bella got the telescope back before we reach the village.'

Billy sat back and thought for a while, passing the crematorium had reminded him again of the big crowd of people at Bella's funeral. He pictured in his mind his last meeting with his Grandmother before she died. The thoughts settled his mind and he began to tell Sarah about Bella and how she had managed to track down Jane and retrieve the telescope.

Jane & Bella, Darlington – Autumn 1919

It is possible that all families have a special ancestor that everyone knows. The Websters do, it is Grandma Bella. In the autumn of 1919 Bella was incensed. This was not unusual; her fiery red-haired character drove her to champion any cause that she felt deserved her attention. This time it was her family. She had learnt from Tommy's Aunt Liza that the family heirloom, a telescope – not something she would normally pay much attention to, but the family's all the same, and more importantly something Tommy had expressed a wish to have, had been given to Great Aunt Mary ninety years ago. Aunt Liza had told her earlier that week that she had once met a young man that she believed to be some relation and possibly the son of her sister Jane. Liza had laughed at the thought of Jane having a son.

'He would have had to have been born already respectable and clean. Jane hated anything messy. Anyway, he was thinking of selling the telescope when I saw him,' said Liza.

'Did you speak to him again?' asked Bella.

'No, but what did happen that was a real coincidence – is that the right word Bella? You know all these big words don't you,' replied Liza.

'Yes, Aunt Liza, I think that's the right word, but tell me what happened?' asked Bella.

'Well, me husband's sister-in law, that's how I got the ticket for the train to Newcastle. Eeeh! It's a big place is Newcastle; good job Harry met me off the train I'd have got lost in no time. I had a real day that day I can tell you,'

Bella stood patiently, outside the store where she had met Aunt Liza. She would get back to the story eventually and in her time as a local councillor Bella had learnt that there was no point rushing people, they would get to the point of their question, or grievance or whatever else it was they bought to her, in their own good time. Aunt Liza was no exception. Bella heard all about Liza's day in Newcastle.

'Oh, but you were asking about Jane weren't you.' Liza paused, not long enough for Bella to speak, but she had got to the point of her story.

'Well as I was saying my husband's sister-in-law's girl took a job as a maid in one of them big houses in Woodland Terrace. It's not easy to get work, well not reliable, safe work as a maid. You have to be so careful, did I ever tell you about the time...' Liza was off on another tale, but at last she returned to Bella's question and paused for breath. 'Well anyway, about a year after she got the job she had a run in with the woman's son, tried to take advantage of her he did. It was just after the man of the house had died. The woman was a right tartar, wouldn't believe any of it and threw me sister-law's girl out. The lass came around to see us later that week to tell us all about it.'

Liza paused; she was rather proud of what she had worked out and wanted to impress Bella who was the cleverest of the family.

'It was a bit later that I thought about it and put two and two together.' Aunt Liza stopped.

'And what did you make?' asked Bella, regretting the ambiguous comment as soon as she had made it.

'What do you mean, what did I make?' asked Liza.

'What was it that you found out or guessed? What was it the girl said?' explained Bella.

'Oh, I see what you mean. Well it was the telescope. It must have been Jane – mustn't it' Replied Liza triumphantly.

'Must it?' said Bella.

'Yes, the girl described a telescope on the sideboard in the house. She had to polish it every day, so she had a real good look at it. From the way she described it I'm sure it was Great Aunt Mary's, the one she got from the old sailor – William Snow I think his name was,' replied Liza.

'I wonder where it is now?' said Bella, almost to herself.

'Well the young man was going to sell it when I left him getting off the train in Newcastle.' said Liza.

'Did you find out what happened to the young man after his encounter with your sister-in-law's girl?' asked Bella.

'Aye, he was packed off to Canada so they said. My sister-in-law bumped into the Housekeeper a few months later and she told her.' Aunt Liza launched into another story and it was a good ten minutes later before Bella was able to thank her for the help and leave her promising faithfully not to leave it too long before bringing that man of hers to Darlington to see them all.

Bella's curiosity was piqued; she wanted to know if the telescope had gone to Canada. Was the young man Jane's son? If it was Aunt Jane even? She loved a mystery and one thing was certain. If it was still in Britain Bella was determined to get it back.

* * *

Tommy, Bella's soft spoken, quiet, unassuming husband had resigned himself to Bella's latest crusade. The two were an incongruous pair. No-one, not even Tommy and Bella, could quite explain how they had come to be married, but once they were they had worked hard at the relationship. Most people assumed that Tommy just did everything his wife asked, but that was not how they lived together. Surviving the Great War – including being gassed – had given Tommy resilience and courage and these two characteristics allowed him to hold his own with his wife and now with one small son and another child on the way they had developed an understanding that enabled them to live in harmony with each other.

'I'm going to see your Aunt Jane tomorrow Tommy,' Bella had announced that morning.

'It's just a telescope pet, must you take on so, I'll not be heart-broken if I don't see it, after all I've never seen it yet anyway,' replied her husband, but he knew it was pointless to argue. The next morning as he left for the iron works, the effects of mustard gas had left him short of breath for all but the desk-bound job of wages clerk, he kissed his wife good bye, wished her luck, and told her to take care. Their young son Joseph was left with his Grandma for the day and Bella set off down the street to travel to Darlington. In 1919 the best way to travel was by train; only very rich people had cars and only large cities like London and Leeds had started to introduce buses.

Bella left the cottage by the back door, open as usual. She turned down the rough unmade lane that led to the end of the street. Several of the wives, struggling on a clear cold autumn morning to hang out washing across the lane called out to her as she passed. When she got to the end of the street the carriers cart from Eston Junction was just returning from the village.

'Jack, Jack!' she called.

Jack's shell-fire damaged hearing worked intermittently, or so he said, so it was several minutes before he was persuaded to stop. It was Mrs Williamson from the other end of California that waved him to stop. The cart shambled to a creaking halt. The old, tired horse lowered its head, weary after the long steady climb up the incline from the junction.

'Jack, can I have a ride to the junction?' asked Bella. She remembered just in time to smile at Jack and drop her eyes as he looked down from his pile of sacks on the edge of the flat wagon, empty now after calling at the school and then the store on the main street.

Jack looked down at the fiery young woman at the edge of the cart. He wasn't supposed to carry passengers, but the smile and the flash of blue-green eyes had worked. He sat up and looked about for an audience – only old Mrs Williamson – no men to score from; he gave in meekly.

'Alright lass, seeing as it's you, and it's downhill, I'll make an exception to me rule.'

Bella smiled to herself. Jack made an exception for all the young women who stopped his cart. She walked quickly to the back of the cart put her foot in the metal footrest and swung herself up onto the back. She knew that Jack would have climbed down to help her, but she was in no mood for his clumsy apologetic efforts to handle her body anywhere he could. He sniffed loudly and picked up the reins.

'Go on Captain, go on.' It was a pretentious name for a horse, even one retired from the mine at the top of the incline after giving twenty years of hard service, mostly underground, hauling tubs from the workings to the top of the tramway. The horse lifted an ear, shook its head and snorted. It leant into the traces. The leather straps squeaked slightly, the metal links clinked and the cart set off slowly at first and then began to bounce over the cobbles and ruts of the downhill slope to the foot of the incline. Jack quite liked to see his female passengers bounce a bit.

Bella was oblivious to his backward glances. She was looking across the valley, picking out the familiar landmarks that had been there all her life. In 1919 Teesside was tired. Flat-out production during the war to make steel for ships, tanks, rifles, guns, barbed wire and all the other needs of a country, fighting what the newspapers called 'the greatest war the world had ever seen' had suddenly stopped. Everywhere there was uncertainty about what would happen now. The euphoric return of the few battered men from four long years of combat had disappeared quickly up in the north. Not only that, during the war many jobs had been taken over by women and they had seen the first signs of freedom. Bella was one such woman. She had gone to work on the railways, cleaning coaches at Eston Junction, with her new-born son Joseph, strapped to her back, feeding him when she could find an empty coach with no supervisor in sight. Unlike many of her school friends Bella had worked hard and had done well at the school in the village. It was another reason for her anger at Jane. A plaque at the school had Jane's name on it marking the time that she had taught there until she was able to escape to Darlington. As a child Bella had been fiercely proud of her relationship with such an early example of a successful woman at work. She had been able to forgive Tommy's Aunt for moving away until she heard from Aunt Liza of Jane's subsequent complete rejection of the Webster family and where she came from. It was another reason why Bella had set herself the task of getting the telescope back for her husband.

As the cart rattled down the track towards Eston Junction she took in her surroundings with absent concentration. She smelt the acrid coke fumes from the works. She saw the dead yellow-grey grass lining the side of the track. When the cart went over an especially big rut she gripped the smooth wooden side of the wagon and felt a rough scratch in the metal runner under the planks. In the distance she could hear the dull rhythmic thump of a steam hammer down at the shipyard beating out the shapes of plate for one of the few ships still being built. They passed a man bent over beside the road, he was retching, an empty beer bottle in his hand, a clumsily made crutch and a rolled up trouser showing a wooden leg, marking him out as another lost victim of the war, alcohol carrying him through the 'land fit for heroes' that he had returned to. Bella could almost taste the rancid hops and bitterness as they passed him, oblivious to the cart. His condition made her think of her new heroine, Lady Astor, hopefully soon to be the first elected member of the British parliament. She shared Lady Astor's concerns for both feminist rights and the dangers of alcohol. Bella had ambitions to become a member of parliament herself.

The cart pulled up just before it came into sight of the carrier's yard behind the railway station. It would not do for the carrier's master to see Jack carrying passengers. Jack hopped down and came round the back to 'help' Bella down. As she dropped to the ground she grimaced and put up with his hand as it slid up her thigh and the other hand as it came round her chest and took hold of her breast.

'Give us a kiss lass, just for the ride,' he whined in the wheedling, grating voice that Bella detested. She pushed him away and laughed:

'No chance Jack Holdsworthy, not while you've arms like an octopus and breath like a midden.' She skipped around him and headed for the station, bought a third-class day return to Darlington and sat down on a platform trolley to wait for the train.

The train steamed into the station and stopped with a squeal of brakes and a loud escape of steam. Bella turned the stiff brass handle of a door on the last coach of the train and climbed in. The coach was empty so she crossed to the other side and looked out over the river as the train travelled along beside it. She had travelled this way a number of times now, her involvement with the suffragette movement and other women's groups had taken her to Middlesbrough, Stockton, Darlington and even once or twice to Newcastle.

The work she did gave her an intellectual lifeline out of the drudgery and survival of California and Eston. She did not resent where she lived or the family she had married into, but she did enjoy meeting and talking to women who were now starting to test the established order of society. Not only had her contributions brought her recognition across the Tees region, she had begun to be asked to visit other groups of women. It was through these contacts that Bella had managed to track down Mistress Jane Beaumont a Darlington society lady that Bella was certain was Jane Webster. Bella was intending to use her experience and the contacts she had made in different levels of society to her advantage when she got to meet with Jane.

None of the Websters had seen Jane since she had left to marry into a higher social status, just as she had schemed for all her life. Bella hoped Jane would remember her father John's sacrifice to get her where she wanted to be, but she doubted it, Jane had left behind a reputation for going through anyone who got in her way. It was going to be an interesting encounter; Bella was looking forward to it, despite being a little more nervous than she had hoped. She settled back onto the hard wooden seat to watch Teesside go past.

Bella was always reminded that travelling from East to West was like going back through the industrial growth of Teesside. The train passed the single busy shipyard where a modern steam vessel was being built; the sound of rivets being hammered was audible as the train went by. The new Transporter bridge, finished in 1911 came into view and Bella, like most Teesside people, was proud of the engineering skills it represented, whether it was practical or not; it was an amazing sight on the Teesside skyline. Across the river the embryonic chemical works was taking shape. Bella wondered if it would become another of Teesside's successful growth industries in the future. From Middlesbrough the train passed over the River Tees on a railway bridge, first built as an unstable suspension bridge in 1830 heralding the expansion of the industrial revolution into the lower Tees Valley. Then on past Stockton and the train was on the historic track of the original Stockton to Darlington railway. Now she looked out of the windows into unspoilt rural countryside. She wondered if Eston used to be surrounded by countryside like this when Aunt Mary was a girl and Old William gave her the telescope. The train passed over the River Skerne, a scene made famous in a picture she had seen of the opening of the railway nearly ninety years before.

The train pulled into Darlington station. Bella got out and walked through the town, stopping briefly at several houses where contacts she had made through the suffragette movement gave her encouraging help in preparation for her encounter with her husband's Aunt. She walked up the street towards the house as ready as she was ever going to be to face Jane.

Bella paused at the foot of the steps of an imposing front door. The feel of her fast-beating heart annoyed her and gave an edge to her determination. She would not be intimidated by this woman. She set her jaw firmly, bent down slightly and lifted the sides of her long black skirt, noticed the dusty-ragged hem and started up the steps. Each step revealed a faded, worn, high-ankled boot; the soles so thin that she felt every ridge and imperfection on the steps as she climbed. They would be hidden when she walked and it made her resolve to stay standing whilst she spoke to Jane. A momentary hesitation as Bella considered the possibility that Jane would not agree to see her; brushed aside with the feisty resolution that marked her out in Eston and would stand by her side for this task that she had set herself.

Bella arrived at the door. She reached out with her right hand, the broken nails and red constantly scrubbed hands a clear sign of what she was and where she came from. She adjusted the bonnet that she wore against the crisp-clear morning and pulled the door-bell knob. There was no sound for several minutes and then the door opened. A small, thin, wispy young girl appeared in the doorway. Bella thought that a strong wind might blow the youngster away. They stood and looked at each other for quite a few seconds before Bella took control.

'Cat got your tongue? Is Mistress Jane in?' she said.

'Yes, but trades people should go round the back, it's down the alley,' the girl pointed with a small, very white hand which when stretched out beyond the long-white sleeve revealed enough red marks to say some form of pox had smitten the girl sometime in her childhood.

'You can go and tell your Mistress that her nephew Thomas's wife Isabella is here to see her; do you think you can manage that?' said Bella without the faintest trace of anything but certainty in her voice and belief that she would get her way. As so often before it worked.

'Yes, Mam,' said the girl who closed the door and disappeared into the house. Bella stood on the doorstep, her heart beating loudly again, a redness had appeared on each of her cheeks and a firm uncompromising look had settled onto her face. She was ready for Jane.

Some time passed before the door re-opened:

'My Mistress can spare you just a few minutes only. She is expecting an important visitor from the town,' the words came out in a jumble of breathless phrases, well remembered, but badly delivered. The edge of Jane's first rebuff was lost as it caused Bella to smile and regain some of her composure. She stepped into the hallway.

'My Mistress says to wait in the drawing room,' the girl said.

'Well lead on then girl, I don't have all day,' said Bella, avoiding having to admit that coming from a two room cottage was not good training for finding a drawing room in a smart town-house. The girl went halfway along the hallway and opened a door on the right. She stood back to let Bella enter a large room, well-lit from the large bay window, that looked out over the front garden. The door was closed behind her as she entered.

The room was like nothing she had ever seen in her life before. She had looked down as she entered and so her first sight was of a Persian carpet, rich multi-coloured with large floral patterns swirling away across the room in all directions. Around the edge of the carpet were floorboards so well polished that you could catch a faint reflection of yourself in them. The olive-green skirting board gave way to pale-mustard wallpaper with Chinese or Japanese characters and scenes painted on it. High up above that a picture rail, painted to match the skirting board, and then higher again a heavily corniced ceiling in white. In the centre of the ceiling surrounded by more of the plaster-moulded cornice was a heavy crystal chandelier. There was no sign of either gas or candles on the chandelier so it must be electric – something Bella had heard of but never seen. There were six chairs in the room, all matching – two in the window. A long sideboard, with several mounted photographic prints placed on top, was along the wall to the left and in front of Bella was a large fire place with a coal fire burning – the heat was very inviting. As she moved towards it Bella noticed the large mirror over the mantelpiece and as she looked into the mirror she realised that someone else had entered the room.

'I don't imagine you've ever been into a room like this before my dear,' said the woman.

Bella started and turned around and was surprised – it had to be Tommy's Aunt, the likeness to his Grandfather was unmistakeable. The same high forehead, pinched long nose, raised cheek bones and a small, thin, straight mouth above a slightly receding chin. Long grey streaked fair hair made up in the fashionable style that was in all the papers at the moment.

'Hello, you must be Tommy's Aunt Jane,' she began.

'And to whom am I speaking young lady,' Jane called on her years of teaching practice to address this pale, rather grubby, badly dressed young woman. 'The maid said something about Thomas and a nephew, neither of which I recognise,' she interrupted Bella with practised ease.

Bella paused before she answered. This was not one of the family or the other women of Eston and California that she could easily get the better of in any conversation. No, this was another thing altogether, here was a woman who was used to having things her own way all the time. So the stories about Jane seemed to be true. Bella would need all her resolve to get what she wanted.

'I am Thomas's wife, Thomas your nephew.' She said.

'Nephew, I've never heard of any nephews,' Jane replied warily.

'William, your brother, he got married and had a son Thomas. I am Thomas's wife,' said Bella firmly.

'Ah, that side of the family. You'll forgive me, since I left the School in Eston I have moved in much better circles so I have been unaware of the Webster family's fortunes... ... are they well?' She added this last remark absently.

'Quite well thank you Jane,' said Bella starting to feel her heart beating again.

'I'm not sure it will do either of us any favours if you adopt such a familiar attitude towards me dear girl. I think it would be better if you addressed me as Mistress Beaumont even for the short while that you are here,' Jane carried on as if Bella had not spoken. 'Do the Websters still live in Eston?' she asked the question as if it was about some other family that she had no knowledge or interest in and certainly no connection with. It was time for Bella to seize the initiative.

'I hear you are hoping to be invited to meet with the Royal Agricultural Show committee when it visits the Hundens next year. No doubt you'll be hoping to be presented to the Duke of York.' Bella paused at that point and waited. In the following few minutes silence she realised there must be a clock in the room that she had not noticed. The pendulum swung back and forth with steady rhythmic accuracy, tick, tick, tick, and then the clock cleared its throat, released the metallic mechanism of the hammer and struck twice – half past eleven. Bella waited.

'You seem well acquainted with events here in Darlington, coming from such a remote, industrial backwater,' Jane began carefully.

'My good friend Clara Curtis Lucas, sadly dead now, kept me well informed of what was what here...' Bella waited again. There was a longer pause.

'Ah yes. We still have a report on her memorial service. I could read some of it for you if you wish,' said Jane busy regaining her ascendancy.

'Thank you but I can read well enough myself and being at the family funeral was sufficient memory for me,' replied Bella.

'I understood the funeral was for family and very close friends only,' said Jane placing some emphasis on the word very as she did so.

'Yes, it was, and yes I was,' smiled Bella thinly, 'I didn't see you there though.'

'No, I believe I had another engagement that day,' replied Jane quickly.

The conversation was diluting Bella's advantage so she turned it back.

'In any event I imagine you would agree that it wouldn't do for a prospective attendee on the Duke of York to be known to be a Webster from a one-room slum cottage in California?' she said.

'What is it you want?' asked Jane.

'I want the telescope back for Tommy,' said Bella quietly.

'What that old relic, it's scarcely worth anything.' Jane paused to consider her options, then continued: 'I was going to throw it out, except it belongs to my son Maximillian. He's out of the country at the moment, so no, I'm afraid it's quite out of the question.' Jane smiled slightly; she would call this grubby little woman's bluff. Although the connection with the Lucas's was concerning for Jane's reputation and her planned attendance at the show next year.

'Does Maximillian know about his mother's childhood?' Bella asked softly. There was another pause and the clock moved on toward midday. Jane glanced at it and remembered that her next visitor was due at Noon. She did not want him to meet this woman under any circumstances – a compromise would have to be found.

'I assume the Websters are still poor and without money,' she mused.

'Without money certainly, but poor no,' replied Bella, sensing some progress. She had noticed the glance at the clock and made the right connection.

'Five pounds would buy a splendid new telescope and leave enough for some proper clothes my dear,' said Jane.

'Old William's telescope would earn my departure and leave enough time for you to receive your next guest. Haggling would leave me here in your drawing room with your visitor, who I understand to be a useful ally in your quest for a royal audience,' Bella waited again. Silently she blessed her husband's ability to teach her patience and the need to know when to be quiet and wait. The clock ticked its way round the face towards the twelve on the dial.

Jane weighed up the consequences of their conversation. Next year's planned visit of the Duke of York so far North was a once in a life time opportunity she could not afford to miss. She could deal with Maximillian, if he ever returned. There really was only one alternative, but how to give in without losing face. Tick, tick, tick.

'As it happens the telescope has been sent to a Marine Chandlers in Newcastle for valuation and possible repair. I have heard this morning that there is little that can be done to repair it, so as a telescope it is of little use. I had intended to have the Chandlers dispose of it rather than go to the trouble of returning it here. If it is of such value to you, I will send a note to them to keep it until the end of the week and if it is not claimed by then, to have it destroyed. Now I really must ask you to leave as I have other business to attend to.

'That would be acceptable,' replied Bella slowly.

Jane carried on: 'I cannot say that it has been a pleasure and I must ask you and your family not to consider visiting here again. I will ask the maid to see you out,' and she turned and left the room.

Bella could hardly keep the smile from her face. She was almost sure that Jane believed the telescope would be destroyed. After all, how could a poor working family from North Yorkshire, be expected to get all the way to Newcastle to reclaim it, in such a short time, but then, if she had kept up with her Webster family, she might have recalled that Liza was married to a railway guard who went to Newcastle every day. Bella was quite capable of writing the sort of letter that would release the telescope to him well before the end of the week. She didn't wait for the maid to see her out. She left straight away and went to meet Tommy's Aunt Liza in Darlington town centre, well pleased with her morning's work. The inevitable hour long stories about Liza's family and all her relations and the same request to visit them all with Tommy soon was a price worth paying for getting the better of Jane.

The telescope was retrieved by Liza's husband and did get back to Tommy. For several years it sat on the mantelpiece and was quite a talking point in the street. Then when the depression caught up with the village, work became scarce and the means-testers began to come visiting. The telescope was hidden together with the family's other meagre treasures in the back of the outside toilet. There it stayed until the threat of war brought work back to Teesside and sent the threat of poverty away from the Webster family. Bella had never thought she would be grateful for another war but she was.

Step three – Ann

Springtime, Innocence
Shattered dreams in leaden death
Hope waits on despair

Sarah, Prospect View – Winter 2014

It was Saturday and Sally had promised to take Sarah into Town to buy her a long-delayed birthday present earlier in the week. Despite her attempt to be cautious about another of her mother's promises Sarah had raised her hopes and although she had gone to stay overnight at her grandparents, she had awoken that morning in the fold away bed in a positive, hopeful frame of mind. Surely her Mam would come, but it was after lunch time by the time Sally drove into California Road, left her car parked in the way and went along Prospect View to her parents' house. She was met at the door by her mother.

'You're too late. They've gone out, down into town, to the library. They waited, believed your promise, much good it did them. Sarah was really unhappy, don't expect you know why, so your father has taken her out, to find out more about her family. See if she's got any reliable relations ...' she left the sentence unfinished.

Through the dullness of the last remnants of her hangover, nothing another drink wouldn't put right, Sally detected the flat controlled tone of her mother's voice.

'What's up Mam? You having a bad day?' There was silence. 'If they're not going to be back for a while I might pop along to the club. You couldn't lend me ten quid 'til Thursday could you?' The silence deepened.

There was a wall clock in the hallway. A present to Billy when he reached fifty years at the steel works, the steel works whose new lease of life, still only four years old, was once again under debate. Where once Britain had supplied the world with steel now it was China. Slowly the metallic click of the pendulum moving back and forth penetrated Sally's brain and her lifelong hatred of the controlling relentless monotonous sound of timekeeping bubbled over.

'When you and Dad are dead I'm going to throw that clock into the Tees.' She paused for a second, savouring the thought. 'Yes, I'll make a day of it. Go down to the lookout point.'

Sally's mother screamed. It wasn't a loud piercing, wake the neighbours scream. It came from the back of her throat, a strangled whine which progressed to an agonised tear-sobbing cry of frustrated anguish. She crumpled slowly onto her knees, brought her hands up over her head and howled into the carpet. Sally laughed, involuntarily, her usual way of dealing with something that she didn't know or want to know how to deal with.

'Mam, you look dead funny down there. What's up? Who's been upsetting you?'

Her mother stood up carefully, deliberately. First onto her knees, then onto a left foot, then the right and finally she straightened up and came towards Sally.

'Mam?' Sally said lightly. Her Mam came closer. Sally backed towards the door and repeated, this time just a little nervously, 'Mam.' As her heel touched the bottom of the front door her mother's outstretched hands reached her and pinned her arms to her sides her face inches from her daughter. A tired almost haggard looking face, pinky-grey, fierce red blotches on the cheeks. Tear tracks ran down past the corners of the thin, tightly compressed lips and two unruly strands of hair, forgotten in the moment, had escaped from the bun on the back of her head and fell across the face.

Peggy struggled with the words in her head. Phrases ran riot in her mind. What sort of a mother are you? Are you really my daughter? What did we do wrong? Your poor daughter – what has she done to deserve you? None of them came out. Instead she pulled the woman in front of her away from the door, fumbled it open and with a deeply hurt, dredged out of her soul reaction, pushed Sally out of the house.

'Get out, get out, get out,' she rasped and shut the door with a fiercely controlled movement and bolted it. Still talking and sobbing she sank once more to her knees, her words tangled up with heart-wrenching sobs and straining tears, 'hate you, hate you, hate you, my own daughter, what have I done.' She stopped at last and curled into a ball. Gradually the silence took over and into it the clock moved calmly and the unfathomable peace that Sarah loved so much returned. The woman lay down on the hall carpet and drifted into a deep troubled sleep.

Outside the door Sally had stood, momentarily gob smacked, until she had shrugged her shoulders and turned away down the path. 'Something or somebody must have really pissed her mother off today.'

* * *

Sarah and Billy returned from town just in time for tea. They both noticed the red eyes and the silent blocked out expression; both wondered at the cause, and for once Sarah did not feel it was right to ask. She was growing up thought Billy. After tea, eaten in the continuing and strained silence, they had washed the dishes. By the time they had finished Grandma had disappeared. Billy said he would go and see if she needed anything. Sarah went into the parlour and curled up in one of the faded nineteen-sixties chairs; big arms and a high back, the patterned cover worn where heads and arms had sat in it. Sarah wanted something to do. The night before Billy had found her some old maps of the Tees Estuary and some pictures of the original railway which ran from the Wear Valley down to Port Darlington. It had reminded Sarah of a question she'd asked her Grandda before. When he came back into the parlour she asked him again:

'Grandda?' she began.

'Yes pet,' he replied hoping she would not ask how her Grandma was.

'Jane's mam Ann, where did she come from?'

His head full of what he had just heard from his wife Billy wasn't ready for the question. Ann was the last person he wanted to think about now. He should be careful with his reply. Sarah had asked this once before and he recalled that he had not really answered her then. Perhaps he should try and divert her with other members of the Webster family. The rumours about Ann's life would not be easy to explain, but this was Sarah and he recalled his determination to face her questions with the truth. She was old enough to be able to make up her own mind and besides, he knew that no information would lead to more questions and he wanted to think, especially after his conversation with his wife. He walked across the parlour to the chair opposite his Granddaughter and sat down, hands held together as if in prayer. Sarah recognised the signs, Grandda was thinking, remembering, pondering Grandma called it. She waited patiently, the exact opposite of her mother. Billy settled his mind and his memory and replied:

'No one really knows for sure. Apparently she never spoke about her life to anyone. No one is really sure how or where she and John met. According to Grandma Bella there was no one from Ann's family at the wedding, only

136

a friend of hers who gave her away. There were rumours that the friend wasn't a very nice person but no one knew for sure. The only thing that most people agree on is that she had some connection with the Wear Valley, but that was just vague stories as well.' Billy paused and wondered what to say next. Then he had a thought, perhaps he could use Sarah's vivid imagination to send her off on her own thoughts. 'Maybe you can think of something; get that imagination of yours working while I have forty winks.' He closed his eye and waited for the next question. None came and in a few minutes he was asleep dreaming that he was a Samurai poet travelling through the paddy fields of Japan.

Sarah snuggled back into the big old armchair with the threadbare covers and the slightly damp-smelling cushions. She curled her legs up under her and glanced briefly at the telescope on its stand on the mantelpiece. She thought about the quiet orderliness of the cottage and the jumbled disorder of the home that she and her Mam lived in. Their house was rented from a Housing Association, she wasn't too sure what that was, but the house had three bedrooms and was too big for just the two of them. When they had first moved in her Mam had a partner; boyfriend Grandma called him, a bit old-fashioned now thought Sarah. They had all moved in together and for a while had been a family. Soon after they moved in a man had come round one evening to see her Mam. Sally had persuaded her partner to be at home when the man came as well as two of Sarah's friends, bribed as Sarah had been, with pizza and a DVD for the evening. Her Mam had spoken to the man in the kitchen, only bringing him to the front room briefly. The other surprise had been her Mam tidying the house.

When the man had arrived it was not at all like it was normally. The man had had a brief look at the three girls before being taken back to the kitchen. There had been no more visits and the only consequence had been a violent argument between her Mam and her partner. The argument only stopped late into the night; after that her Mam and her partner were at it all night as Sarah and her friends called it. He left in the morning and the two of them were left alone in the house again, well not quite just the two of them – the man had left his dog, a vicious animal. Sarah thought about the life that she and her Mam lived. Her Mam was very disorganised. She compared their home to the reassuring comfort of her Grandparents' home and wondered what sort of childhood her ancestor Jane's mother Ann had had. They'd had some history lessons about mining in County Durham at school. Perhaps Ann came from one of those lead mining villages in the Wear Valley. The school was having a trip to a museum, Killhope she thought, yes that was it, Killhope Wheel. It was fifteen pounds, no chance of her Mam having that sort of money. Maybe Grandda would treat her. She looked over at him, he was sound asleep already. It was warm in the parlour; Sarah went off to sleep as well.

* * *

She did manage to persuade her Grandda to pay for her to go to Killhope. Grandma grumbled about it, said that he spoiled his granddaughter and he ought to be careful – after all look what had happened to their daughter – but Sarah got to go. They visited everything; listened to talks by the people at the mine; ate their picnics and tired themselves out in the forest behind the museum. On the way back on the bus as it travelled along the bottom of the Wear Valley, through the many small towns and villages, Wearhead, Westgate, St. Johns, Eastgate, Stanhope, Sarah dozed and as she did so she thought about Ann and what her life might have been like and how she could have come to have met John. Sarah's dream and Ann's life ran in parallel, they followed the same route but, from very different sides of a harsh divide. Sarah's dream was not Ann's life.

Ann, Wear Valley – Summer 1850

Ann Rookhope, wife of John Webster, was born in a rented cottage up one of the steep-sided tributary valleys of the Wear Valley in County Durham. Her childhood was untroubled and happy. She lived in a small mining village that straggled along the steep valley that a burn had carved through the Northern Pennines as they rose from the overwhelming weight of a previous period of global cooling. Her father was a lead miner working up the main part of the Wear Valley. Every Sunday evening he left home to walk over the fells to the mine bunkhouse where he slept in a bed that he shared with the opposite shift. The work was hard and unremitting all week, until he walked the eight miles home at the end of his last shift on a Saturday to spend just less than a day with his children until they went to bed after supper on Sunday. So Sunday was a very special day for Ann. On a Sunday she and her two brothers, young sister, and Mam and Da went to Chapel together, ate dinner together, and played together until her Da packed his bag and left for his work.

The week after her fourteenth birthday Ann's Da did not come home. He was working the last remnants of a sill when the roof collapsed. He was dead when they dug him out of the slip. They buried her Da in the small Chapel graveyard and as they did so the sunshine began to fade from Ann's life.

Stanley Jenkinson was nondescript to look at; the kind of man that passed unnoticed, third from the left on the third row of a sepia photograph of a village outing in the museum archive at Beamish. He had used his ability to blend into the crowd and disappear to avoid the retribution of a string of broken hearts in his life. He arrived in Rookhope on the day of the funeral. He had been staying in Stanhope on his way from somewhere west to somewhere else. He read about the funeral in the local newspaper and saw straight away the opportunity that a lonely, bereft woman and her four children might offer. He paid his respects, hat held submissively in front against his chest, head bent slightly, shoulders slumped and face impassive. An inveterate gambler Stanley Jenkinson was easy to misjudge and dangerous to trust. In her grief and desperation Ann's mother would do both during the course of that summer and autumn.

After the funeral Stanley invited himself to the wake in the institute and then, having paid his respects to the bereaved widow and heard from the village gossip the likely fate of the family, left to return the six miles to Stanhope where he had found himself a convenient place to stay with a well-intentioned widow – Stanley settled down to wait for the family to arrive.

What had happened to Ann's Da was not uncommon in the lead mines of County Durham and the consequence was predictable as well. He wasn't from Rookhope; his wife had met him at Westgate fair. He was from further up the Wear Valley and although they set up home in Rookhope after they married he had continued to work at Killhope. So when he died, although the village was sympathetic to the widow and her family no help was forthcoming for them. The eldest boy worked for the Iron Smelters at the top of the village. Already ill from the work, by the end of August he was unable to carry on working the hours needed to support the family. Until then his wages were just enough for them to get by with the washing and sewing that Ann and her mother took in. The widow used their small savings to pay a week's rent in case he should recover, but he was no better by the end of the week and they were evicted. The nearest Workhouse was in Stanhope down in the Wear Valley and it was to the Workhouse that they all went one September afternoon in eighteen fifty. They packed up their few possessions, or at least those that they could carry and left Rookhope for the last time. They walked up over the brow of the moor. It was a glorious autumn day, the sun rose into the clear sky across the valley as they climbed up out of the narrow valley. The children wanted to stop at the top so they sat beside the narrow track and ate their meagre dinner of bread and a smear of dripping – the family were just beginning to become undernourished. The three youngest children were able to walk unaided but the eldest boy had to be helped on anything but the flattest of the ground. His time at Lintzgarth lead smelting works was catching up with him. His job, one of the most lethal in the industry was to go into the big horizontal chimney viaduct that spanned the narrow valley of the Rookhope Burn and scrape the lead soaked residue from the walls of the chimney. He was poisoned beyond help and that autumn would be his last. The children sat on the hillside and looked down into the busy sun-drenched valley below them. Everywhere it was busy, in eighteen fifty the Wear Valley supplied large quantities of lead ore and lime to Britain and beyond. The railway had not yet reached Stanhope down to the east of where they sat, so there was a constant noise and bustle of horses and carts travelling up and down the valley bottom to the nearest rail head at Frosterley. Ann sat with her knees drawn up under her chin – she was heart-broken. She had heard the expression before and had wondered what it had meant. Now she knew, the dull ache in her chest was painful and she could imagine that her heart really had broken – she didn't play with her younger brother and sister as they chased about the grassy slope, she sat next to her elder brother as he tried to recover from the long climb up out of the valley.

When he was able to breathe again they left their resting place and headed along the brow of the hill and on down into the Wear Valley. As they crested the brow they had their first view of Stanhope – it seemed enormous, who could imagine a town with over seventy businesses, not to mention five public houses. The track joined the main road, a busy dusty streak of brown across the valley floor. The Workhouse was at the far end of Stanhope and they arrived as dusk was darkening the streets of the hard-working town. They were met by the Workhouse Master, a fiercely severe man who interviewed them and completed admission tickets for them all. They were put into the probationary ward to await the arrival of the Relieving Officer and then formal admission by the Board of Guardians. Their first night was a traumatic experience; Ann and her sister clung together all night. They were not likely to fare too well in the Workhouse. This one was contracted out to a mean couple who provided a poor diet, worse even than the minimal 'bill of fare' that was in the governing rules. They had no rest from the morning after they were accepted for admission; the influence of local Quakers meant that all those who were fit enough were expected to work. Ann was sent to serve in one of the town's pubs and it was there that she met Stanley again.

Stanley had returned from the funeral to his rented attic room with the widow in The Butts to await the arrival of the family. He was sure they would arrive as the woman he had spoken to at the funeral had assured him that all evicted mining families from the Rookhope valley went to the Stanhope Workhouse. He just had to wait. Stanley had always lived a frugal life so the money from his last scheme in Brampton over in Eskdale was sufficient to keep him in modest well-being while he waited. In the third week of September his patience was rewarded. He had taken to having a drink in a pub near the junction of the main street and the road up to the Workhouse and it was there that he found Ann as she collected beer tankards from the tables in the lounge bar. When she came up to his table he spoke to her in his under stated but compelling voice:

'Good day young lady, what has brought you to this public house so far from your village?'

When she heard his voice and recognised the slightly overweight, somewhat dishevelled man from her Da's funeral Ann jumped and almost dropped one of the tankards she had gathered up. She wasn't sure why she jumped; she had no reason to dislike him. This man who had made such an impression on her mother when he had appeared on the day of her father's funeral and yet, deep down, Ann felt an unease that she had no experience to name or identify, but she had to admit that she did not like him. Despite that Ann had been brought up in the chapel to seek the best in everyone so she smiled and said politely:

'Good day to you too sir. I trust you are well.'

'Most well my dear young lady and infinitely better for seeing you,' replied Stanley. 'Tell me; are you in Stanhope on your own?'

'Oh no sir, I am here with my family,' Ann paused, she still hated the stigma of their fate and found it hard to admit it to anyone, but this man had been most polite to her mother and so she continued: 'We had to leave the village and are now in the Workhouse.'

'Your mother, a fine brave woman, is she well? Stanley asked, concern in his voice, calculation in his eye.

'Yes, Sir, as well as can be expected given our circumstances,' said Ann.

Stanley was struck by the maturity of the young girl's speech and of her demeanour. His thought moved down from her face to her body, which although hidden by the Workhouse uniform was developed enough to hint at a growing young woman beneath.

Ann stepped back involuntarily under his gaze and he stopped his inspection, embarrassed that she had recognised the object of his glance and keen not to unsettle the girl.

'And your brothers and sister are they well too?' he changed the subject and she responded to his apparent concern for her family with a catch in her breath:

'My eldest brother died two weeks back, in the Workhouse Infirmary – it was the lead poisoning, he worked in the chimney flue,' she stopped for a minute.

Stanley waited, this was a key point in the conversation; he had learned when to wait and did so now.

'But my other brother and my sister are well, thank you.' Ann stopped, and for some reason, which she never came to terms with, she blurted out her worries and concerns to this stranger. A stranger that deep down she was unsure of and when she gave it some thought, did not like at all. 'We hate it in the Workhouse, my mother cannot cope, she needs to be out, but we cannot see anyway that can be.'

'Get those pots back here girl or you'll be back in the Workhouse sharpish,' came a voice from behind the bar.

Ann jumped again and with a brief 'good day' disappeared with the tankards and did not return that evening.

Stanley sat and finished off his warm ale, he was well pleased, the woman had been right. He could see how his scheme, the seeds of which had formed when he first saw the widow and her children at the funeral, could become a reality. Stanley had first recognised the possibilities of the scheme a year before. He had found himself in Bellingham in Northumberland during the collapse of the Bellingham Iron Works. He had gone there as a temporary clerk to the Union Bank. Whilst he was there he had got to know the wife of a contractor who had been employed by the Bank to rescue as much of the machinery and assets as he could. The young woman, left alone for much of the daylight hours by her work driven husband, had confided in the soft-spoken sympathetic man that Stanley portrayed to his victims. He had amused her with tales of the Ironworks original Owners, Messrs Campion and Batson and their wild scheme to make Bellingham a centre of Victorian entrepreneurial endeavour. Their vision had been short lived, lasting just short of ten years from its grand launch in eighteen thirty nine. Circumstances had compelled Stanley to leave before he could complete his scheme – the husband found out, and Stanley escaped with only a fraction of the money he had hoped to make.

Now though, a year later he was sure he could make it work. He had persuaded the Widow he lodged with that she should invest in railway stocks and that the best place to do that was in the North's railway town of Darlington. In his pocket he had a letter of introduction to a solicitor and stockbroker in Darlington signed by Mistress Thompson from Stanhope and an authority to draw funds from Backhouse's Bank. To make use of these documents Stanley needed to arrive in the Town with Mrs Thompson. He needed to arrive without arousing any suspicion; especially from the eldest girl, who he knew would be the most difficult to persuade. He decided that he would have to appeal to her imagination; he suspected that she was a bright imaginative girl given to romantic ideals – Stanley knew just how to make the best of people like that.

Over the next few weeks he began to build up Ann's trust. He resisted the urge to look at her in anything other than his light innocuous way. She began to relax and he was able to confirm that she was bright, imaginative and a romantic. One evening a visiting mines inspector from the London Lead Company head office left a copy of the London Gazette on the end of the bar. Unlike many Victorian itinerants Stanley Jenkinson could read – he picked up the newspaper and sat at his table to read about the world outside the Wear Valley. He was rewarded almost at once by an article describing what was being called a Great Exhibition of the Works of Industry. It was to be the Victorians' statement to the world about Britain's ability to produce manufactured goods of all sorts. It sounded very grand, even to Stanley, and more importantly for his plan, it sounded romantic, especially as it was described by the enthusiastic reporter. It was just what Stanley needed. He tore the account out of the newspaper and put into his pocket until the young girl, Ann he thought her name was, came to work the next morning.

Ann was surprised the next morning as she walked through the smoke-stained rooms collecting the previous night's empty glasses. Her bare feet stuck to the nicotine and drink-stained floors. Sitting at his table in the dullest corner of the lounge bar was the man from the funeral – she still did not know his name. She had got used to him now; her early wariness had lessoned as he spoke to her of trivial things and teased her mildly about her job and the way her long hair got caught between the beer tankards that she bent over to pick up from the tables. She was surprised and curious, but not concerned. Stanley had made his first move successfully – now for the next.

'I came in early as I could not sleep – I'm going off to London – to see the Great Exhibition,' he began.

'What's the Great Exhibition?' asked Ann.

'I've been reading about it in the newspaper,' said Stanley unable to avoid sounding grand as he said so, few ordinary people could read, certainly not a young girl from the end of nowhere up in a County Durham valley – she was bound to ask him to read what it said. She surprised him.

'I can read,' said Ann, I learnt at chapel, the Minister's wife taught us. Do you have the newspaper, can I read it?'

Stanley hesitated. His plan had been to read the account of the Great Exhibition to the young girl and capture her imagination with his words and embellish them to suit his plan and make it possible to persuade her to help him convince the rest of the family to travel with him to Darlington – there was no plan for them after Darlington, Stanley would be long gone before they suspected.

Ann asked again. She had a tenacious streak in her from her Da's side of the family.

'Please sir, may I read the newspaper?' Ann's life in the Workhouse and the pub were dull and repetitive and she yearned for some excitement and this seemed like a way to at least read of some excitement, she asked again: 'Please?'

Stanley acquiesced, to give him time to revise his plan. He reached into his jacket pocket and brought out a crumpled, folded sheet of newsprint and handed to the girl. She took it from him and said:

'Can I take it and read it to my family. I'll bring it back tomorrow, I promise.'

The hint of an idea began to form in Stanley's head.

'You can take it with you if you promise to help me Miss,' he said.

'Oh!' said Ann, surprised and for an instant suspicious, but again she had nothing that she could say she was suspicious about. She compromised. 'That depends on what you want me to help you with Sir?'

'Well,' said Stanley, 'to tell you the truth I'm a bit embarrassed to say. It's just, well, I best say what I think I suppose. It's your mother, I'm quite taken with her, ever since I first saw her, first time I was quite overwhelmed with feelings. Feelings of...' Stanley watched the girl carefully. He didn't want to go too far, but he wanted to get her on his side so that she would agree to help him in his plan. He continued with a few more heartfelt phrases until he sensed that he had said enough. 'Well anyway, if you could see your way to saying a word on my behalf – to your mother – I would be most grateful, and you can borrow the newspaper account.'

Stanley had succeeded with the next stage in his plan. Ann took the newspaper account back to the Workhouse and read it to the family. She also relayed Stanley's clumsy endearments to her mother, who agreed, with little persuasion, to meet him down by the ford the next Sunday afternoon. Ann's mother had always been prone to accept both hard luck stories and flattery in equal measure. Stanley gave her both. She accepted his request that she go with him to Darlington to help retrieve his inheritance from a solicitor who needed proof that the black sheep of the Jenkinson family had mended his ways and was now a respectable man. Stanley promised that if she would help him in this simple task then she and her family would be free of the Workhouse and that he would set them up in Darlington where an accomplished woman such as she was would have no trouble getting work and lodgings. Ann's mother accepted his plan without question. In her mind she was already planning a future life for both herself and her family in the care and hopefully the love of this kind and generous man.

Stanley visited the Workhouse Master the next day and explained his plan to look after the widow and her family. He repeated his story that he had come into an inheritance and needed to go to Darlington to collect it. The Workhouse Guardian that he approached was sceptical but an opportunity to have one less family to house was not to be passed, over so his request was accepted especially as Ann's mother was unusually vocal in her support of the plan. The family were allowed to leave at the end of the week, by helping the brewery drayman to unload barrels for a week he negotiated a ride for them all on a brewery dray returning to Wolsingham.

Ann, Witton Park – Autumn 1850

Ann's memory of their arrival in Witton Park and their journey from Stanhope was hazy. She recalled that they had stopped overnight twice, once in Wolsingham and then in Witton le Wear. Stanley had appeared with some bread and ale at Wolsingham, but there had been no food in Witton le Wear so it had been a big surprise when Stanley had found some money to feed them all when they reached Witton Park. After their meal Stanley announced that he was going to look for somewhere to stay and to arrange for their onward journey to Darlington. He ignored their pleas to go with him and left quickly, relieved to be away from the constant questions and clinging reliance of them all. Stanley headed for the nearest pub, he needed a drink and to make some contacts.

Inside the pub, seated by himself, his corduroy railway-uniform jacket unbuttoned and his peaked hat on the table in front of him sat Harold Winterburn – engine driver. In some respects another ordinary man. Away from his work, in the same sepia photograph of a group of the men of his time he too would not have stood out. Third row, second from the right this time. Outside the photograph, dressed in his railway uniform, five feet eight, ten stones, size eight feet, slightly splayed he could stand with little obvious effort, balanced on the foot plate of the engine that he drove. The hint of an oily black stain across his right cheek, left handed then, that was rare.

His face windblown to a thin vein-lined red where he had spent years peering out past the engines he drove into the distance, the few routes on his rota imprinted on his mind so that he could drift off between the signals into a fantasy world. A world that Stanley Jenkinson was about to stumble into with Ann. Of the three of them only two would come out alive, of the other two one of them would fall into a life right outside their imagination.

At the beginning of the eighteen fifties rail travel in Victorian Britain was starting to become popular and accessible as more and more track was laid across the country and people began to explore their country. Even at this early stage of development consistent speeds of twenty and forty miles per hour, frightening to many still, meant that journeys all over Britain could be done in unimaginably short times. For the first time it was possible to travel from Darlington to London in a day. In this new age of steam the men who drove the smoky, spark-spitting, noisily-monstrous machines that epitomised Victorian engineering achievement had an aura about them that attracted respect. Harold Winterburn stepped out of his railway cottage door at the start of each shift an ordinary man; he climbed up onto the footplate of his engine a figure of influence. He had learnt to make the most of his position and had his fingers into all sorts of schemes – he was a man with a lot of contacts along the railway route from Frosterley to Redcar; people who needed things moving with no questions asked and with no trail left. There were not many things that Harold had not been paid well to transport up or down the railway.

Stanley noticed Harold as he pushed open the pub door just down the street from Witton Park station. He went up to the bar and bought a pint of the same ale that he had been unloading the week before to earn a ride to Wolsingham. He stood at the bar for a few minutes savouring his first drink for a few days and considered the engine driver. He had reckoned that it would cost about four shillings and six pence to get himself and the family to Darlington from Witton Park. He needed to get them there, well at least the mother anyway, as soon as he could, to take advantage of the papers in his inside pocket. Not only that, he would have to get rid of the family as soon as he had completed his business with the solicitor. The last thing Stanley wanted was to be stuck with the clinging woman and her family. First though he needed to get them all to Darlington quickly; by railway they could be there tonight, but not without money, unless. He picked up his half empty glass and walked over to the engine driver's table and sat down opposite him. Harold watched him as he approached. He was used to people coming and asking for favours, mostly requests to travel somewhere. He sat back and filled his pipe from the tobacco in his jacket pocket.

The two men began their conversation carefully; weather – good; the growth of the railways – impressive; the growth of the Iron works – uncertain; each tried to work out the others character and way of thinking. The first break through to a shared experience was an answer to Stanley's question:

'Any work around here for a man with ambitions?' he asked.

Harold drank from his dirty pewter mug. 'Depends on his ambitions', he replied at length.

'Profit,' said Stanley, 'no point in working unless it's for profit.'

'Depends on what he has to offer as well? On what assets a man might have to invest for profit,' continued Harold, 'do you have any assets that you could invest?'

Stanley thought about the papers in his pocket; about the money he hoped to realise from his visit to the solicitors. He decided to see what the other man might suggest.

'What type of assets might secure a good return would you say?'

Harold looked across at the man opposite him. On which side of the law might he lie he wondered? He took a well-tried route.

'All sorts of things get transported up and down the railway, so I'm told.' He paused, 'not all get transported for the benefit of the railway. I have to be ever watchful on the company's behalf.' He added.

Stanley, felt he could take a chance:

'You must get paid well, it's a responsible job. The company must rely on your integrity,' he said.

'Yes, but as you said yourself; no point in working unless it's for profit,' Harold waited.

'So what are the most profitable assets that travel along the railway,' asked Stanley.

'People,' replied Harold. There's always a demand to transport people, the businesses of the Tees are always looking for people. Some people will pay well to get there themselves and other people will pay well to have people brought to them. Are you thinking of travelling alone; you do want to travel don't you? Do you have any others with you who need to travel as well?' Harold drained his ale and sat back to wait.

The two men sat looking across the stained table at each other. Their sleeves stuck to the surface of the wooden table. Stanley hedged; he wasn't in control of this conversation, an unusual experience for him. He needed to know more about this man. Instinctively he knew he had the end of an opportunity in his hand if he didn't snatch too fast. He decided on more time to consider. 'Your glass is empty can I stand you another?' he asked.

'Don't mind if I do,' replied Harold, non-committal and content to wait. A free drink would pass the time. He studied Stanley as he left for the bar. First watching as he approached the bar and then through the mirror behind it as he ordered the two drinks. The three piece suit was not his own; the sleeves were just too long and the trousers were too short. The waistcoat struggled to contain the pot belly even with more than the customary bottom button undone. The hair matched the colour of the walls he thought. He glanced to the right to check. Yes, a dusty musky off-white yellow, both hair and wall long neglected. His eye stopped at a cupboard in the corner, both doors half open, half lit from a dull light coming through the front windows. Two shelves were overflowing with packets, boxes, bags and loose items placed with no apparent care or plan for space or access. It offended the neat man's being. Without getting up and moving closer Harold was unable to tell what the contents of the cupboard might be.

Harold turned his attention back to the man at the bar. He was at home at a bar. He leant easily against it, foot balanced on the metal rest that ran along it. He was talking to a tall well-dressed man. The man smiled, without his eyes, and left the bar with his two drinks. Stanley was next to be served, he turned his conversation to the barmaid, he was a natural talker. He raised his thumb towards the man who had just left to emphasise a point he was making to her. She smiled, no eyes involved there either. Harold drifted past the two of them to the other corner of the room where a silent focussed game of dominoes was in progress. He squinted to be able to see the row that was facing him and was briefly concerned to realise that he could not really make out any of the patterns.

* * *

Ann and her family did not stay in the eating house very long. The woman who ran it needed the table and it was obvious they had no money. She turned them out despite their plea that they needed to wait for Stanley.

'He'll be likely in the pub – the one near the station.' She took pity on the anxious-looking woman and continued, not unkindly, 'You can sit in the park just up the street; if he comes back I'll tell him where you are.'

'He's sure to come back,' said Ann's mother, 'But if you would tell him where we are I would be most grateful.' They passed a pub on their way to the park and Ann suggested going in to check if the man was there. She still hadn't been able to bring herself to refer to him as anything other than the man.

'Alright, but don't disturb Mister Jenkinson if he's busy. He might be talking to someone about how we can all get to Darlington so come away if he is,' said her mother.

'Yes mother', said Ann, and crossed the street and went into the pub; Stanley was standing at the bar. He did not appear to be talking to anyone specifically so Ann went straight up to him.

'Mam says to say that we'll be in the park, sir. It's just up the street on the left. We'll be waiting there for you. The woman in the eating house said we couldn't wait for you. Will you be long?' She asked.

Stanley looked a bit annoyed. He had not wanted to be seen with the family yet. He glanced across at the engine driver. He was looking the other way, maybe he hadn't noticed. Stanley hoped so.

'You best not leave your family too long. I'll not be long so run along now I'll be there as quick as I can.' He took her arm and led her to the door, keen that she left before the other man saw her. With Ann gone he ordered two drinks and returned to the table. Harold had noticed Ann.

He took a drink from the tankard, set it down carefully on the table and looked over at Stanley.

'Is that lass with you then?'

'Stanley took a drink too, a longer more reflective drink. His next answer could be his opportunity or his downfall, he gambled and as was often the case he won.

'Yes, she's the eldest daughter of a widow that I have agreed to help on their journey.' He laughed, self-consciously, but not well enough to fool Harold. 'The woman has taken a liking to me and I am now unsure how I might leave her without too much heartbreak on her part.'

There was a definite pause as the two men drank their ale. It was now mid-afternoon and the sun was beginning to move across the floor of the bar. It had reached the edge of the domino player's table so that one player had to hold his hand up to shield the row of ivory pieces so that he could read them properly. Harold began the final move.

'I might have a solution to your problem. It may be possible to transport you and your 'family' (he emphasised the word slightly) to Darlington for a price that will suit us both and leave you able to continue your journey without them.' Harold paused. 'I suspect that you have an asset, as yet not invested, but ready to use... ... ripe for investment you might say.' He stopped.

Stanley was taken aback. How did the man know what was in his pocket.

'What kind of an asset do you believe I might have that would be worth investing in?' he asked.

'The girl,' said Harold.

Stanley had been raising his tankard to his mouth; it took all his self-control to continue without showing any sign of surprise. Stanley Jenkinson was an itinerant con-man by trade. He had survived for the past ten years by tricking a string of unsuspecting widows out of their meagre savings across the North of England. It was an unpleasant occupation, he had left despair and anger in his wake, but it was what he was good at, he had never thought of any other way of exploiting the people, especially women, that he knew he was able to take in with his innocuous, appealing manner. Making money from a young girl though was different. Stanley was surprised to find that he was not sure if he had either the courage or the wish to do so and yet, the idea had aroused his interest and he felt compelled to find out more. He wanted to know more:

'What kind of investment did you have in mind?' he asked.

'Nocturnal entertainment, fresh, untouched ripe for someone who prefers a first-time investment,' Harold floated the idea and stopped to see the other man's reaction.

'Ah,' said Stanley and paused.

Harold continued: 'The right contacts could maximise the investment for the owner; contacts who know how to realise the investment, who know the right people and the right place. The rewards could be significant for both the contact and the owner.'

Stanley realised that he needed to make a decision now. Two investments, the widow's papers and the young girl could make him a sizeable amount and sitting opposite him was a man who could help achieve both. He wondered what the price would be, and yet, the widow's inheritance was already his, after all he could walk to Darlington if he had to, now he came to think about it. The girl, she would be a bonus, profit that he had not even thought about, anything he could get would be a bonus. He committed himself; he felt it was well worth the risk:

'Hypothetically, how might the owner realise his investment?' he asked.

Harold smiled to himself, the bait had been taken he just needed to bring in his fish. 'The person with the contacts would need to have sight of the asset – a proper sight.'

'Of course,' responded Stanley, 'the sort of thing that could perhaps be arranged during a train journey?'

'Why not,' replied Harold, 'a ride on the footplate for the owner and the asset, both could be arranged.' He paused again awaiting a response. None came – Stanley was holding his breath. Harold held all the cards in this deal, he went on.

'The train will stop at Heighington station. An acquaintance of mine is the station master there. He could organise a visit to the engine and perhaps a short ride,' said Harold.

Stanley took another drink from his tankard and moved the negotiation on:

'That would seem to be an admirable plan. It just leaves us to agree on remuneration for the owner.'

'Ah,' said Harold, 'It always comes down to money.' He sat back and waited for the other man to make the first move. He had learnt that it put him into a position of advantage if he waited at this point. This time though, he was surprised by the man's first offer.

'I would see it as more than adequate recompense if the transaction made it possible for the widow and her family to travel, without cost to Darlington. I believe that she has relatives in that town and I consider it my duty to see that the family would be safely delivered to their destination,' Stanley paused, he wondered how much he could ask for, but thought the risk was worth it, he went on, 'I myself am intending to travel on to London. So a suitable ticket from Darlington to London would be quite sufficient recompense.'

Harold was amazed that the man did not recognise the potential value of the young girl to the right investor. Harold knew just the person to contact and had a good idea of what sort of money he could make. He just had one thing to sort out. His contact was not in Darlington it was in Port Darlington, or Middlesbrough as it was being called. He would need to get the girl there without raising her suspicions and that meant that she must agree to travel on past Darlington – this man would have to help.

'That seems a reasonable request, I have just one other thing I would ask in return.' He said.

Stanley, sighed inside, he'd gone too far, what else did this man want?

'Name it and I will do my best to comply,' he replied.

'The asset needs to travel to Middlesbrough to complete the investment. You would need to ensure that happens before I could see a way of providing you with your ticket to London. You need to accompany the girl to Middlesbrough as I think it unlikely that she would agree to travel on from Darlington by herself. Your ticket to London would of course be from Middlesbrough. I think we have a deal if you are agreeable,' Harold sat back and waited.

Stanley agreed, he had little choice.

'Excellent, when does your train depart.' he asked.

'6.30 pm prompt.' said Harold.

'We'll be on the platform,' said Stanley still unsure how he would be able to leave the family at Darlington and yet stay on the train with the girl to Middlesbrough.

'May I wish you good health then, and here's to a successful investment,' Harold drained his tankard and placed it down on the table in front of him. He picked up his cap to go, but before he did so he gave Stanley a clue as to how he might get Ann away from her mother and family. 'You need to get into the front four carriages, the back two will be left at Darlington. They are part of a special that came up here last week. We are taking them back to the depot. Is there anything else we need to discuss?'

'No,' said Stanley.

'I will see you at Heighington station then. Good day to you sir,' Harold rose to leave.

Stanley completed his drink and went to find the family. He had a whole afternoon to fill in with them but he was not too worried about that. For a small outlay he would buy ice creams for them all. He found them sitting together on the grass in the park in the late autumn sunshine. They had been befriended by the local-minister's housekeeper. She and Ann's mother were talking in animated fashion about the difficulties of getting the working men to go to chapel. It was a clear still warm day; perhaps the last before the winter began to encroach. As he had approached them he had no doubt that they would go along with his wishes. He felt sure that none of them would have ever seen a train before let alone travel on one. They would have no idea of where they might be, they were totally reliant on him, especially as it would be dark before they began their journey, there would be no light in the carriage as they travelled to Darlington.

Ann's mother greeted him with grateful surrender in her voice.

'Oh Mister Jenkinson, I'm so pleased to see you. I had begun to wonder where you had got to. Ann said that you were in the pub. I trust you were successful with your business,' she said.

Stanley scowled briefly as he turned to take off his coat. None of the family noticed his grimace, just as well given how bright the eldest girl was. He would have to be more careful, still not long now to keep up his caring face.

'Now then my dear lady, there was no need for you to be concerned, I was always coming back for you, you have never been far from my thoughts all afternoon.'

Ann's mother blushed at this compliment. The pale spots on her face matching her weather-marked cheeks and nose for a few seconds and momentarily making her look less careworn than usual.

'What's going to happen to us all sir?' asked Ann, nowhere near as bemused by this strange unnerving man as she could see that her mother was.

'Now then young Ann just you wait while I sit down here on the grass with you all and then I'll tell everyone our plans,' Stanley laid great emphasis on the word 'our'. It was something that the housekeeper remembered when she was questioned by a tall serious and sombrely dressed man a week later in Darlington.

'He told them that he had just agreed with a business acquaintance – she had to be helped with the word acquaintance – that they were all going to go to London,' the housekeeper had explained. The man he had met represented a charitable organisation – more stumbling over this phrase. The man had heard of the conditions of families in the North-East and had determined to come north to help families who had fallen on hard times. The man they called Mister Jenkinson had apparently and very graciously put forward the family as a worthy cause and his suggestion had been accepted. The only problem seemed to be that to take advantage of the offer they all needed to get to Darlington. It had been at this point that Stanley had managed to allay the doubts in Ann's mind about his intentions towards her mother. The housekeeper had recalled his words to the family.

'He said that they were not to object as he had arranged to get them to Darlington that very evening. He had obtained the means for them to travel on the next train from Witton Park station, so they all needed to go with him to the station', she had reported. 'Wasn't that a most kind and generous thing to do,' she had added.

Stanley had stood up and shepherded the family towards the station. When they arrived he had recalled the words of the engine driver.

'We had better get into this first carriage,' he advised. 'I'm not sure when it leaves so we had best take our seats now.' He opened the door of the first coach and ushered them all onto the train. 'Now you all wait here while I go and check when the train leaves. I'll be back in a few minutes.' As he walked up the platform he glanced back at the last carriage and saw a look of excitement and wonder on Ann's face as she leaned out of the window – Stanley knew his plan would succeed.

Ann, Middlesbrough – Winter 1850

When the train arrived in Darlington it stood at the platform for some time. Ann's mother had to pacify her two youngest children as they grew restless. She had complete faith in Mister Jenkinson so she waited patiently for his return. After what seemed like a long time there was a crash behind them and the carriage they were in jumped forwards, knocking the two young children onto the floor. Several more crashes could be heard before the coach began to move backwards. It swayed and rattled along for several minutes before coming to a stop again. They could see nothing from the carriage windows in the almost total darkness of the cloud-filled winter sky. The woman drew the two young children closer to her as the night stretched out and no one came to see them. Fearful of leaving the carriage they stayed where they were huddled together to keep warm. They were found the next morning by a railway workman checking the line. By the time they were taken back to the station, warmed up and their story pieced together there was no sign of Stanley Jenkinson or Ann. Everyone came to the same conclusion – he had travelled on to London, taking Ann with him. Ann's mother never saw her daughter again.

* * *

Harold Winterburn was now in charge and in full control of the asset and its owner. As the train had pulled out of

Darlington station he had produced a dark brown glass bottle with a corked top. He pulled out the cork and offered it to Stanley.

'Here, this'll warm you up, have a sip of that.' he'd said.

When it was offered to Ann she had choked on the bitter tasting mixture only partly disguised by a sweet liquid. They had persuaded her to drink a little to stave off the cold, but she had spat it out and refused any more. Her Mother's saviour had no such inhibitions and as the train crossed the Durham countryside he had let it take control.

Stanley had never felt like this before and he was showing off now. He was balanced on the foot plate almost leaning out over the edge, his coat open, blown back by the wind. Ann watched, horror in her heart, yet transfixed by the throbbing pink-red thing that stuck out from the mass of hair at the top of the man's legs. She tried to look away but couldn't pull her eyes away, until Stanley said the wrong thing.

Stanley wasn't in control of himself. It was an unusual state of affairs for him but the events of the last day had changed his outlook on life. Until now he had taken only a passing interest in women, satisfied by the comfort of conning vulnerable women out of their savings with the guile of his voice and demeanour, but the scheme that the engine driver had suggested to him had aroused in Stanley an animal like desire for the young girl that they had kidnapped onto the train. His latest antics were driven by an uncontrollable sexual urge. The frightening exhilaration was leading him to abandon his normal controlled approach to his scheme.

'Bet you liked your Dad to do this eh Lass?' he shouted over the noise.

The thought of her caring, sensitive, modest, considerate father doing anything so, so vile as this man was doing, tipped Ann from horrified disbelief to uncontrolled anger. She ran at the man with unbridled rage. As she ran forward the engine passed over a loose join in the track, where the line went onto the bridge over the Tees at Stockton. Ann pitched forward; she stretched out her arms to catch herself. Stanley staggered and clutched at the side of the cab with one hand. He half caught it and might have recovered but at that moment Harold grabbed the young girl by the nearest outstretched arm. She twisted around and her other hand, already bunched into an angry fist caught the exposed penis of the off-balance man. He screamed, doubled up, lost his grip and disappeared.

Harold pulled the distraught young girl towards him and enveloped her in his arms. She sobbed hysterically and clung to his coat.

Stanley hit the ground half way across the bridge. His head struck a stanchion and he lost consciousness as he rolled under the fence and dropped into the icy river below. The shock revived him and in a moment of self-preservation he struck out for the shore, unable to see but instinctively moving towards the nearest bank, away from the safer bank of the Stockton coal Staithes where some help might have been found. The tide took him up and down the Tees for several days before he was found and pulled out by two poachers. Undiscovered and unknown he was buried in a pauper's grave in Stockton churchyard.

* * *

Ann slowly began to stop crying. As she did so she began to notice where she was. She realised that in her anger she had allowed the engine driver to put his arms around her and hold her tight against him. Faintly, at the back of her mind, Ann began to be aware of a sense of foreboding that she could not identify – until she looked up and into the eyes of the man who held her. Ann had always been unsure of Stanley. She had been wary of his intentions, but she had never been frightened of him. Even when he had begun to behave in such a strange and horrible way on the footplate of the engine her initial disgust had turned to anger – at no time had she been afraid of Stanley. When she looked up into the eyes of the man holding her she moved from fear straight to terror. There was no light in the eyes that looked down at her; through her clothes; across her innocent untouched body, and deep into herself. Even before Harold moved his hand down from her shoulder Ann felt cold terror – abject terror, and complete vulnerable loneliness – a feeling that she was never able to lose from her soul for the rest of her life.

* * *

She lay on the bed. Not her bed, just the bed she used when the men came. It was early morning, she recalled her last visitor. He had been too drunk to know too much about what he was doing. He had only just managed to undo the buttons on his trousers as he had fallen on top of her. As he did so semen had sprayed up the inside of her thigh and across the bottom of the crumpled dress that she had been trying to pull up ready for him. Her second best dress, used for regulars, not specials. She didn't get too many specials. The man had sprawled across her, his thing – after her first encounter with a man's penis, Stanley's, she shuddered at the memory, that's what she called it – had only just entered her body when his drink sodden ejaculation drained his spirit. He had belched, an acid, rancid smell of stale food that had drifted into her face. His last conscious act was to slide a nicotine tasting lick, it wasn't a kiss, across her mouth and cheek, and then he had passed out.

Ann couldn't move to start with. She had struggled, which had made him grab hold of her arm in his soporific drunken state. Eventually he snorted and rolled off her. She had sat on the side of the bed until he woke. He had staggered off the bed pulling up his trousers with clumsy disjointed tugs; he fought a disoriented, ineffectual battle with his buttons – he had only managed one. He had searched in an equally disoriented yet determined fashion in his pockets for the coins that she needed then left, crashing into the end of the bed, the door, the banister and the hat stand, a curiously refined object, in an otherwise abject brothel on the corner of Gray Street in the dampest end of Middlesbrough just where it reached the docks.

* * *

Ann lay on the bed. It was early morning and the north-facing window showed a loom of light and no more. She waited, the usual knot of anxiety in her stomach. Angelique would be in soon. To collect the night's takings. Ann hadn't checked to see if she had made the minimum needed before she got anything. She knew she hadn't. Her short life as a prostitute had taught her the essentials quickly. Six punters and she could be warm and eat, five and she could eat, four and Angelique could be paid, three and Angelique would beat her, two and Archie would beat her, one; well one wasn't an option really. She was still there and so far she had only had three beatings. Two from Angelique and one from Archie. The cracked ribs had excited a few of her clients when she cried out in pain; although not as they thought or hoped from the excitement that their drunken state had brought on them. Ann had been lucky so far.

She thought of the advice that Lizzie had given her, but it was all pretence. She couldn't enjoy it, she hated it, she wouldn't encourage them, and she would survive them; so she only got the drunks that were too far gone to care; to notice or to choose. Ann hadn't yet learned how to work to thrive or even survive.

Ten o'clock and she awoke briefly. She thought again of Lizzie's words.

'Moan, when they get inside you, arch your back, whisper in their ears, tell 'em how good they are, tell 'em they're the only one that gets to you. Then they'll ask for you and Angelique will ask 'em for more and you'll get better clothes, well a better dress, no sense wearing anything else is there.' Lizzie had cackled at her joke. Ann sighed, the day faded and she slept again.

* * *

The girls sat round the table in Angelique's kitchen.

'Lizzie!' said Ann suddenly, her courage finally seized, 'how do you moan for a man?' The others laughed. Lizzie leant back, tilted her head behind her, hitched up her dress, spread her legs apart and put her hands between her thighs. She moaned a low sound from the back of her throat. Ann hated it when the girls touched their own bodies, but sometimes, like now, it was a hatred tinged with a guilty desire to try the same thing on her own body.

'Go on Annie,' said Millie. Ann hated being called Annie, Angelique had called her that, and the first time she had met her. 'You try.' All the girls joined in. The moans were all different, the chairs creaked and their hands rubbed back and forth between their thighs. Archie walked in and stopped to look.

'Need any help girls? Getting in some practice?' He smiled, a leering, ugly disturbing smile that touched nothing but his cruel mouth. They all stopped abruptly. Archie didn't need any invitations, they all sat back at the table and went back to their bread and watered ale – the one 'free' meal of the day. Angelique came in.

169

'Let's check you all out then,' and disappeared into her 'interview' room as she called it.

'Need any help Angie, I can put me hand to anything,' smirked Archie. The retort from Angelique explained graphically how she could keep the girls in control and handle Archie for all his size and temper.

The girls went in, one by one, to be 'checked' for lice and fleas, bruises and the clap. Any one of these could mean a visit from 'the doctor' – he took his payment in kind, part of the internal investigation he said. Angelique's was a 'good' house, not like the ones right close to the docks, where the dark, damp, decaying houses drew the worst and the desperate and the dying and yet seemed able to produce new unwanted life with depressing frequency.

* * *

Ann lay on the bed. Angelique had given her a warning, a final warning, one more beating and she'd be out. She fought with her conscience and her fading, damaged principles. She recalled again Lizzie's advice on how to encourage a man. Despair and revulsion fought with the terror of being alone in the smoke-filled, dirt-stained, noisy iron town that she had been brought to. Why hadn't her mother come looking for her? Where were they? The familiar anguished debate raged in her head as she curled into a ball and wept dry tears. How could anyone do those things? She sat up, held her head in her hands, her lank, greasy hair tangled between her fingers. The first thing she had lost had been warm almost comforting tears. No one had come to comfort her, to wipe her eyes, to hold her close. Well plenty had come to hold her, but none in loving safety.

Ann & John, Commercial Street, Middlesbrough – 1851

Ann lay on the bed. Four miles away John Webster was being taken to task by his two brothers.

'John lad,' said Ned, 'I don't believe you've had a woman yet and you're a man now, twenty one this year.'

'Leave him be Ned,' said Jeremiah, the middle brother anxious to keep the peace one minute and cause grief the next. It depended on his mood. The two brothers had come up from the farm to take John to the Ship Inn for a drink. It wasn't something that John would have done on his own, but he agreed so that he could spend time with his brothers; there was still no sign of any reconciliation with his sister. They sat in the corner. The Spaniard's corner it was called now; the only recognised memory of Mary's ill-fated husband who had disappeared the previous winter. The farm was doing well and John was finally getting the knack of filling the ironstone tubs and therefore getting paid consistently for them. The three brothers had some spare money of their own and a half day off – what to do? The devil came into Jeremiah's head and he let it play.

'Let's go to Middlesbrough – see the sights,' he paused,' maybe we can find John a girl.'

Ned grinned at the idea and banged his pot down on the table.

'Now that's an idea Jeremiah,' he said, 'Come on John, what do you say, we could go down there on the train, we can manage third-class day returns.'

John protested, he had things to do, he had to be up early the next morning, he'd promised his landlady this, the neighbour that, but his two brothers were insistent and determined and they wouldn't take no for an answer. They caught the afternoon train down to Eston Junction and then on to Middlesbrough. The town seemed enormous; nearly eight thousand people had arrived in the rapidly growing town in just twenty years. There was street after street of houses all joined together in long terraces criss-crossing the flat land on the south bank of the Tees; new buildings going up everywhere. It was clear to anyone from the town that the three brothers were visiting from the countryside and a series of new friends helped them to spend their money on ale, fortune telling and a trip across the river and back. The three of them became by degrees, happy, uninhibited, morose and disorientated so that when, in the late evening, they arrived at the railway station they were just in time to see the last train disappearing towards Eston Junction. They were stuck in Middlesbrough. They would have to walk home, but to three fit hard-working men the four mile walk was no problem – an hour at the most. They got some directions, which they vaguely understood, from the station porter as he chased them off the platform and set off eastwards, along the north side of the railway, the wrong side to get back to Eston easily. They followed the edge of the noisy bustling rail yard and in the fading evening light found themselves at the end of Commercial Street. The darkness and noise disoriented them even more, but it seemed to be a straight road so they set off along it.

They had found themselves in the east end of Middlesbrough close to Port Darlington. This was where the town and the Port shared its red light houses. As they walked down the street they noticed a shadowy figure in the dark ahead of them walking up the middle of the road with a red lantern. The shadow stopped outside a house and left his lantern in the doorway. The three brothers stopped outside the doorway. Jeremiah took the opportunity to empty his bladder against the house's side wall. A large woman was standing in the doorway; Angelique had been thinking of closing up, until the railway man with his lantern appeared along the street, trade had been poor that night. Then she saw the three lads, clearly brothers, clearly drunk, clearly from the country walking down the street towards her. She waited to see what they would do. They stopped while one of them, she guessed it was the middle brother, pissed against the wall. He finished and began to button up his fly before they moved on.

'Shame to put it away without making good use of it; handy looking thing like that, needs a woman's touch lad,' she said loudly.

The three of them jumped. No one had spoken to them since they had left the station and they had settled into a steady companionable stride as they walked home sobering up as they did so with the cool night air and exercise.

'Well come on boys, aren't you coming in. The girls are waiting and ready to make your dreams come true,' said the woman.

Ned and Jeremiah glanced at each other. They both remembered their promise to their brother and without saying anything, instinctively came to the same decision.

'How much Missus?' asked Ned, boldness prompted by the need to be the eldest?

'Two shillings deluxe, shilling for a straight fuck and for a half a crown we'll give you all a night you'll never forget,' replied Angelique carefully. She didn't want to frighten them off and she suspected they might not have much money left after a night in Middlesbrough.

The two elder brothers felt in their pockets. The night had made big holes in their money.

'How much you got John?' asked Jeremiah?

John came out of his shocked reverie, brought on by the sight of the woman, her blunt speech and most of all by the thought of her offer which excited him much more than he wanted to admit.

'No, not me, thank you madam, we'll be on our way,' he said hurriedly.

'Come on John,' said Ned, 'this is your chance, have yourself a good time with a lovely lady, bet they'll know how to make a man of you.'

Angelique sensed the moment. 'Yes love, I've got just the lady for you, well respected, and in demand from my more discerning clients' – she'd heard that expression at the fair once and had used it ever since, whatever it meant. She could tell they would struggle to raise even the shilling but money was money and Annie had had no visitors that night. For some reason she took pity on both of them.

'Tell you what,' she said to Ned, 'if you can raise a shilling between you I'll introduce your young brother to Annie, special offer, can't do better than that can I.'

The devil prodded Jeremiah and he reached into John's pockets knowing that he would have more money than he and Ned would. Before John could react he pulled out two coins. He added one from his own pocket and prodded his elder brother. Another coin emerged and was added to the small pile in his hand. The deal was done.

Ned and Jeremiah half carried John through the door and, guided by Angelique, up the stairs and along the passageway to the smallest, dingiest room at the end. Angelique opened the door and said loudly:

'Special customer for you Annie – give him a good time.' She leaned over the bed and whispered, 'make him happy and you'll not get the beating you deserve, you've had no-one tonight have you? This'll be your last chance, so make the most of it.'

They pushed the still protesting John through the door and down onto the bed.

'Take his boots off then,' demanded Angelique.

John's boots were removed and thrown into the corner and the three conspirators retreated to the kitchen to sample some of Angelique's ale with Ned and Jeremiah's last few pennies.

Ann had retreated to the head of the bed when the four people had come through the door. She knew she had no choice, she had to do her job, she had to make this man happy, to let him come into her body, to – she still couldn't bring herself to talk the way that Lizzie and the other girls did about the sex that was their every day job. The man who had been left in the room had rolled away from her on the bed. He sat up half way along the right hand side of the bed and Ann noticed his tight, hunched shoulders, he was frightened too. He made no other attempt to move or speak. There were several minutes of silence in the room and then Ann made up her mind. She sat up and tried to remember what Lizzie had told her to do and how. She hotched across the bed on her knees, came up behind the man and paused. He was young, maybe in his early twenties. Ann's powers of observation had improved in her time at the house. He had the familiar country-workers clothing; an old cloth suit of worn trousers and shiny elbow-polished jacket with a greasy collar that was level with her chin. The collarless shirt was dirty white cotton with faded blue stripes, just visible between his neck and the jacket. Unlike many of the visitors to the house this man was clean. He smelt of dust, a bit like her father had when he had come home from the mine, a strangely comforting smell. It helped to give her the courage and determination to place her hands on his shoulders – he jumped.

'You don't have to do this, I won't mind,' he said. His voice was quiet and unhurried, the words came slowly but clearly and were easy to understand, the Yorkshire accent soft, yet strong enough for her to recognise it. His hair was quite short, cut close to stop the dust from the mine matting into it as he worked under ground. Ann felt a sudden unwilling sense of compassion for the man and pressed her fingers into his taut muscles and began to massage his shoulders and neck. He was wrong, very wrong; she did have to do this. If she didn't she faced two beatings, one from Angelique, it would be hard but with no lasting pain and another from Archie, a different, long lasting pain that she might carry for the rest of her life. She had no choice she must do it.

John shivered; this wasn't at all what he had expected. Guiltily he found himself thinking of his sister, of the deep relaxing shoulder massages her strong fingers used to give him after a long day in the fields hoeing or planting potatoes. This was different; the fingers were tentative, but he could feel care coming through them and into his body. He'd expected to feel aroused as he and his brothers had done when they had looked through a magic lantern that afternoon at a partly clad woman, everything and nothing in a black and white, jerky frenzy of blurry movement. Instead he began to relax and almost involuntarily he moaned and said:

'That feels good, my sister used to do this for me, it's good.'

Ann stopped abruptly, her father and mother had told her long ago, in a different life, of the dangers of too close and intimate contact with her brothers and sister and its sinful nature, but then she laughed, a soft quiet tinkle of sound that surprised both of them. Her sins were well past sibling affection, she had a permanent place in purgatory by now. She needed to avoid a beating not shorten an already interminable stay between heaven and hell. She started again and took her next step towards total damnation.

'Why don't you take off your coat, so I can rub you better,' – it didn't sound right, but she wasn't yet ready for Lizzie's more brazen and direct approach to her customers.

John did as he was told. Gradually Ann massaged John's shoulders and then after helping him to remove his waistcoat and shirt she moved down his back and then his chest as he obediently, almost trance-like, followed her request to roll over on the bed. By now John's reticence had parted company with his loins and his now eager penis stood up happily to admire this angel of desire that straddled its owner.

Ann now faced a dilemma. Lizzie had described in graphic detail the various ways that men liked their sex. She couldn't bring herself to use the brazen descriptions that Lizzie did. So as she moved slowly back down across John's chest and across his stomach with her hands she had to ask the next question:

'How do you want it?' she asked hoarsely. Her words and tone were governed more by her nervous uncertainty than by Lizzie's advice, but she had outdone even Lizzie in the man's response. The low, husky sound of her words helped John to lose all his inhibitions and he knew that he wanted this woman, however young she looked, however unskilled she seemed and however unsure he had been himself.

'Can I take off your dress?' he asked. His voice was kind and strangely compelling. Ann surprised herself; she arched her back and let him pull off her dress. She raised herself up off his chest as he struggled to take off his trousers. In the end their instincts overcame his reticence and her expectation of a painful entry and they joined together easily. Although Ann felt no lasting reaction the passionate response of the man to her body gave her a surge of totally unexpected pleasure, she was simultaneously excited and disgusted with herself, it was something that she had never experienced before.

Angelique had kept watch through a crack in one of the door planks and was surprised to find that she was pleased for Annie that she had managed at last to save herself a beating by giving a man what he had paid for. She had no doubt that Annie would get another beating from herself and sooner than later she would receive the inevitable beating from Archie. The job was hard, to attract enough customers regularly the girls had to get a reputation for some sort of deviant sex that men would talk about. Then the girls would attract more visitors. Nothing that she had seen from Annie gave her the slightest belief that the terrified young girl that Archie had carried into the house three months ago would survive as a prostitute, let alone outside of the house when she was thrown out. If Angelique had been capable of it she would have feared for Annie's survival.

The two inexperienced young people that Angelique had watched had managed to satisfy each other's needs without either understanding what those needs were. Ann, coloured by her rude education from Lizzie, believed that the man needed the release of his body's demands brought on by drink and bravado. That wasn't quite how

Lizzie would have described it, but it satisfied Ann and amazingly the man hadn't hurt her, he had been almost gentle. For John, the young woman, he couldn't believe how young she looked, had taken him by surprise. He had sat on the bed terrified of what he was supposed to do. He knew the sensation, had enjoyed it himself in the privacy of the hay loft on a warm summer evening when his brothers and sister were away, but for it to happen inside a woman, the where and how of which was still, even in his manhood, still vague and unclear. Yet between them they had succeeded beyond John's muddled imagination; he tried to understand his emotions. The sort of feeling he had for his sister, of care and concern, a different compelling, instinctively animal feeling to push deeper inside the girl as she lay beneath him unresisting and silent, but not, as far as he could tell, frightened or obviously unhappy. The two sensations had caused him to want to take care of her and in doing so he had started to feel the beginnings of something that he didn't recognise at first but would turn into devotion.

On a fusty, stained, creakingly hard bed in a drab brown and cream-painted room sparsely furnished with no other decoration except two torn and faded blue curtains at the wrong end of Commercial Street in the new town of Middlesbrough, John Webster fell in love, hopelessly in love, a love that would consume his life and determine the fate of his family for the next three generations.

John stood up and pulled on his trousers and shirt, buttoned them up, put on his waistcoat and jacket and then sat back down on the bed to pull on his boots, stiff now before the warmth of his feet made the coarse leather supple again. He stood up again, checked that everything was in place and went to leave – a small voice stopped him at the door.

'Please, you need to pay me.'

He stopped flustered and embarrassed; the short flat statement sent a harsh slap across his sense of warm contentment a sense that he had so far not shared with the girl on the bed. It made the experience a bit unpleasant, a bit tarnished, messy even, and yet that was what it was, sex for money. He reached into his pocket and brought out the four coins that he and his brothers had found in their pockets. He felt that he didn't want to touch her, to break the spell, so he put the money on the end of the bed and tried to think of something to say, something to express his feelings, to prolong his dream.

'Well good bye then, and thank you so much,' came from his mouth. Not the most romantic start to a relationship, at that point totally one sided, but it was as much as he could think to say at that moment and then he left.

* * *

Ann lay on the bed, drained. The usual tearing pain in her body from the often rough and painful entry by a man wasn't there, but even so her small, undernourished frame was easily tired, exhausted even and the emotional trauma she had imposed on herself hadn't helped. The man's visit had allowed her to make a first small effort towards survival and to accept that to be able to survive in the house she had to do and act as Lizzie had said – so Ann was grateful to the man. Beyond that gratefulness she had experienced a sensation that she didn't want to acknowledge. As they had lain together and he had filled her body with the heat from his thing she had felt something other than the fearful, terrified guilt that normally came to her when a man pushed into her body. She had felt a faint but undeniable longing for something more; the feeling frightened her. She thought instinctively that such a longing must be bad. She wanted it to be bad – it must be bad. Ann didn't want to see him ever again.

Her wish was granted for a month. Her wretched existence improved marginally, her newly practiced tentative and timid approach to her work attracted a few paying customers, enough to make her life an existence rather than just survival. Angelique was pleased and Lizzie was glad that her strange friend was at least now trying to stay alive, albeit still clinging on by a thread.

* * *

It took John four weeks to amass the money he needed to return to the house. He knocked at the door with a hesitancy that belied his eager and mounting excitement at the thought of seeing the girl again. As he waited for someone to come to the door – no one would – most customers just walked into the hallway unannounced, he suddenly realised that he didn't know her name. Naively he thought they would recognise him – nobody did. He stood there for perhaps half an hour. In that time three men went in and two came out, one of them a man who had only just gone in – not ten minutes before, sex can be a high turnover business. At last John realised that no-one was coming to meet him or to help him, he had to do this himself. He cleared his throat, adjusted his jacket and walked through the door.

Even from the outside the house, which wasn't more than ten years old, looked run down. The roof slates had started to come away where the cheap wooden battens and cheap iron nails were unable to hold in place the cheap heavily formed slates; an almost inevitable symptom of the rapid growth of Teesside's new industrial age. The bricks rushed through the moulds and kilns were useable without being evenly shaped and every so often one from the last make of the shift or from the corner of the kiln would be crumbling in the already acid air of the smoke filled winters of Middlesbrough. The short-seasoned window frames didn't quite fit and the glass, with hastily made blemishes, was streaked with dust and ash and the grime of the wrong end of the street. The door that John went through may have fitted at some point, but not anymore; it was seldom shut and even when it was it didn't stay closed. All the woodwork had once been painted with a colour that was now the same as the caked dirt that made up a strip of ground to one side of the house where visitors relieved themselves after their brief often unsatisfied urges had been paid for but seldom delivered. John went into the house.

Inside it was already dark. The faded, dull red and brown canvas strip along the floor merged into the brown and cream walls and ceiling of a hallway and passage with a flight of stairs leading up to the rooms above, there were four, one for each of Angelique's girls. Downstairs was the kitchen at the end of the passage where they waited for their customers and lived their harsh transitory lives. Angelique lived in the other two rooms. One was a bedroom, the other, a once respectable parlour was available for her few top paying customers and their friends to wait. John stood in the hallway, the light from the flickering, badly trimmed oil lamp threw vague patterns onto the walls and faint unidentifiable sounds came from upstairs. This time Ned and Jeremiah were not there to help him. John was rapidly losing his small store of confidence. He was saved by a scream, or more accurately a high pitched moan cut off by a dull thud from one of the rooms above him. He went to climb the stairs to offer help but as he did so he was pushed aside roughly by a woman whom he recognised to be the owner or matron as he seemed to recall her being referred to as.

Angelique had come out of the dingy parlour quickly; she had recognised the sound and the room so she knew who it was and why. She couldn't afford to lose her best earner again and if she didn't get there in time she would do. The customer was a man who liked violent sex and was a friend of Archie – she would need to be careful. There was a young worried-looking young man at the foot of the stairs. She would deal with him later, if he was still there. She pushed him out of the way, not roughly, a customer was a customer after all, but firmly and for a big woman went up the stairs quickly and surprisingly quietly, in the dull light she almost looked as if she had floated up the stairs. The door to the room was jammed shut, as she had half expected, experience and weight combined to force it open and she crossed the room just as another metal belt-buckled blow was being landed on the cringing, cowering female shape on the bed.

'Come on Harry, that's enough, Archie won't like it if you damage the goods will he,' she said; carefully and firmly taking the man by the arm and pulling him away from the bed. The man stopped and stood still for a moment, seemingly at a loss, surprised by the interruption. While he stood there Angelique bent over the body on the bed and whispered: 'just let him do it Cassie, or he'll smash up your face again.'

The girl on the bed spat into the fireplace, blood and saliva spattered onto the blackened iron back plate and a sharp ting sounded as a tooth bounced back into the room. She wiped her hand across her mouth and swore at the woman leaning over her:

'I'll kill the bastard, that's what I'll do, if he lays another hand on me.'

'Yes love, and then Archie'll kill you, so do yourself a favour and let him have his way,' said Angelique in a louder imperative whisper, conscious that Harry had recovered himself and was ready to start again. She turned towards him: 'Here Harry, use this.' She handed him a length of canvas strapping with no buckles and took his heavy leather metal-buckled belt before he could object. She left the room, shutting the door behind her, and went down the stairs before the man had a chance to react. She had read his reactions well, as she most often did with the wretched, often drunken men who came to the house. Cassie would be bruised, but not damaged beyond healing repair.

The young man was still at the bottom of the stairs.

'Well,' said Angelique, 'what do you want?'

The man hesitated, then said in a rush: 'I want to see the girl I saw last time.'

'I'm sure you do son, but who was that? I've got lots of girls.'

John realised again that he knew nothing about the girl he had visited – he couldn't bring himself to say had or the more graphic words that his brothers used – and worse than that he realised that this woman didn't recognise him so would have no idea who it was he had seen before.

'She was young, very young,' he tried.

Angelique was suspicious. Although her house wasn't of the quality of those in Stockton it was, by her rules, respectable, so children were not on offer. She looked at the young man more closely. Was he an elder brother, or a relative come looking for a lost sister or worse a snooper paid by an anxious parent trying to find their lost child.

'What do you want with this girl that you think you saw here?' she asked.

'To talk to her,' began John, he stopped, embarrassed, that was stupid, 'to, to lie with, to have sex with,' he said finally admitting to himself what had drawn him to return.

Angelique looked hard at the young man in front of her, not much more than a boy really, she made up her mind:

'It'll be Annie you've come back for – she's in the room at the end of the landing. What do you want straight or special?' she asked.

John almost jumped as the reality of the arrangement struck him, up until then he had not considered what this visit was – he stood, indecisive, the woman's eyebrows came together and he knew he must decide.

'It was a shilling last time,' he said quickly, 'I came with my brothers,' he added, for comfort rather than necessity.

Angelique remembered the three brothers; from the country, it had been this lad's visit that had prolonged Annie's existence in the house. She still wasn't good, but at least now she paid her way. She looked at him with more care now, trying to decide if he might be a threat to Annie or even... She stopped and let her thought continue. Annie had never said anything about the man, but then she never spoke much anyway. She would have to talk to Lizzie – Annie did talk to Lizzie – about the only person she did talk to. Angelique could not afford to lose Annie. Archie had brought her to the house himself and had threatened Angelique with dire threats if the little girl – she couldn't be much over sixteen – was to disappear.

'A shilling'll do,' she said abruptly, 'you pay the girl after, but I want to see your money first.' The man shoved his hand into his jacket pocket and fetched out two silver sixpences, where he had got them from Angelique had no idea and she didn't care, he looked like he might be a farm labourer or one of those new miners from up in the Eston Hills. Whatever he was he had the money. She pointed up the stairs.

'She's available now, you best go up. No hitting her mind,' she added, unnecessary with this customer she was sure, but force of habit none the less.

John went up the stairs. He walked slowly along the landing, terrified that he might choose the wrong room, he was especially anxious not to meet the man that he had caught sight of when the woman had gone up the stairs before. He got to the end of the landing and stood at the door; he hesitated; then knocked, far too quietly. Nothing happened; so he knocked again, not much louder, his tentative tapping barely went through the wood of the door despite the crack in one panel. The panel that Angelique had used to check on Annie's efforts the last time he had visited. Luckily for him the woman in the room had heard.

* * *

Ann lay on the bed. She had heard the cries and blows coming from Cassie's room and had sunk lower into the stained mattress. Sometimes she had prayed that a violent man would ask for her and beat her to death, but according to Lizzie to get that to happen she would have to fight and yell a bit – was that what Cassie was doing – to get the man going Lizzie had added. Ann knew that she would never be able fight and swear like Lizzie and the other girls. Since she had taken Lizzie's advice she had attracted more customers, enough to avoid any more beatings and enough to eat. She wasn't as tired now, but her greater strength had allowed her to dwell more on her life, on the wretchedness of her existence and the trap that she had been lured to the house with. If anything she felt worse now than before she had tried out Lizzie's advice. For some reason she thought back to the young man who had come to her that night, it seemed a life time ago, she could not remember how long ago it was. She hoped he would never return; the thought that he might filled her with horror. It was her memory of the reaction she had had when they had been together. Ever since the engine driver had forced himself into her body she had hated sex, she loathed it, abhorred it, detested it. She had thought back through her mind to now receding memories of the teaching that she had had in her previous life, a life that she now felt detached from. In that life she had learnt to read and to write and from that learning she had dragged all the words of disgust that she could remember to describe the feelings that she had when a man entered her through the opening in her body between her thighs. Her horror was that when she thought back to the time with the young man, there had been a tiny, undeniable and dangerously persistent part of her that had responded to him. She never wanted to see him again.

Ann got off the bed and crossed the room, she opened the door and she gasped. She went to shut the door, but he smiled and that tiny undeniable persistent part of her, that small flaw in her armour shivered and gave way a fraction. They both stood, speechless, motionless and looked at each other – Ann let him in. She decided to set herself a test. To repeat what she had done with this man before – she grimaced inside, she had no choice anyway, she had to do it, Angelique would make sure of that, but she would test to see if she could retain the sense of comforting revulsion she used to cling to her sanity with since she had been in the house.

It nearly worked. She rubbed his shoulders and removed his clothes. She watched as his thing – what did Lizzie call it; she didn't want to think about it. She watched as it came to life and rose from his loins – she thought how clumsy the words from her childhood were to describe the language of sex. He had entered her body with the same almost painless care as he had the last time and now he lay on top of her breathing slowly and he was starting to become heavy. She moved and winced as she did so, the hairs at the top of her thighs pulled as she moved. He spoke in a soft caring voice, his mouth close to her ear, the words pushed the tiny chink in her armour apart again and after this time she was never able to close it again.

'You're the nicest woman I've ever known. I want you to say you'll let me come and see you again, but I don't know your name. My name is John,' he stopped, holding his breath, waiting to see what she would say.

Ann had never noticed the names of any of her customers. She blotted them out. She could do so very successfully. All the while they were anonymous, nameless men, who just used her body for sexual release she could deal with her life, with her existence, but this man, his face, his memory, it wouldn't fade and with wretched painful sorrow in her mind she began to look forward to his visits.

Ann & Mary, Commercial Street, Middlesbrough – 1852

The one-sided courtship progressed well in John's mind. He was a patient man and besides it took a lot of effort save the shilling he needed to visit Annie. He had fallen in love with her name too, once the matron of the house – Angelique he thought her name was – had revealed it to him on his second visit. He had started to make plans for them both. He had found out how to get a cottage in California, there was one coming available in Prospect View. How to get banns read at church. How to get married. He had everything sorted out, except the most important thing. He had said nothing to Annie and in truth, when he thought about it he had no idea how she felt. He was frightened to ask. Finally, he did what he had always done when faced with a big decision in his life; he went to see his sister. So in the end it was Annie who brought Mary and John back together and in so doing gave Mary a sense of purpose and put her own, her family's and Lizzie's lives in great danger.

'You need to ask her,' said Mary. Her initial revulsion at the story her shy diffident brother had told her had subsided as his obvious infatuation with the girl had come through. Mary thought back to José; to her own behaviour, to her oblivious reaction to everyone around her and her determination to go through with their marriage.

At first it seemed to Mary that Annie should seize any opportunity to escape from the house that she assumed the girl had become trapped in, but that was before she talked to Lizzie. They met quite by chance a year after John and his brothers had first visited the house at the end of Commercial Street.

Mary decided one day, on a whim that she wanted a new dress. There was talk of an annual holiday at the mine and a fair to be held at Cargo Fleet the same day. The news coincided with Mary using John's dilemma as a way out of her mourning for José or his jilting her as the village had taken to describing it. Whatever it was, she decided to accompany John on his next visit to Middlesbrough to buy a dress while her brother went off to visit Annie. Mary promised faithfully that she would not interfere and would wait for him at Cargo Fleet Junction before they returned home.

Mary quite enjoyed her visit to the new town. She could remember when it was just a village of forty people and now its eight thousand people lived in a bustling, growing, confident place full of hope and plans and opportunity. All that was offset by the smells and disease and loss and desperation all jumbled together in a frantic rush to live a Victorian dream of hard-working prosperity and 'getting on'. With her shopping finished, Mary had bought her dress from a traveller's stall in the market place; she visited an eating house for a meal and then set off to walk to Cargo Fleet where she had agreed to wait for John. She knew a woman who lived there and she had told her brother that she would pay a visit. She didn't set out to walk down Commercial Street it just happened. When she passed a corner shop a tall gaunt woman came out in a hurry, and bumped into Mary. Mary apologised and the woman swore.

'Why don't you look where you're going,' said Lizzie. She looked at the large stocky woman in front of her and was struck by her resemblance to someone she thought she knew, and then the woman smiled, tentatively and Lizzie was sure she recognised something about her. Faced with Lizzie's direct stare the woman smiled again, this time more direct with her look and then Lizzie knew, instinctively who this woman might be, she must be a relative of Annie's young man. They all called him Annie's young man. They teased her about him and by now, the small chink in her armour had widened so much that Ann went red whenever they did so and Angelique would make sure, as soon as he had dipped his wick and paid his money that he left on his own before she felt confident that Annie would not do anything silly. She had enlisted Lizzie to help, if nothing else as a way of ensuring that Lizzie did nothing silly either. Angelique was worried about the girls in the house.

'You got a brother' – what was Annie's man called, John, that was it – 'a brother called John?' Lizzie asked – blunt and to the point as usual.

'Yes I have,' replied Mary, surprised, but not put off by the woman's direct approach, and then something about the look of the woman jogged her memory of something John had told her and made her pause, she took a guess. 'You're not a friend of Annie are you?' she asked tentatively.

Lizzie looked round hurriedly. Archie controlled everything around here and nothing was said or done without him finding out, one way or another. 'Keep your voice down woman. It don't do to let your mouth go round here. What if I am? What's it to you?' she hissed at the woman.

Mary was taken aback, she could not understand why her question had scared the woman so much, but it had and as much for John's sake the reaction worried her. There was something not quite right here, something not quite safe, her natural protectiveness towards her young brother asserted itself.

The two women eyed each other carefully, neither sure of how much to reveal. There was no question of trust as both of them had experience of the frailty of trust and neither of them was prepared to put it to the test. Mary the more stable and confident of the two spoke first:

'It's alright; I'm not looking for any trouble. I came to Middlesbrough with John. I wanted a new dress, haven't had one for a long time. There's going to be a fair in Cargo Fleet. I fancied dressing up for it. So I came down with John,' she paused, sizing up the other woman, making up her mind, she decided to take a risk. 'He's quite taken with Annie,' she paused again, not quite sure what she wanted to say next. 'Don't suppose she thinks anything of him, just another customer I suppose?' She stopped, leaving the question hanging, waiting for the woman to speak. She did so, but not at all as Mary expected.

'There's a pub on Stockton Street, other side of the market, Ship Inn it's called, meet me there in a quarter of an hour,' she raised her voice and cackled with laughter, tense, nervous laughter, 'you'll find no lodgings round here, not as would suit you. Now clear off, I've things to do,' and with that she disappeared through a gap between two houses.

Mary stood dumbfounded for a few minutes, until a giant of a man came out of a door across the street, a drinking house she realised, and came towards her, a look of malevolent determination on his face; he stopped and towered over her.

'What did you want with her,' he demanded harshly, gripping her arm tightly as he spoke. Despite her strength Mary yelped with pain and tried to break free, with no success. She drew a breath to give herself time to gather her thoughts.

'I was asking about lodgings, that's all,' she said.

'What would a woman like you want with lodgings round here?' he growled tightening his grip as he did so.

'My husband died recently and I'm to be thrown out of the cottage so I need somewhere to live,' Mary said quickly.

He looked at her; he looked through her, filling her with dread as he did so. She held her breath. He released his grip and laughed; a deep menacing growl that had no humour about it. He put his face down next to hers and said: 'You take my advice and look elsewhere and don't come back,' as he spoke his mouth reeked of tobacco and stale beer, 'do you hear?'

Despite her strength of character, when he released her, Mary jumped back and stammered: 'Yes, I'll do that.' She turned and walked back the way she had come quickly, towards the centre of Middlesbrough, not looking back until she was amongst other people and the comfort of better looking buildings. If Mary had been concerned for John before; she was fearful now. She felt sure that there was some connection between him and Annie and the woman and the man who had come out of the drinking house. She thought several times before finally deciding to keep the appointment with the woman. She stood across the street from the pub for several minutes looking for any sign of the man before she crossed over and went in. She went into the lounge. There were several groups of men, and to her relief some had women with them, sitting at the tables – she decided to stay. She found a chair by the fireplace and sat down, she felt safer with her back to the wall where she could see who came in and out of the pub door. There was no sign of the woman. Mary could see a church clock through the smoke-stained window across the bar. She began to think she ought to leave soon and meet up with John and had got as far as gathering up her parcel when suddenly the woman was there beside her.

'I'm not stopping long; Angelique's expecting me back with the stuff.' She spoke quickly, breathlessly, with short hesitant words, looking around her all the time. 'Your John's really taken with Annie, but she's not interested in any man. Thinks they're all evil, she's not wrong, most of 'em are, most we see anyway. He wants to take her away; asked me to help. Archie'll kill both of 'em and me if I help. Tell him not to come and see her again. It's best for everyone. Annie won't go with him. She wants to die. I've got to go. Take my advice keep your brother away. Archie'd find them where ever they went. Anyway, Annie won't go. I've said too much.'

Mary glanced round to see if anyone was watching them. Everything seemed normal; the groups of people were behaving normally, taken up with their own business, ignoring the two women by the fire. She looked back towards the woman – she had gone. Mary gathered up her parcel and left the pub as well. She made her way to Cargo Fleet, avoiding Commercial Street, and found John waiting for her, a bit anxious that he had arrived first, but pleased to see her. For the first time in several years, at least since the violent end of her marriage, Mary drew John to her and hugged him tightly – she urged him to hurry home with her, she was anxious to get away from Middlesbrough.

John was pleased. He was pleased with his hug. He was pleased with his visit; he had convinced himself that Annie had responded to him this time and he was more certain than ever that he wanted to take her away from the house. It was how and when that he was unable to work out in his mind.

They reached the farm before their brothers had returned and sat down at the kitchen table in companionable if nervous silence. Mary spoke first:

'John,' she started.

'I want to marry her Mary,' interrupted John.

The clock ticked in the hallway.

'What does she want, do you know? Have you asked her?' asked Mary gently. She did not want to destroy their reconciliation so soon after it had happened.

'She doesn't know,' said John, 'but she responds to me. I can tell. I could take her away from that place; give her a good life. I'd be kind to her, look after her, treat her as she should be. She'd never have to do that, to have men like that ever again. She's the woman I want Mary, I've never felt like I do with her ever before. I love her. I love her.' The last two sentences were muffled as John put his head down into his arms on the table and his shoulders heaved. He was crying.

Mary reached across the table and ruffled his hair; it was something she hadn't done for years, but it felt right.

'John,' she started again.

'What?' he said, he raised his head and looked across at his sister suspiciously. She had a way of saying his name before telling him something he did not want to hear.

'I met two people today; I think it was not far from where you go to see Annie. They knew each other and I think they both know Annie. They're not very nice people John, and the man is dangerous, very dangerous,' she stopped, wanting to see if there would be any reaction from John. The clock struck the quarter past and ticked on

– he stayed silent, watching her. 'The man threatened me John, told me to go away and not come back. The woman told me to keep you away, to stop you going to see Annie, not to build up her hopes and to leave her where she is. The woman was terrified John. Who are these people, what have you got yourself into?'

'Nothing,' said John quickly.

Mary recognised the closed up word for what it was. She would get no more from her brother unless she was patient. She waited a few minutes then asked:

'How did you three come to visit that house?'

John smiled, remembering how his brothers' efforts to embarrass him had turned out. They hadn't expected him to fall in love with a girl from a brothel. Mary waited.

'It was a dare, a joke. Ned and Jeremiah thought I needed a woman. It was about time I became a man. Prove I could do it; prove there was nothing wrong with me. We'd lost all our money, well nearly all of it, to drink and swindlers in Middlesbrough. We missed the last train and had to walk home. We ended up on Commercial Street and Jeremiah stopped outside this house, it was a brothel, to relieve himself. While we were waiting for him the woman who runs it – Angelique she calls herself – asked us to come in. Ned said I needed a woman. We hadn't much more than a shilling,' John stopped, embarrassed, 'but it was enough.'

Mary had trouble suppressing a snort of annoyance at the degrading thought, not to mention the cost, the waste of good money. John didn't seem to notice and continued his story,

'They took me upstairs to Annie's room and she helped me out. She was gentle and thoughtful and we did it,' he paused, 'and I wanted it again, with Annie, and now I've fallen in love with her. So whenever I can save the money

I go back. I want to ask her to marry me. Mary, I need to take her away from that house, I love her.' He raised his voice and almost croaked the last sentence.

'Have you ever seen a man there, a great big evil-looking man,' asked Mary.

'That'll be Archie; he owns the house, and all the girls. He probably owns Angelique as well,' replied John.

'Have you ever upset him?' asked Mary.

'No, I've only ever seen him once. He's scary, but he didn't bother with me, just went to see Angelique. Why?' asked John.

'If he owns the girls he wouldn't let you take Annie away John.' She went on: 'is one of the girls tall, gaunt with black hair, red and blue dress.'

'That sounds like Lizzie, she's Annie's friend. She looks after Annie, taught her how to,' John stopped, not wanting to admit out loud what Annie did. 'She helped her out when she first went to the house.'

'How did Annie get to be in the house?' Mary asked.

'She won't say, she won't say anything about it at all, keeps it all inside. If I took her away, she could tell me, it would help, help her to be happier, I know it would,' said John, his voice rising as her spoke. 'Will you help me Mary? Please help me to rescue Annie from that house.'

'Lizzie said that Archie would kill you both if that happened John, and I believe her, he's an evil man.' Mary stopped. She had made up her mind, as she walked home with John, to persuade him to give up Annie; to forget her. Whatever he thought, a woman from a brothel was no sort of a wife for her brother, but now; now seeing his longing and steadfast commitment to Annie Mary wasn't so sure. She compromised. 'I'll think about it John. I'll make no promises, that man is dangerous, very dangerous.'

They didn't speak about Annie for a while. John continued his visits, the date of the holiday and the fair grew closer. Then two weeks before the big day, he arrived at Mary's door in a state of great excitement. He had to wait until his two brothers went off to the pub that evening before he could speak to her on her own.

'Mary,' he said excitedly as he sat at the kitchen table. 'Lizzie gave me a letter. She pushed it into my pocket on the stairs as I was leaving. She told me not to stop and read it until I got home. Can you read it for me?' He pushed a dirty, crumpled piece of paper across the table towards his sister.

Mary was the only one of the Websters that could read. William Snow had taught her. She did not read well, but she could read. She picked up the paper and spread it out onto the table. She concentrated on the words. Mary hadn't read anything for a while so she had to remind herself what some of the words were. She began:

'This message –she had struggled with that word to start with – is from Lizzie, Annie's friend. Annie says she will run away with John. When we go to the fair at Cargo Fleet. John must come to the fair and fetch Annie away. Lizzie will start a fight. Annie must not come back. This man says he can write so I hope you can read it. Goodbye, Lizzie.' There was a scratched cross at the foot of the paper.

Mary read the note again; the second time more fluently and filled in some of the gaps.

'Lizzie's taken a big risk getting someone to write a letter like this for her,' she said, 'still I don't expect Angelique or Archie can read, so it's a good way of sending a message. Lucky one of us can read though.'

'I told Annie you could read, she can write too. She learnt at chapel when she was little. She told me about that last time I was there. It's the first thing she has ever said about her life before she went to the house. Will you come with me Mary, to the fair? I said I'd go if Annie was going and if she'd agree to come away with me. She said she'd think about it and let me know somehow. This means she wants to come. I can't let her down can I.'

Mary made up her mind: 'No John you can't, but we'll need some help for this; you and I can't deal with that Archie on our own. I'm going to tell your brothers John, we're going to need their help. You better go now. I'll speak to them and let you know what we decide. You best not go and see Annie again before the fair, best stay away until then,' she looked across at him pleading for him to accept this last piece of advice. He sighed and nodded and after giving his sister a big hug he left to go back to his lodgings full of more hope than he had ever had in his life.

The Webster boys were treated with some respect and caution in the places they were known in, Eston, Stokesley, Guisborough. It was obvious they were brothers when they were together and it was not a good idea to upset one if you could not deal with all three. John had thought about getting his brothers to help when José had died but in the end he had wanted to protect them. Despite their constant teasing and fighting they would protect each other without any thought to what might happen afterwards, but Archie was a dangerous man and they would need to stick together to stay safe.

Ann & John, Cargo Fleet Fair,
Summer 1852

Archie and Angelique had hired two covered wagons from a gypsy for the fair. They needed to take two girls for the trade so Angelique had decided to take Lizzie and Ann, if nothing else she could keep an eye on them, they always seemed to have their heads together at the moment. She dressed all of them as gypsies to tell fortunes – the only way Archie could get permission to be at the fair. The fortune telling was just an excuse for the real purpose of their visit – to sell sex to any customer who asked for it, or could be persuaded to ask, once they got into the wagon. The two wagons were parked behind the drinking tent to avoid the curious eyes of what Archie called trouble makers with nothing else to do but complain. Despite their position away from the main arena they did a good trade. The first few visitors spread the word about what sort of fortunes were being told in the wagons and soon Lizzie and Annie were being kept busy with a steady stream of men. It was Lizzie who spotted the Websters. They had brought the small cart with food and bundles of firewood to sell. They arrived late and had to make do with a space in the farthest corner of the fairground from the two wagons. Between customers Lizzie ran over to the window of Annie's wagon, on the opposite side from where Angelique had set up a table and chair to sell fortunes. She warned Annie to be ready and told her where to look. She finished by adding fiercely:

'Once you start to run don't stop and don't look back. Don't fret about me; I expect I'll get a smack or two from Angelique but that won't be nothing new will it. Don't let me down Annie girl; I'm doing this for you so you make sure you get away.'

But Ann was in a state, she jumped at everything.

'What's up with 'er,' asked Archie when he came back from the beer tent to check how they were getting on, and to get some more money. He'd met up with a man with some contacts on the London colliers and unbeknown to the girls he was negotiating to sell one or two of them to the man. They would do alright in London; Archie was sure he could get some replacements easily enough. In the rush to bring in new working families to the Tees it was not difficult to grab what you needed if you knew how. Besides these two were causing Angie some problems at the moment so it would not do any harm to move them on. He went back to the tent to fetch the man to come and look the girls over, try them out if he wanted.

Lizzie was beginning to get worried that they would not get a chance when she saw the two men coming back towards the wagons. She realised she needed to do something straight away. While her latest customer was reaching for his trousers to get dressed she called to the other wagon through the window away from where Angelique was sitting:

'Annie, you ready?'

'Yes, I suppose so' said Annie her voice betraying her nerves.

The man was stepping into his trousers now and was on one leg when Lizzie kicked him between the legs. He was a small man and went down onto his knees in agony. Lizzie screamed loudly to cover his groans and to draw attention away from the other wagon.

'You dirty bastard,' she shouted, 'I'm not doing that, we're respectable gypsies, and she smacked his face with her hand and kicked open the wagon door. Her efforts were working. Angelique had left her chair in front of the wagons and was coming round to the steps. Archie was running the short distance from the drinking tent. If Annie went now she might just get away with it. Lizzie turned back towards the man, still on his knees in the wagon, and screamed again:

'Leave me alone; what sort of a girl do you think I am.' She hit the man again and threw a vase through the window just as Archie was nearing the wagon. He had to duck as the vase hit the edge of the wagon window and disintegrated, showering pieces of pottery all over him. His naturally short temper snapped as he reached the steps to climb into the wagon and collided with Angelique. The two of them fought to get in front and Lizzie came to the top of the steps. At the top of the steps of the other wagon Ann stood indecision all over her face. Lizzie waved at her frantically. At last, as Archie threw Angelique to the floor and came up the steps Ann ran, down the steps of the other wagon and away across the fair ground. Archie reached the top of the steps and threw Lizzie back into the wagon. She flew across the inside of the wagon floor, crashed into her erstwhile customer and cannoned into the corner of the bed which knocked her out; Lizzie crumpled onto the floor unconscious. Archie grabbed the man by the collar and belt and threw him down the stairs of the wagon where, probably fortunately for all of them, he landed on top of Angelique who was still picking herself up. Gradually things settled down. Archie took one look at Lizzie and swore loudly, he left the wagon and looked round for his prospective business partner; seeing no sign of him he set off back towards the drinking tent. As he left he growled at Angelique:

'Get this lot cleared up, we need to go. I'll deal with that girl later.'

The last thing Angelique did once order was restored was to cross over to the other wagon to check on Annie. She had assumed that the frightened young girl would have hidden in the wagon at the first sign of trouble so she hadn't bothered to go and check. She had helped Lizzie's customer to his feet and given him a half a crown to persuade him to avoid any more trouble with Archie by leaving quietly. She found a pitcher of water and threw it over Lizzie who came to eventually, a vicious scratch and bruise across her forehead where her head had hit the wooden bed frame.

'What on earth made you do that you stupid cow,' said Angelique. 'You've ruined the day and lost me a lot of money. Worse for you though. You've probably lost Archie a good deal he was working on. There'll be hell to pay now. You best keep your head down for a while. We'll have to pack up now and leave before we get any bother from the town. Come on get all the stuff together, I'll go and sort out Annie.'

Lizzie watched apprehensively as Angelique climbed the steps of the other van and shouted inside to Annie, had she got away?

'Annie, Annie, come on out, we've got to go.' There was no reply. Angelique pushed open the wagon door. 'Come on Annie you stupid little bitch, get out here now, we've got to leave, and now.' There was no sound from the wagon. Angelique went inside. Lizzie heard her banging about presumably searching the wagon – not that there was much to search, just a bed and a chair, but she took out her frustration and mounting fear on the search and by the time she had finished both wagons had been wrecked. Angelique was now panic stricken in her efforts to reduce the damage that this last discovery would do to both her and Lizzie. She hadn't been too worried about Lizzie up until then. A beating from Archie would be careful especially as it was Lizzie and Annie who were to be sold to the man in the drinking tent, but a badly scarred Lizzie and a missing Annie spelt disaster for everyone. Angelique was terrified by now.

'Lizzie,' she squeaked her voice out of control, 'where's Annie, where's she gone?'

'Don't ask me. I've been out cold on me back in this wagon. I don't much know where I am meself let alone Annie. Isn't she in that wagon?' said Lizzie with as normal a voice as she could manage.

'No she isn't you silly bitch. The fucking silly cow's buggered off,' Angelique yelled back. She didn't know what to do. They needed to leave before any sort of authority came to cause more trouble, but to leave without Annie was unthinkable. She couldn't imagine what Archie would do.

Archie was calm when he returned a few minutes later, dangerously calm, much too calm for safety.

'The miserable bastard changed his mind,' he said. 'Come on we've got to go. I'll get the cart and we'll be off. Romany Jack said he'd collect these two tomorrow. Come on Angie get them two stupid cows and follow me.'

'Archie,' began Angelique.

'Didn't you hear me woman get the girls, we've got to go, before anything else goes wrong,' he shouted at her.

'She's gone Archie.'

'Who's gone?' he demanded.

'Annie, she's disappeared,' Angelique's voice tailed off as she saw the look on his face. The man laughed, an evil, guttural, foul smelling laugh from deep down in his belly.

'You're having me on. That's good. I needed that. Trust you to think of something daft to say. Now pack it in, we've got to go.' he said.

'But she has, she's run off, no idea where, should we look for her? What shall we do Archie?'

There was a silence between them. By now the fair had recovered from the outbreak of violence, not uncommon, there were often outbreaks of fighting at the few public events working people were able to go to. Everyone made the most of their rare days off – heavy drinking led to arguments and inevitably fights – it was an accepted part of the fair. By now people were laughing and talking and passing them by. One or two glanced at the three people by the wagons but no one stopped. Music was still playing and the smell of hot food hung in the air. All round them the raucous conversation from stalls and tents was still in full flow, it was only early in the afternoon, but there was no sign of Annie and there was no possible way to know where she had gone in the mass of people around them.

Archie struggled with his hot temper but at last after a few half-hearted attempts to see the girl in the crowd he shrugged and growled:

'She'll not get far, I'll find her, someone will have seen her go, when I do she'll pay for this same as the bloody daft stupid cow as started it all.' He looked round for Lizzie who was seated on the bottom step of one of the wagons holding a piece of bloody rag to the cut over her eye, still groggy from her fall. 'Come on you two we need to go and now.'

Ann & John, Eston – Summer 1853

They would have got away with it. Lizzie did get her beating, but strangely Archie left it to Angelique to give it to her. Lizzie had two cracked ribs for a few weeks, but after that the house returned to normal. There was no sign or word of Ann despite all Archie's contacts and favours being called in. No one had paid much attention to the cart load of sacks that a woman in a shawl had driven away from the fair. Ann had nearly suffocated under them but they had got away and after four weeks were confident enough to begin to relax their vigil at night outside the farm where Mary had persuaded John to leave Ann while he went back to work. At first Ann spoke to no one but John, but Mary persevered and bit by bit Ann began to talk to her. Mary started by getting her to help with the chores, first in the farmhouse and then around the farm itself. As they worked Ann started to talk about her early childhood when she had helped her mother. Mary's two elder brothers were very protective of the tiny, frail girl, they all now realised just how young she was – she seemed to get younger as she relaxed and the gaunt care lines subsided. Ann even started to put on just a little weight, but she would never talk about her life between leaving the Weardale lead-mining village she was born in and when she first met John. She was so determined about it that they all gave up trying, even John.

Ann agreed to marry John. She was so grateful to him for rescuing her from the house that she was prepared to agree to anything he asked. He was a religious man and perversely he told her that he wouldn't sleep with her again until after they were married. The banns were read at the church for a second Webster wedding and the day was set for March. John got his cottage in Prospect View and they planned to move in soon after the wedding, but before that they would have to deal with Archie.

Archie was never able to find any trace of where Annie had gone even when Ann had decided that she wanted Lizzie to be at her wedding, to give her away, a very unusual idea for a Victorian wedding even without anyone in the village knowing what Lizzie did to earn her living. No amount of advice from Mary or John could persuade Ann of the danger that her wish would bring to them all. Ann was determined and for all her frail timid outward appearance her steely inner strength, the strength that had helped her through her time in the house was brought to bear on the Websters and she got her way. Ned was despatched with a message for Lizzie and so on the 5th March 1853 when Ann and John were married there was one guest on the bride's side of the church – Lizzie.

It wasn't this risky meeting that led Archie to find out where they had gone; it was a chance encounter with a man in Stockton that brought Archie to Eston four months after the wedding. Ann had been a dutiful wife and allowed John to consummate the marriage. Ann never recovered from her experience on the train to Middlesbrough and in the house on the corner of Gray Street – she submitted to sex with John as her duty. She never wanted it and never enjoyed it throughout their marriage, but she owed her life to her husband and so she complied with her religious vows, and to the surprise of John and his family she conceived within weeks of their marriage; when Archie caught up with them there were three of them to protect not just two.

It was the man that had written the letter for Lizzie who gave them away. He had some spirits that he wanted to get rid of and he needed somewhere near Port Darlington to keep them for a while. Archie offered him the use of Annie's old room in the house in Commercial Street and they struck a deal. As soon as the man arrived at the house he recognized it, he said so to Angelique when he met her at the door.

'I've been here before, have you got a tall girl with black hair and a red and blue dress?' he asked.

'Yes,' said Angelique, 'that'll be Lizzie, she'll be here soon, do you want her, Archie said to say you could have one of the girls if you wanted.'

The man laughed: 'No I was drunk that night, I'm working tonight, and besides, your girls have seen better days,' he said as Cassie came down the stairs and went into the kitchen.

Angelique did her best not to react to his jibe and concentrated on completing the arrangements for receiving and storing the spirits, she promised herself a couple of bottles in payment for the man's slur on her house. It wasn't until later that week that she remembered the conversation and mentioned it to Archie. When the man returned for the spirits Archie was there to collect his money and he joked about his comment to Angelique.

'She's proud of her girls; that lass of yours,' he said.

'Aye, she is,' said Archie, 'too soft with them by far if you ask me.'

'Did she let that young lass run off with her man then,' the man continued as he sat and counted out the money in Angelique's front parlour.

Archie grabbed his arm and swore.

'What did you say?' he growled.

'Steady lad no need to get excited, I just asked about the young lass,' replied the man.

'What's it to you? You got something to do with her,' demanded Archie.

The man paused and looked at the giant of a man across the table from him. He considered his options, he was a useful contact, not too bright, but a good contact for the sort of business he wanted to do on the south bank of the Tees. No harm in telling him what had happened. He was not frightened of Archie; too many street fights to remember had taught him the wrong side of fighting and he could tell that the giant lumbering man would be easy to deal with for anyone who knew what they were doing.

'I wrote a letter for her, the one called Lizzie asked me to when I spent a drunken night here last year,' he said.

'What did the letter say,' asked Archie in the deep menacing voice that came out when he was getting angry, what did you write for the silly bitch.'

'I can't recall too much of it, it's a long time ago and I was well drunk that night,' replied the man.

'Think man, I'll make it worth your while, I don't like to lose a girl, it's bad for business,' growled Archie.

The man hesitated; he wondered briefly what might happen to the two girls who had crossed this volatile, angry man and then he decided it was of no concern to him. Girls who ended up in brothels had only themselves to blame, the one called Lizzie would probably get a beating and the other one, the young one was most likely long gone by now if she had any sense.

'It was to a man, John I think his name was; he was to meet them at a fair. That's about all I can remember.

Now here, this is your money. I need to go. I think the lads have finished loading up the wagon. We can do business again. I need a reliable contact this side of the river. Don't do anything stupid to them girls though. I don't need any attention being paid to people I work with.' The man stood up, nodded good night and left.

Lizzie's body was washed up on the beach south of the Tees estuary a week later. It was too far from Middlesbrough for anyone to recognise, especially after a week in the strong tidal waters of the North Sea. Archie got nothing from her, not even the satisfaction of her death; his first blow broke her neck so he was left to take out his temper on Angelique. Despite her loud protests and eventual pleading he still believed that she knew something about where Annie had gone, but it was not until he went back to Cargo Fleet that he made any progress. He found a shop keeper who had bought all the firewood bundles from the Websters and remembered them. Jeremiah had always been open with everyone and had told the man they had come down to the fair from their farmhouse near Eston.

Archie set off the next evening armed with a wicked looking cudgel to fetch Annie and to teach the interfering Websters who they were dealing with. He had a reputation to keep, but the man who had sat in Angelique's parlour and concluded that Archie was not a serious threat was right. Instead of using some thought and guile to find out where the Websters lived and then take them by surprise Archie crashed open the door of the Ship Inn in Eston and demanded to know where they lived.

'Who wants to know,' asked Ned, sitting in the corner of the bar, on his own for once.

'I do,' said Archie, 'they've taken something that belongs to me and I've come to fetch it back,' he added as he walked over to the tall young man sitting at a table in the corner.

'Oh,' said Ned, 'what might that be?'

'None of your business sonny, I just need to know where they live. I can make it worth your while, here' – he reached into his pocket – 'I've a crown here, it's yours if you can tell me,' growled Archie, his voice deep and menacing.

'I could do better than that,' said Ned, leaning back and gauging the man's strength as he did so. He was certainly big, but like the man who had written the letter, Ned could tell that if he was handled right he would not be difficult to get the better of. It was what to do to make sure he never came back that made Ned pause to consider what he might do next. He leaned forward towards the man and said: 'for a sovereign I could take you there myself.'

Archie looked at Ned suspiciously: 'Why would you want to do that?'

Ned laughed: 'I could do with a sovereign and besides,' he paused again, testing the man's interest, 'I've a debt I need to settle with one of them Webster boys from a while back.'

Archie looked down at the well-built, fit-looking man. He was suddenly suspicious of his willingness to help so readily, Archie had survived for years on his wits and now his wits were telling him to be careful of this man. People didn't normally want to help Archie with anything willingly; it was usually after a threat or two or because of his reputation.

'Do you know who I am?' he asked his voice dropping a tone or two.

'No,' said Ned, Should I?'

Archie made a decision, he was more than a match for a simple country farm worker, but it would be as well to be on his guard. He transferred the cudgel from one hand to the other, easily, demonstrating his strength and then turned towards the door and growled: 'Come on then let's go.'

'You're in a great hurry, said Ned, 'What's your rush. I've this ale to finish.' For a moment or two he thought he had pushed the big man too far. He already had an inkling of who he was, but he needed to keep him in the dark about who he was talking to. The man growled an oath and started back across the room. Ned stood up and drained his pot. 'Come on then, I can see you're in a hurry to go.' He walked past the man, put his tankard down on the bar winking at the landlord as he did and left the pub. Without turning back, but hearing the man following behind him, Ned started down the lane towards the village.

Although it was July, there was a mean, cold north westerly wind blowing in breath-stopping gusts across the flat sundried grassed estuary as Ned walked down the road. He disturbed a blackbird which chattered away in front of him adding to the nervous uncertainty of the day. Ned was in a hurry now; he still could not believe how stupid his youngest brother had been. He glanced across at the giant, shambling man beside him gripping the heavy club in his hand like a twig. The girl was a trollop from a brothel, how could he have fallen for her like that and now everyone was involved and just as he had suspected this man had tracked them down. He kicked at a broken branch blown onto the road by the wind which was pushing and pulling at a tall elm tree in the corner of the field where a farm track led off to the right.

Ned stopped and turned to the lumbering man beside him:

'It's down there, the farm, you can't miss it, there's nothing else down the lane. Now where's my sovereign?' he demanded.

'Not so fast, you're too clever for my liking; you might get your money, it depends. You can come along with me, them Websters'll know you I'm thinking,' said Archie. The more he looked at the tall man the more he thought there was something familiar about him and he kept getting flashes of memory that made him sure he'd remember and he needed to remember before he was ready to give up his money.

Ned too was beginning to think the man might be close to putting two and two together and sooner rather than later would guess who he was. He wanted to be at the farm before that happened so that his family could help deal with this man that he now recognised from the fair when they went to fetch Ann; the man at the foot of the wagon steps in the chaos that had allowed Ann to escape across the fairground to where they waited with the old cart.

'As you like,' he said, 'this way, it's just down the lane.' He turned down the lane and began to whistle. As he approached the yard Jeremiah heard the timeless noise – Ned never could keep a tune – and was about to shout some brotherly abuse when he caught sight of Ned and the shambling man that was with him. Unlike his elder brother Jeremiah recognised the giant man straight away. He took in the menacing walk and the mean looking cudgel. He ran to the barn and picked up a half empty sack of chaff from the floor. He stopped in the shadow of the door and as the two men entered the yard he shouted across towards the wall of the kitchen; the sound of his voice echoed in the confined space of the yard and seemed to come from several different directions.

'What do you two want?'

Ned recognised his brother's voice and from experience knew where he would be. 'Over there,' he said to Archie, 'there's someone in the barn.'

'Hold on you, wait for me,' growled Archie, still not sure where the voice had come from. For a big man he moved surprisingly quickly and Ned only just made it through the door of the barn first. As Archie chased after the man the snatches of memory joined up and he realised that this was one of the brothers of the man who had persuaded Annie to run away.

'Stand still you bastard,' he yelled, and raised the heavy cudgel to crack Ned across the back of the head just as he disappeared into the barn. Archie followed and ran from the daylight of the yard into the deep gloom of the barn. As he did so he ran into a face-full of dusty chaff thrown by Jeremiah from where he stood half way up the steps by the barn door. Archie put his hands to his face to shield his eyes from the dust-filled choking cloud; he retched as he took in a mouthful. As he did so he tripped over a hay rake that Ned knew leant against the wall and had pushed between his legs, Archie fell to the ground.

One on one Archie could have beaten both of them senseless, but the brothers were skilled at fighting together and shameless in their tactics. They took turns to beat the man on the floor with the hay rake and the cudgel that Ned had retrieved from the floor. They hit him about the head and kicked him in the ribs, but he still he managed to get to his feet. He chased first one of them and then the other until his strength began to fade and eventually he collapsed to the ground. He lay breathing heavily, semi-conscious and bleeding from a broken nose and two livid cuts, one across his forehead and the other behind his right ear. Before he could recover they tied him up with twine. They pulled his hands behind him and down towards his feet, already trussed up behind him. They were skilled at dealing with fear-crazed bullocks so the man, once down on the floor again, was no match for them. Their enemy safely bound up they paused for breath, leaning against each other, gasping for air and nursing a cracked rib and a broken finger between them – it had been a close fight despite their half blinding and knocking him to the floor to start with.

When Archie came round they gagged his mouth with a potato and an old rag. They needed to stop his bull-loud bellowing roars of frustrated anger and threats while they decided what to do. It was one of those rare occasions when their sister Mary was out so they had to come up with a plan themselves. When the threat from Archie had first been explained to them by John they had spent several evenings in the pub coming up with a number of schemes until they had settled on a simple idea that they now put into action. They were pleased that neither their brother nor their sister were about and resolved between them not to tell either what had happened. At first Ned was sure that Archie would not be stupid enough to come back, given the beating they had given him, but Jeremiah knew differently. He could see the black determination in the man's eyes as he heaved and struggled on the floor; uncontrolled anger that would only be satisfied by taking violent revenge on the two of them and on John and his girl.

They had a heated argument which crashed around the barn and out into the yard, but Jeremiah managed to persuade his older brother and they finally agreed on a plan to get rid of the man forever. Ned saddled up the old pony and hitched it to the cart. Used to the weight of the beasts they took to market they hoisted the still groggy man into the cart. Jeremiah, still concerned by the man's brute strength took the cudgel along with them as they prepared to drive out of the yard and up towards the rail head. They had some potatoes to deliver so they piled some full sacks on top of their red faced, starey-eyed prisoner now lying on the floor of the cart. They set off up the lane with an apparently valid reason for going up to the mine head. Part way there one of the sacks was lifted into the air as Archie tried to kneel up. Jeremiah stood up on the side of the cart and hit him a savage blow to the side of the head with the cudgel. The big man collapsed silent and did not stir again.

That night the two brothers went into the pub, their bruises from the blows that Archie had managed to land obvious to everyone in the bar. Their story of the fight and the man's dire warnings to them before disappearing back towards Middlesbrough were accepted readily enough by everyone and Archie's visit to the village became just another story in the turbulent growth of the mine workings around Eston.

A week later an ironstone wagon from Eston was upended at Witton Iron works in the Wear Valley. Out of the bottom of the wagon rolled the body of a giant man who appeared to have suffocated under the weight of the rough ironstone blocks piled up on top of him. The supervisor notified the manager who shrugged his shoulders. He had too many worries already. The rapid decline of the works, already unable to compete with the growth of iron smelting in Teesside. He had little time for the death of an unknown man that nobody recognised. The body was bruised and still smelt faintly of strong spirits – they found two broken bottles in the bottom of the wagon. They assumed that he had either been thrown into the wagon or climbed in himself to sleep off a drunken brawl. The consensus was that he had fallen into a drunken sleep and been unseen by the shift when they began to fill the wagon. The first tub of ironstone would have covered him and most likely knocked him unconscious before he could wake up and shout for help or climb out.

Angelique did not look out for Archie. The man who had written Ann's note for Lizzie decided that she would make a much more reliable business and occasional sleeping partner so made her his contact south of the river. They moved the brothel from the house in Commercial Street to a better part of the still rapidly expanding town and never gave Archie another thought. When Ned came to see how Lizzie was the house had been turned into a warehouse and no-one knew or would say where any of its former occupants had gone. Ned, who had been a tiny bit sweet on Lizzie, shrugged his shoulders and returned to the farm. Neither he nor Jeremiah ever told Mary or John about Archie's visit to the farm just as the two elder brothers never found out what happened to José.

Ann gave birth to a girl in December of that year – they called her Jane. Their sex, Ann's experience never allowed her to call it love making, resulted in three still born children over the next seven years – Mary wasn't at all surprised – and then, just as everyone thought that Ann would never bear another live baby, in 1860 they had a boy, William. By that time Jane had received seven years of unrestricted attention from two devoted and protective parents and as a result grew up to be an over indulged and thoroughly spoilt child. It was exactly the wrong upbringing for Jane and her parents bore the consequences for the rest of their lives – neither ever complained.

Step four – Mary

Oyster Catchers call
On silent mud lined Tees
Farm and fish provide

Sarah, Redcar and Eston Nab – Spring 2015

They had come to Redcar first by bus and then by train from Middlesbrough. Grandda wanted Sarah to see the blast furnace from the beach to get an idea of how impressive it looked, sounded and smelt. He had not been disappointed by her reaction and had been surprised at her understanding of the effect of the international price of steel and the possible impact on the steel works. Once more he was reminded that she was no longer a child. Sarah's optimism for the future had made him smile and cherish his granddaughter's determination to see the best in everything.

The walk back along the beach on the sand had tired Grandda out, so now, after buying their dinner from the pier vista fish and chip shop they were sitting across the road on the esplanade, sheltering from the cool wind whilst they ate. Sarah eating quicker than her Grandda had finished first and was peering out to sea, through the misty lens of the telescope. In truth it was easier to see without the old telescope, but much less exciting.

The rumours of more trouble at the blast furnace and talk of its closure and the possible end of iron and steel making on the Tees had reminded Billy of his delving into the family history and he thought about Mary. Mary Webster had lived in Eston before iron and steel making had begun on Teesside, still less than two hundred years ago. Mary, from the little he had managed to learn about her from stories his own Grandma told him, was just as imaginative and romantic as Sarah. Mary was a mystery; the stories passed down through the family raised more questions than answers about her. One thing for sure Mary would find it difficult to recognise Teesside now from how it was when she was young.

'Grandda?'

'Uh-oh! here comes a question,' Billy thought. He prepared himself for three at once, but this time there was just one, but it was right in tune with his thoughts.

'You know Mary, our first relation on the gravestone, do you think she ever came to Redcar?' Sarah asked.

'Probably not, there were no trains or buses then and Redcar was just a small place. What made you think of Mary pet?' asked Billy.

Sarah held up the telescope that she had been looking at the wind turbines with:

'Perhaps she came to Redcar with William Snow the old seaman to look for ships going up the Tees.'

'No, I don't think so. The spit where the blast furnace is wasn't there when Mary was alive. The best place to see ships would have been from the old watchtower up on Eston Nab. There was a beacon there before that and I would think William Snow would have known about that. Perhaps he went up there with Mary,' said Billy.

'Oh, I didn't know about the watch tower and beacon. Can we go up and have a look?' asked Sarah.

'Well we can go up and look, but the only thing left is the ICI monument. The watchtower was knocked down when I was your age,' replied Billy. 'Teesside was all farmland and only a few houses when Mary was your age, apart from a tiny port near where Cargo Fleet is, she would just have seen fields and salt flats – it was a giant estuary.'

* * *

A week later and they are back up on Eston Nab and Sarah has remembered why she had wanted to come back.

'So, Grandda, tell me again, how did Mary get to have the telescope? Who was William Snow?' asked Sarah.

'You always ask too many questions at once lass', said Billy. 'Tell you what, look down at the village through the telescope, pretend its 1829 and tell me what you can remember.'

Sarah balances the big telescope on the rocky outcrop, peers down at the wide river valley below and tries to recall what Grandda has told her about Mary and the old sailor. Apart from his descriptions, there is not much known about Mary or William, just old stories, handed down and no doubt embellished by the family. She looks out across the Tees Valley below her. She looks to the right, out over the almost flat flood plain towards the sea. A scene forms in her mind of a broad, silent, breeze-swept, featureless estuary. Beyond to the east, there are several ships all with sails set in a fresh westerly wind. They are moving slowly along the coast. Empty collier brigs bound for the North East's coal staithes. A group of fishing smacks far out to sea, hazy, at the furthest reach of the telescope's range. As she moves the glass unsteadily westwards the mouth of a wide mud-lined river is revealed. There is no shelter in the deep inlet for ships waiting to follow the tide upstream to Stockton, where the coal staithes have been built. As Sarah concentrates she is pulled back into the past. She forgets about the telescope, about herself and her Grandda, it is 1829.

Mary & William, Eston Nab – Spring 1829

In 1829 Eston was a small agricultural hamlet with a few farms and a pub, the Ship Inn, on the road from Stokesley and Yarm to the coast. It stood alone in the North Yorkshire countryside about four and a half miles from the river Tees and about 65 feet above sea level, at the foot of Eston Nab which rose behind it 800 feet above the sea.

It was late spring on a warm, clear sunny morning. The pungent, breath-taking smell of gorse filled the air on Eston hills. The bright sunshine made the butter-yellow flowers hard to look at directly. William Snow could still feel the sharp spikes of the bushes that he had pushed through, as he climbed the hills behind the tiny village. His hand rested on the wind carved, grit sand, grey-mauve rocks that stuck out of the bracken and gorse-strewn hillside. Through the feel of the rock sand on his hand he could almost taste salt. Salt that he would always associate with the hard physical job of holystoning the decks of the 'Penelope' when he had been a sailor forty years before. A sound interrupted his thoughts, a subdued thud. He searched the estuary below him.

A flash of light caught his eye and a second dull thud followed it moments later. He reached into his old, faded pea-jacket pocket and pulled out a brass telescope. With a deceptive, almost lazy movement he snapped it open, raised the glass and scanned the valley below to pick out the source of the noise. In a farmyard half way across the flat plain a man was cutting wood. William watched and listened for a while and realised as he did so that this was the only 'man-made' sound he could hear on an otherwise peaceful morning.

No one in the village knew how old William Snow was. This was perhaps because William couldn't remember either. He had an ageless weather-worn leathery-skinned face that was tanned the colour of varnished wood. Two faded red blemishes marked his cheeks and one bright blue twinkling eye peered out from under bushy white eyebrows. His hair was long and white with a sailor's queue, even his long beard was white, except for a splash of ginger down the centre. William was always barefoot and wore patched blue trousers torn off at the knees and a dirty white shirt.

Earlier that morning he had been driven from his bed by the birthing pain cries of Liza Webster delivering her fourth child, John, who was born finally at eleven thirty that morning. William's bedroom was a straw palliasse in the only dry corner of a small lean-to shed attached to the Webster's farm just outside Eston. He had washed his face under the farmyard pump and stomped off up the path towards the old signal station at the top of the Nab. Although he was no longer a young man William could still walk the two and a half miles to the top in an hour carrying his old polished telescope in his pocket.

The telescope was his most treasured possession. He had been promised it by a grateful naval captain during the Napoleonic wars for spotting an approaching French ship coming out of the sun-blinded mist in 1796. William had been discharged as being unfit for service after losing a hand and an eye in a skirmish following the Battle of St Vincent, 1797. He had taken his telescope with him.

After discharge William had made his way back to North Yorkshire from where he had been press-ganged as a boy 15 years before. Then an orphan he had lived with his Aunt in Staithes. One evening a press gang, travelling up the coast from Whitby, caught him out on an errand and that was the last he saw of his Aunt who had died shortly after he left home. When he returned home to Staithes no one remembered him so he had travelled on up the coast arriving eventually in Stockton where he found work on the coal staithes helping to moor and unmoor the collier brigs that travelled to London and back. Eventually, unable to pull the wet hawsers up from the river with just one hand, he had moved inland and taken a job as a farmhand in Eston. Maybe it was the pub's name that had attracted him; for whatever reason it was in Eston that he would spend the rest of his life.

On his occasional day off and with his ties to the navy, William was drawn to the bronze-age fort cum Napoleonic lookout post from where he could look out over the Tees estuary. He stopped looking at the woodcutter and raised his glass towards the river; he picked out a small collier slowly edging its way along the river Tees towards Stockton. He took in the rigging and the miniature stick-like figures working the sails as the ship struggled to make way against the increasing current of the river, pushing downstream against the failing incoming tide. The ship would have to anchor soon and wait for the next tide to progress further up the river. He watched as it did so, the sound of the anchor running out reached him across the still day as a faint but clearly discernible roar.

With the ship anchored, William, followed years of habit and panned his telescope round from the far East where the sea's horizon met the sandstone outcrop of the Eston Hills to the far West where the same hills disappeared in the heat haze near Stokesley and then beyond towards the far distant Pennines. About two thirds of the way round he picked out the farm that he stayed at. He lowered the glass and as he did so he spotted someone coming up the path towards him. It was Mary, at eight years old the youngest of the Webster children – that is until the baby arrived. He sighed, his peace would soon be broken, but then he smiled, he had a soft spot for Mary. She was enthralled by his stories of the sea and his life in the navy and would sit at his feet, hands wrapped around her legs with her chin on her knees, listening in silence as memories rambled through his life. Memories that came and went now, so that each time he told her a story, different combinations of people and events would change the picture she would dream up in her mind whilst she took in his words. He watched as she half ran, half walked up the path.

'Mister William, I've a new brother, he's to be called John. I won't be the youngest anymore,' Mary shouted in short, squeaky breaths as she hurried the last few hundred yards up the steep path below the rocks.

'That's grand lass,' called William, his voice long practiced, carried down the cliff easily to the small straggly haired girl in a ragged brown dress and bare feet.

Mary reached the boulder that William was sitting on and dropped down onto the warm rock beside him. She lay on her back, breathless as she looked up into the sky. 'What's that bird Mister William?' she always called him Mister William, it was a special name that she had decided on as soon as she could make herself understood.

William squinted up into the sky and then unable to make out what the bird was peered at it through his telescope. 'It's an Oyster Catcher lass, it's got an orange beak and legs and makes that loud squeaky noise.' On a sudden impulse he reached over with the heavy telescope and said, 'here take a look through the glass.'

Mary didn't breathe for a second or two. She had dreamt of looking through Mister William's telescope ever since she had first seen him using it to look at the ships out to sea and up the river.

'Can I?' she whispered.

'Aye, lass, long as you're careful. Mind its heavy so best let me help you out first time,' he replied.

'First time!' she whispered to herself; maybe that meant there might be more times. She sat up next to William and with his help peered through the eyepiece. Eventually after more help from the old sailor she was rewarded by the sight of the bird, suddenly much bigger and clearer, and its bright orange beak and legs, wings flapping madly as it flew across the sky above them.

'Whaaa,' she exclaimed, the sight overwhelming. The two of them sat in silence for a while. It was the silence and her clear and genuine excitement at being able to see the bird's flight that set an idea into William's head. He decided at that moment that when he died the telescope should be left to this simple young girl who had captured his heart and lifted his spirits.

'Mister William, do you know about the new railway?' she said at last.

'Yes lass I do,' he replied. He had been drinking at an Inn in Stockton on his last half day off and had listened to the stories about the new port to be built near the small village of Middlesbrough downstream from Stockton. That and a new railway that would be built to link it back to the railway which ran from the coal fields in County Durham to Stockton.

'Things are going to change around here Mary, you mark my words. There'll likely be more houses and villages and people along the river towards the sea. Not in my lifetime I'm sure, but most likely in yours. Look over there, by the river, a point or two west of north, that's where the new port is going to be built. Them Quakers from Darlington are going to build it. So the colliers won't have to go so far up the river or take so long. You see where that one is anchored now. The new port will be just near there.'

They took turns to look at the spot where the collier had anchored, near to Middlesbrough a small village, where maybe forty people lived. William remembered someone reading from the newspaper in the Inn; something that a man called Joseph Pease, a Quaker from Darlington, had said; something about empty fields being full of people and a new seaport full of ships.

William sighed, 'nowt'll be the same once they build that new port Mary.'

He stood up and put the telescope back into its case and then into his pocket. He took one more look across the valley and then turned to set off down the path towards the village. Mary, excited by what she had seen through the telescope and the idea of the port and the railway, neither of which she had any idea about, danced around him as he walked along. William was content in his knowledge that at his age, he would not have to adapt to much more change in his life. Mary's mind was racing, imagining, imagining what? It was unimaginable, too difficult for her simple uncluttered mind to think about so she stopped thinking and concentrated on skipping down the path with the old sailor.

Sarah, Eston Nab – Spring 2015

The opening of Grandda's back pack brought Sarah out of her dream and back to the present. It was mid-morning. They shared the biscuits and drinks they had prepared in Grandma's kitchen earlier that morning. As they sat and ate and looked out over the valley Sarah thought about how William might have come to be a sailor and how he had come to be on the same spot as she was now.

'Grandda?' she began.

'Yes, lass,' he replied, knowing more questions were coming.

'How would William Snow have got to be a Sailor?'

'He was probably press ganged in those days.'

'What's a press gang?' asked Sarah.

Billy bit off a piece of his apple and chewed it carefully. He didn't like to get the little bits of skin under his false teeth.

'In the early nineteenth century Britain fought a lot of wars against France. In the history books now they are called the Revolutionary Wars but William would have called them the Great Wars. For a long time they were fought at sea by the British Navy. The navy had a lot of ships, hundreds, but never had enough men to serve on them. So they used press gangs', he said.

Sarah thought of Jimmy, Uncle Joe's grandson who was thinking of volunteering for the army. The uncertainty at the blast furnace had made him apply and once enlisted he was full of enthusiasm for it:

'Did men volunteer like Jimmy has Grandda?' She asked.

'No lass, some, not many volunteered, but most, men and boys were rounded up from the ports and towns near to the coast and taken off to sea without any choice. It was allowed by law then, "being pressed into service" it was called,' explained Grandda.

'So they had no choice?' Sarah said.

'No lass, they had no choice at all.'

'Is that what happened to William Snow?'

'Well no one knows what happened for sure, but it's likely that William Snow was pressed into the Navy.'

'I wonder what it was like and I wonder what he did in the Navy. I expect he told Mary about his life as a sailor.' This was more to herself than to her Grandda. Sarah lay back down on her back, snuggled her shoulders into a patch of long warm grass she had found and closed her eyes. It didn't take her long to imagine that she was listening to the old sailor telling stories about his life at sea.

William, Staithes – Winter 177?

William Snow paid for his ale and walked over to his chair in the corner of one of the rooms in the Ship Inn in Eston. He had sat in this chair since he had first arrived in Eston. Like everything else about William the exact date of his arrival and indeed that of the chair was not clear. The chair, a discarded ball and claw corner chair rather suited the sailor with its bowed legs and sturdy shape. It had come to the alehouse from a sale of furniture at a stately home near Marton, one of a part set. The chairs had been sold off to satisfy the fashions of a new wife – the first having not survived a trip to London. This surviving chair was well used and bore little of the polish and upholstery that would have made it a rare and expensive luxury when first made. Along both arms ran a line in the wood carved by generations of thumbnails driven by anxious memories of unsettled worries. Next to William, on a small wooden shelf was a pot of ale, waiting patiently whilst his hand carried on the absent labour of thumbs long since departed. William's anxious movement was tracing his earliest memory of going to sea. The thumb was digging deep into the groove of recollection.

* * *

Two small feet were running. Not as fast as they had been, as they were tiring. They slipped occasionally on the wet, fish scale greasy cobbles, but they were running as fast as they could. Two heavy booted feet were catching them. The small bare, dirt-engrained feet with bruised and broken-nailed toes were wet and mud stained now. They had fled from the booted feet which crashed down onto the cobbles behind them.

The narrow street began to rise up through the houses at the end of the village. Houses all built close together, no land to spare, shutters battened and doors bolted. No help for the desperate, scared feet as they tried to reach the cottage at the top of the hill. They might have done it, but a slip on the edge of a mud-lined puddle, a gasp of pain from a heaving rib-lined side and the stagger it caused allowed the boots to catch up. Ten feet from the door, ten steps from safety, ten years of hope all disappeared as a large weather-beaten, cruel unrelenting hand reached a scrawny, drooping, heaving shoulder. Escape was gone and the boy's life changed forever.

'Get another boy, Thomas, if you can. There's another shilling in it if you do so' the captain had said. Thomas heaved the small wriggling bundle up over his shoulder and started back down the street, well satisfied. He felt the three guineas sewn into his jacket collar with his free hand. His reassurance. Another two and he'd be set, a place in the country, far from the sea, a bit of land, clear of the press. Just a few more boys and some luck. The boy had cried out. A harsh cuff across the face, he'd get used to them, and silence. No doors were opened, no shutters pushed back. On the wet, cold evening just after dusk no one cared, no one ventured out to help. Darkness fell as Thomas returned. They all boarded the Pinnace, press gang, volunteers – two this time, returning sailors bereft of dreams and money, five pressed men and a small, shivering, frightened, heart-broken boy. William was taken off to sea.

William's quirky Aunt had sent him to the ale house for a jug of light ale. She was partial to some ale with her supper and she steadfastly averred to anyone who would listen that the later the ale came from the cask the better it tasted, so in turn William had to go as late as possible to the public ale house on the quayside, it was the only place to get ale, according to his aunt. That was how as the press gang slipped across the bay and tied up at the quay William had run down the street and in through the back entrance of the pub. He had gone up to the corner of the bar carrying the small brown earthenware jug and the few coins entrusted to him by his aunt. The barmaid had glanced over at him as the three naval officers came in through the front door and up to the bar. William had looked over at them, wide eyed and admiring; it was the wrong reaction and a cold shiver had run down his back. He had backed into the corner of the bar and waited for the bar maid to fill the jug. She never did. A whispered word and a shilling to the landlord and the barmaid was 'escorted' up the stairs by the third lieutenant. Of the two remaining officers, the man with the plainer of the two uniform coats had moved around the bar and smiled, a lopsided leering grin at the now terrified boy in the corner. William had forgotten the ale, the jug, and the coins and fled from the bar – the big, swarthy, black-haired man had come after him and William had lost his freedom.

* * *

William awoke from his day dream to an empty pot and the banging of the outside door. It was young Mary bringing eggs to the Innkeeper's wife. Leaving the eggs with the girl who collected the pots and bought fresh ale Mary walked across to William's corner and sat on a bench next to his chair. Her feet rocked back and forth as she sat on her hands:

'Mister William?' she began.

The old sailor sighed momentarily, but then smiled – a question was coming:

'Aye lass,' he said.

'Will you tell me a story about the sea?' she asked.

The sigh disappeared and the smile lingered.

'I'll need a good wet first,' he replied. William waved his empty pot at the girl who took it away to get a refill, a fresh pot of ale. Unlike most retired sailors William preferred ale to rum – besides it was cheaper. He sat back in his seat, pushing it against the wall behind him. He stretched out his battered, dirt grained feet and looked at the little girl through his one good eye; he winked and said:

'What story should you like to hear?' he knew the answer but asked anyway.

'About the telescope – how did you get to have it?' Mary replied.

He paused while the girl brought back his refilled pot, took a long drink, closed his eyes and before long the story, or at least the latest version of it, filled the room. The only person who didn't follow the story without break was Mary. Eight years old is too young to be tied by just one thing, especially when you've heard it already, several times, but Mary liked to listen to the old sailor's voice. It helped her to imagine her version of a seaman's life. Mary's imagination was full of her own stories. She drifted in and out of the old sailor's tale.

* * *

William Snow stood by the ship's starboard bulwark next to a line of marlin spikes stored in a wooden rack at the foot of the mizzen mast shrouds, his hand gripping the first of the ratlines. The ship was a frigate in His Majesty's navy. He was in that state of detached readiness that ensured survival in the hard, often cruel life of the eighteenth century British navy.

There was some excitement amongst the officers on the quarter deck just astern of where he stood. They spoke of a fleet, an enemy fleet, French they said. It didn't really matter to the men whose fleet it was. They would fight when they were ordered to and stop when they were told to. With luck they would be alive and unhurt at the end of it, with poor luck they would be dead, over the side in a length of canvas with a cannon ball for company. With really bad luck they would be wounded and still alive – at the incompetent mercy of the ship's surgeon, sawbones. If it didn't look right cut it off, if it bled wrap it with scraps of whatever was to hand and then wait – either to die or to be discharged or, sometimes, to recover. William touched a worn rabbit's foot tied to his belt and waited patiently. Naval service taught patience in abundance to all its servants; patience or punishment for the men, patience or angry retribution for the officers.

'Damn it, where are they? If we don't find them it'll be the end of my career,' fumed the captain, standing about ten feet away from William up on the quarterdeck, in reality a million miles away. The captain looked down:

'Here Snow take this glass and get to the main mast head. Find me some ships and look sharp about it.'

William was instantly reattached to the moment. He touched his forehead with his fist and ran up the few steps to the captain. He took the magnificent brass telescope from the proffered hand and put the fine leather strap carefully over his shoulder.

'If you find them you can have that glass at the end of the commission,' said the captain.

William paused for just a second before common sense took over and he ran to the main mast shrouds to begin his climb, as he climbed he grimaced at the captain's words. The captain's *telescope was safe, William's back was not, he needed to find one ship at least and at best a fleet ...*

* * *

Mary had noticed a cloud, shaped like a cow floating slowly across the window as she looked out. She recalled the first time Old William had described searching through the cloud filled horizon for ships. As she did so she missed how William managed to find the tiny pale sails against the hazy distant horizon ...

* * *

'Deck there, sail three points on the larboard bow,' he hailed.

The muffled sound of conversation below sent the first lieutenant up the ratlines with the big watch telescope over his shoulder. He confirmed what William had seen. As the sun left the cloud's partial shade the lieutenant wrote on a slate in his painstaking hand. Three maybe four sail of the line and three others, transports maybe with two frigates and the brig ahead of them. William had found the enemy ships.

A year later, off Cape St. Vincent, the last shot of battle took off the captain's arm at the shoulder. The impact spun him round and he crashed into William at his station by the quarter deck nine-pounder. William caught him and lowered him to the deck. Shock from the injury made the captain bright and alert and surprising clear in his memories.

'Snow, isn't it?' he said.

'Aye aye Sir, that it is,' said William amazed that the man recognised him.

'You found those ships Snow, the ships that made me famous.'

'Aye sir, that I did,' replied William carefully. You could never tell how this captain, even after three years of knowing, would react.

'Jackson?' cried the captain with a concentrated effort. The captain's coxswain dropped down on his knees by the captain's head.

'I promised this man my glass if he could find those ships in ninety six.'

'Aye aye sir, that you did.' It was a well-repeated story below decks and until now most men had the same belief as William; a story that would have no happy ending.

'See that he gets it man, when and however he leaves this ship. Do you hear that Parker;' the captain looked directly up at the first lieutenant, standing anxiously at his feet.

'That's an order, Parker, d'ya hear Sir?' added the captain fiercely.

The answer came reluctantly, 'Aye aye Sir, I'll see he gets it when he leaves the ship.'

William did get his freedom, eventually, and surprisingly his telescope as well.

Sarah, Eston Nab – Spring 2015

'I think William Snow must have been a very brave man,' said Sarah, 'but I still don't understand why he gave the telescope to Mary.'

Billy smiled to himself; it was a question he remembered asking his Grandma Bella when he was about the same age as Sarah. He wondered if there was any truth in the answer Bella had given him, no harm in trying it out on Sarah.

'Apparently he never spoke of any relatives. He had a soft spot for Mary and would have been unlikely to have made a will so no-one would have questioned it if he had said he would leave the telescope to Mary.' he stopped. There was no response from Sarah; perhaps she would be satisfied.

'So when did William Snow die and where was he buried, there's nothing on the gravestone about him is there?' she asked.

No, thought Billy there isn't, not surprising really given the conclusions that his Grandmother had come to when she had tried to find out in the nineteen twenties. No harm in telling Sarah where William was buried though.

'William Snow died in eighteen thirty two; Mary would have been twelve by then. He was buried in Eston cemetery, in a pauper's grave, so there would be no trace of it now, but your Great, Great Grandma, Bella found an entry about his death in the parish register so we know he's there somewhere.'

'Mary would have gone to his funeral, even if it wasn't very grand,' said Sarah. She reached for the telescope and pointed it down towards Eston cemetery, to the north west of where they sat, down in the valley bottom. Before putting it to her eye she thought of something else to ask her Grandda.

'Grandda? What happened to Mary after William died? Why didn't she get married?'

Billy had been thinking back to his conversations with his own Grandma and was caught off guard by Sarah's question.

'She did get married,' he said absently, 'she married a man from Spain.'

'That sounds very romantic and exciting, was he a sailor from the Spanish Main?' asked Sarah, closing her eyes and remembering the holiday brochure for the Caribbean her Mam had brought home the other evening. 'I'd like to marry a sailor and sail off to the Spanish Main and find a white sandy beach with palm trees on a warm evening at sunset.'

'You'll just have to see what happens won't you,' replied her Grandda carefully.

Sarah looked across at her Grandda who was now lying on his back, eyes shaded by his hand looking up at the sky. Grandda said things like that when he wasn't saying everything he was thinking. She wondered what else he knew about Mary's husband.

'What was her husband's name?' she asked, keen to get more information from her Grandda.

Billy sighed, he was getting drawn into a conversation he wasn't sure he wanted to continue, but he knew his granddaughter, once she started she was like a blackbird with a worm, she wouldn't let go; she would tug away until it all came out. He reached for his little tattered black notebook where he kept notes about things he wanted to remember. There were various pieces about the Webster family that he was collecting for a possible story, a story not to be written, just to be planned. The note book had a bent spiral wired spine to make it easier to open. He turned to the back.

'Here we are: José Domingo Santa Cruz,' he read out.

'We didn't see his name on the family grave,' said Sarah sitting up quickly. 'Only Mary, and her name was still Mary Webster when she died. Did they get divorced? Did you find out what happened Grandda?'

Billy paused, as usual his granddaughter had led him to a point where he could either lie or explain something he still wasn't sure she was ready to hear yet. He smiled to himself again, with rueful honesty. He had already told himself that at fourteen she was old enough to be treated as an adult. He admonished himself for starting to repeat the over protection he had given his daughter and the consequences that had brought. His pause was probably a mistake.

'What happened to him, to José or whatever his name was? Was he murdered or something?' asked Sarah excitedly, 'perhaps he was murdered protecting Mary from attackers, it was quite a wild sort of a place then wasn't it? Wasn't that when the mining started?'

'Aye lass, it was, 1850, just when the ironstone mining started, all sorts of new people came here from all over. People thought it was like a gold rush. That's why they called our place California, after the great gold rush in America the year before. All sorts of things probably happened then, until the place settled down.' He hoped that Sarah would not ask him to tell her any more. He was lucky; she was off, back into her imagination. She picked up the telescope and looked down towards California where the first mining settlement was built in the early eighteen fifties. She was away into gold prospecting, romantic tall swarthy sailors; her imagination in full flood, had rescued Billy. He didn't need to explain how Mary had come to have a short and disastrous marriage, something his Grandmother had found out eighty years before.

Mary & William, Eston Cemetery – 1832

William Snow was buried in the pauper's corner of Eston cemetery on 15th February 1832. The telescope would have paid for a proper service and gravestone but his instructions had been insistent and clear; Mary was to have the old glass. She stood at the foot of the mound of fresh earth holding it in her hands, tears trickling down her cheeks, her brother John besides her clutching a handful of fast wilting wild flowers they had picked that morning. Mary's eldest brother Ned was handy with tools and had fashioned a small cross onto which, on Mary's instruction, he had carved:

'William Snow 17?? – 1832 – retired sailor'

By the time William died the railway had been completed from Stockton to Middlesbrough and coal was being shipped from the new port to London. In 1850 Iron ore would be discovered in the hills just south of Eston and John, Mary's youngest brother would go to work in the new mines, a far different life to his farm-working elder brothers and sister. Life on Teesside would change for ever.

* * *

Mary stayed working on the farm after William died. In the early eighteenth century change was coming to agriculture as well. The traditional almost subsistence life style of cultivated strips and common land was being replaced by enclosures and a new European system of four crop rotation, wheat – roots – barley – clover was to become a tradition itself over the next one hundred years. In the far north east corner of Yorkshire though change came slowly and the shared labour of both men and women that characterised pre-revolutionary agriculture gave women a measure of equality that they would soon lose for at least the next two hundred years. The death of William left Mary and her elder brothers, already without any surviving parents, to run the farm themselves and because Mary was better organised than her brothers she came to be the head of the household. They continued to farm their few acres much as their ancestors had done for centuries before them. It was only the discovery of ironstone in the hills behind their farm that caused their lives to change. Mary grew into a strong, fit healthy woman. The hard physical work and exposure to the weather gave her a muscular body and sun burnished arms. Mary was quite tall, five feet seven and wide shouldered, her long fair hair was always tied back with a length of twine and her bright blue eyes shone against the red brown complexion of her face. She was not a beauty but she did become a striking woman; yet all through her twenties and early thirties she never married, she laughed off the offers from the village's few eligible men. The truth was that deep inside Mary's imagination was the memory of William Snow and his stories. There was one in particular that she clung to; an almost subconscious dream of a tall dark handsome sailor, a man who would appear one day and carry her away on his tall ship. William's stories were many and always changing but this one was constant and involved a voyage he had made to the Caribbean Sea, to the British West Indies.

* * *

Standing as he did so close to the quarter deck William was often included in shore parties and this day was no exception. The ship needed fresh water and as a result was close hauled on a starboard tack heading for the north end of one of the Caribbean islands where the master and pilot assured the captain that water could be had. The captain had hoped to make landfall, anchor and be gone before dusk but the wind dropped away as they neared the land and the afternoon drifted by as the ship headed slowly towards land. They anchored finally in the bay half way through the first dog watch, not long before dusk, which came quickly in the Caribbean. The cutter was already loaded with the great empty casks. Pushed by anxious officers they reached the shore with time still left to scrub out the casks and fill them from the master's stream, which they found in the small cove. William was posted as lookout rather than helping to fill the casks so he had time to take in his surroundings.

* * *

It was William's well-remembered picture of a Caribbean sunset that Mary carried about in her head. It was still clear in her imagination when a dark swarthy man called José appeared in the village and told her that he had just arrived from the West Indies and that he was a sailor from the Spanish Main. It didn't really matter much what happened to her after that, her dream had come true.

* * *

'We landed on the beach as the sun was moving down towards the horizon. A thin line of cloud dampened the glare from the deep red orb so you could look west out to sea towards the sunset.' William started his tale the same way every time. He had been up on a rocky outcrop behind the small cove they had rowed into. The cutter was drawn up onto the beach, it leant

245

over on its port side so the barrels could be unloaded and then reloaded on two thick planks dug into the silver sand; sand that the sinking sun was turning gold with a hint of red. Either side of the boat waves, maybe a foot high, squished into the sand with pink framed crests that sank into the beach as they swirled up the slope. Across the small cove the blue grey meander of a clear freshwater stream rippled down to the sea and then spread out into an estuary of pebbles and shells where the sand was unable to settle in the constantly moving current. The sea was a changing pattern of light blue, turquoise and in the distance a darkening royal blue as it neared the horizon. When the sun's rim reached the sea a wavering line of red and mauve stripes stretched towards the land. Behind the beach palm trees and rich green undergrowth grew in a dense uncontrolled pattern around the bay. Behind William the greens were turning a dark purple black as the sunlight lost its battle with the night. Where the undergrowth faced the sea, water holding leaves reflected the reds and gold that the sunlight found in them. What sound there was, was subdued. The undercurrent of the waves on the sand, the bubbling gurgle of the stream, evening birds calling from the trees, a soft melody of noises that became less and less as the light faded.

The final piece of William's story was a Spanish crew man, José – all Spanish sailors were called José according to William. This one had been taken prisoner two years before and rather than face a Caribbean jail he had volunteered for His Majesty's Navy.

He stood silhouetted against the sun, stripped to the waist his wet clothes hugging his lithe muscular body. The sweat of his efforts scrubbing weed encrusted casks was a sheen across his chest and shoulders and the sun brought a golden, almost auburn tan to his already brown skin. His black hair had the sun's rays shining through its ragged ends and his angular looks and pool black eyes were framed in the blue red sky behind him.

* * *

William's sailor was a handsome man and Mary had fallen in love with him from the first moment she had heard him described, but she had to wait another eighteen years to get a chance to live with her dream.

José Domingo Santa Cruz went through life by chance. He attracted things to him like a magnet and once attracted they had to be pulled from him forcibly and often painfully in order to survive. Until he met Mary his attractions had not survived long after they had left him.

He arrived in Eston in October eighteen fifty, a few months after ironstone had been discovered in the hills behind the village. He was a descendent of a Moorish Andalusian family with silky black hair and dark brown predatory eyes, eyes that complimented his smooth olive skin and lithe slender body. José was a handsome man and knew how to use his looks. He wasn't sure how he ended up in the hold of a returning collier brig tied up in Port Darlington that autumn, but he did know that he had been forcibly removed from the brig and thrown onto the quayside. He definitely knew why he had come to Eston. He had heard about the mining 'gold rush' and wanted to make some easy money to get him back home; which was why, late on a cold October evening he was sitting in the corner of the bar in the Ship Inn, Eston, drinking a fellow prospector's money and trying to come up with a way to make money from the ironstone gold that lay in the hills above the pub. Whilst he thought out a plan he needed somewhere to stay and as he sat there wondering into the bar walked Mary. She was bringing eggs to the pub as she did every afternoon.

As she went up to the bar to give the eggs to the landlord she noticed the man in the corner and said to the landlord:

'Who is that man in the corner?'

'Oh just another useless prospector, come to seek his fortune. This one reckons he's a Spanish sailor, Josey Dom... something I think he said his name was. We're getting all sorts in here now, yesterday we had...'

The rest was lost on Mary. She had heard enough and she turned to look across at the man in the corner again. She took a deep breath and sighed right down inside herself. She paused to take in the moment that was giving her a glow from the pit of her stomach down to her thighs, her long wait was over, he had come, her sailor. Here, to Eston. When she turned he looked up and smiled. She thought about pinching herself but instead she beamed at him with incoherent surrender; she knew that her dream had arrived. Here was William's Spanish sailor from the Caribbean. She fell hopelessly in love, first with his smile and then with his broken English voice enquiring about shelter for the night.

Mary spoke with a husky voice that she and the regulars in the bar didn't know she had:

'You, you could come and stay with us, we've a hayloft you could sleep in.' Her words came tumbling out, tied together with hopeless adoration; he made her repeat them:

'Not understand too well,' he said.

Mary's bed proved much more comfortable than the hayloft and her strong muscular body stimulated José – he had found his place to stay. He just needed a quick way to make some money.

As well as a comfortable, accommodating place for José to lie his head Mary also provided a source of income to José. He found out from the family that the route of one of the wagon-ways and of the new railway branch line touched on some of the Webster's land. Being a woman Mary was finding it difficult to get any benefit from the opportunity. A lucrative sale of land rights was just what José wanted. Rather than explain to Mary that Ned her elder brother would have no trouble in putting forward the family's claim José came up with a safer plan for himself – he offered to marry Mary. It was a marriage that suited them both, sealed with years of pent up longing in Mary's body and the aggressive physical reaction she brought out in José – he liked aggressive sex. They were married six weeks after they met.

His fortune sealed José decided to increase the excitement in his sex and on the third night of wedded bliss he tied Mary face down to the bed and beat her with his belt until she cried out. Her cry was what he needed and their marriage was consummated with pain. With nothing to compare it to and no close female companions to confide in Mary accepted their relationship. She was a strong resilient woman used to a hard physical life with three rough farming brothers who sometimes did hit her when the occasional visit to Yarm or Stokesley markets brought them home drunk and they would knock her about themselves. She took her treatment as a part of her life with José and the enjoyment of the violent sex that he wanted was how it was meant to be. In any case he was her dream sailor, she was sure that she had the right man after thirty years of waiting. She accepted the beating as a part of the prize.

The only thing Spanish about José was his natural grandfather's brief stay in Deptford forty years before. Joseph Tideswell grew up the spitting image of his Grandsire; everything else about him was firmly rooted in South London. Joseph's other trait was his ability to make the worst of a good thing; it combined with his attitude to John, Mary's younger brother, the one person whom she would protect above anything else. John had grown up with Mary as his mother – their real mother died when he was eighteen months old; he had no memories of her. Mary was always there, always looking after him, Mary was his mother and he had a fierce uncompromising love and sense of protection towards her.

It was a burnt hand that brought the marriage to an end. As well as the fate of the money they made from the sale of the corner of land for the new railway branch line. José spent Mary's long and carefully gathered savings on schemes to make quick and above all easy money out of the 'gold' rush. He invested, with three other new arrivals in a new seam on an outlying part of the Eston Hills. They were assured of its credence, late one night in quiet whispers, in their corner of the bar at the Ship Inn where José had set up his investment business. For the price of a night's drinks anyone could become a partner and share in the eloquent and so far elusive search for return on investment that characterised José's ventures. None of the men had any skill or knowledge and definitely no strength of body or character to hew into the rock and dig more than eight to ten feet into the rocky outcrop they had bought the rights to. A half heard comment from some of miners from the Bold Venture drift mine convinced José's three new partners that their investment had been wasted and after exacting some retribution in the form of a sustained but largely ineffective drunken beating, which José took out on Mary, the investors moved on – it was that sort of uncertain transient time in Eston in the early eighteen fifties.

José was not deterred and used the last of Mary's savings to buy a 'new' cart and a string of 'four of the finest horses' this side of Appleby. The four when they arrived at the farm, were just able to walk and only capable of pulling the cart if all four were harnessed to it and it was empty. José had neglected to consult Mary about his investment. With winter coming four ravenous animals would eat

250

their way through her winter feed. The horses had arrived from Liverpool where the four worn out carriers' nags had been sold to four immigrant Irish families who had come over the Pennines to find work on the new railways. It wasn't just the health of the horses; it was the timing of José's new venture. The new branch line was due to open in the New Year. The demand for horse drawn transport disappeared almost overnight and José was left – or rather Mary was left – with a cart that was too big for the work they had on the farm and four broken horses.

To compensate for the four horses eating into the winter feed the farm was doing well. Food was in demand from all the new immigrant workers and their families, especially now as a new settlement was being built by the foot of the mine workings incline – California they were starting to call it, after the 'gold rush' in America, not that too many people knew where that was. With the care and resilience built up over the years the Websters would survive just as they always had done, but José was a failure and he began to look for a way out. He heard in the Ship one night that a great exhibition was going to be held in London the next spring and José convinced himself that he could make his fortune from the thousands of unsuspecting visitors who would be visiting London from all over the country. After all London was his home, he had associates – José tended not to have too many friends, just people that he could use to help set himself up again. So on the night of the 12th December eighteen fifty José determined to leave Eston, and his wife of four weeks, and return to London. Whilst he sat in the pub that evening drinking other peoples' money he managed to sell the four horses to a horse dealer from Guisborough for a share of the profit from their meat and hides. He sold the cart to a newly arrived carrier from Sheffield who was convinced he could make a business out of it even after the railway arrived. José didn't make much, just enough for one third class rail fare from Middlesbrough to London; he just needed to get to Middlesbrough the next day. Ever the optimist José decided that he would work that out the next morning. He drank the last of the carrier's ale and left the pub to spend one last night with Mary.

Joseph Tideswell staggered out of the pub door, slipped and rolled down the slope to the road below. He picked himself up and wandered back to the farm, half singing, half dreaming. It was market day in Stokesley next day; the two eldest Webster brothers had driven the last two of the year's bullocks there that morning. There was no sign of the youngest brother John when Joseph came into the yard and crossed to the kitchen door, Mary was baking when he pushed open the door. She was bending over the oven with the door open checking the loaves that were just about ready to come out, she didn't hear the door open. Joseph realised she hadn't and despite his drunkenness was able to cross the room without her hearing. He reached down and lifted up her dress with his left hand and gave her right buttock a fierce open handed slap that stung both his hand and her bottom. Mary staggered forward and put out her hand to stop her fall. Her open palm touched the open oven door and the heat took the skin off. It wasn't a serious burn and with enough time and goose grease it would heal, but it took off the top layer of very sensitive skin on the palm of Mary's left hand – she screamed in agony. Normally Mary's cries were a part of their sex, but not this one. The pain drew an uncontrolled scream as the pain from her exposed nerve endings seared up her arm and deep into her core. The scream was shrill and loud and penetrating. This wasn't the dull almost husky scream that normally accompanied their sex; this was a howl of pain, pitched straight at the ear of Mary's young brother out in the cow shed settling their two cows for the night. He was still holding the hay knife in his hand as he ran through the kitchen door.

Joseph was leaning against the kitchen table laughing, a deep drink sodden belly laugh, not quite in control. He was holding on to Mary's long hair as he pushed into the crack between her buttocks; she was trying to balance on one hand while she put burnt fingers of her other hand into her mouth to sooth the pain.

It wasn't a focussed vicious fight between two men trading deliberate blows in an attempt to get an advantage. It was faintly comical. They each struggled, one with blinding temper, the other to stay upright, balance affected by his drunkenness. It was a melee of missed punches and rage driven slashes of the hay knife interspersed with desperate attempts by Mary to stop the two men she loved most in the world coming to harm, she wanted to save them both. Left to themselves it would have ended with one of two outcomes, either neither would have managed to inflict any harm on the other or one of them would have been seriously hurt.

'You Spanish bastard,' shouted John, 'what are you doing to my sister?'

'That's my wife,' Joseph laughed, 'a cow ready to be mounted,' and he reached for the buckle of his belt to add more spice to his last night of sex with his wife.

Despite his opponent's drunkenness John was no match for Joseph. The tall powerful London street fighter towered over the smaller man even without his once elegant leather boots worn to lift his heels another inch. He had long rangy arms so he was well able to hit John without being hit back. Even drunk Joseph had enough advantages to tackle the enraged John. The hay knife didn't help, it was heavy and unwieldy, once sent swinging through the air it had a momentum of its own and swung John round. His latest swing ended with him facing out of the kitchen. He sobbed in frustration and turned back towards the room. His next attempt struck the kitchen table and buried the blade deep into the table top; it jarred and numbed his arm. He jerked it out and the effort nearly brought him to his knees. As he got to his feet Joseph caught him with a glancing blow to the side of his head. John staggered back and Joseph caught him again on the chin a blow which knocked him backwards propelled by the blow and the weight of the hay knife that he was once again trying to raise over his head. The knife crashed against a cast iron pot hanging on the wall by the back door. The ringing and vibration made John drop the knife and it crashed onto the stone slabbed floor. John continued backwards and hit his head on the pot. He dropped to the floor stunned. Joseph, beginning to sober up, was angry by now and adrenalin took over. He reached down and picked up the knife, he lifted it over his head to hit the dazed young man attempting to get up onto his hands and knees.

The copper sleeve on the telescope that William had used to shield the sun all those years ago caught the drunken man on the side of his head just in front of his ear. It was the weakest point of his skull and with the blow the marriage was over. José Domingo Santa Cruz, otherwise known as Joseph Tideswell, con man, womaniser and erstwhile husband of Mary Webster was dead. She was inconsolable.

Nothing happened to Mary or John after Joseph Tideswell was killed. It was Joseph himself who had ensured that there were no questions asked about his disappearance from Eston. When Joseph had a drink or two he tended to become loose tongued and would share his thoughts and plans with whoever would buy him another drink or listen. Having thought up his plan to return to London and struck deals to ensure it happened he decided he could afford to celebrate and had spent the rest of his night at the Ship Inn sharing his plans with anyone who would listen to him. By the time he had rolled out of the pub door at least six people knew about the sale of the horses and the cart and his determination to catch the afternoon train from Middlesbrough to Darlington and then on south to London, never to return.

When Mary's two elder brothers Ned and Jeremiah returned from Stokesley market the next day they decided, as it was midday, to call in at the Ship for a drink. They felt that they had done well selling the two bullocks and wanted to celebrate. They came through the door to the bar in good temper, although mindful that if they stayed too long or drank too much they would incur the wrath of their sister – she could be quite aggressive when she had some cause – but they were determined to have at least one pint of ale to celebrate their good deal.

'He's gone then,' said the landlord cheerfully.

'Gone, who's gone?' asked Ned.

'That no good brother in law of yours,' replied the landlord.

'What do you mean gone?' said Ned.

'That Josey, your Mary's husband, sold his horses and cart and gone back to London. Good job too if you ask me,' said the landlord. There were several growls and grunts of agreement from around the bar. The Webster boys were not to be messed with so none of the comments was loud enough to understand or place with a particular person, but there were enough to be certain that the regulars all agreed. José was a waste of time and no one could quite understand how Mary could be so hopelessly besotted with him and in particular why she had agreed to marry him.

The two brothers looked at each other. They were fiercely loyal to their sister. Without Mary the farm would never have survived so their first instincts were to defend her without any thought. Neither of them could understand why she had fallen for the Spaniard either, but she had, so they would defend her decision. They had seen the bruises though, and had heard the occasional thud, muffled shouting and loud moans or even cries from Mary's room at the end of the landing in the farm house.

'How do you know he's gone?' asked Ned.

'He was here last night,' said the landlord, 'He sold the horses to a farrier from Guisborough, over here visiting his sister. The lad's coming over today to collect them from the farm. Then he sold the cart as well, to a man up from Sheffield, wants to set up a carriers business from the new station by the mine when the line opens after Christmas. He gave Josey a down payment on it, more trusting than me, that's for sure. The man had a London newspaper with him. He could read it as well. He read us all a bit about a great exhibition in London next year. Josey wanted to know all about it so they sat in the corner talking about it until Josey left. The man told us afterwards that Josey had decided to go back down to London, didn't know that's where he came from, anyway that's where he's off to. You two best get home quick if you want to see Mary before they leave. She's bound to want to go with him, she's besotted with him – break her heart if he went without her – I'll miss her though, and the eggs.

The two brothers forgot their plans for a drink and left the pub. They ran from the village down the lane to the farm. They reached the farmyard just as John appeared from the barn. He jumped when he saw them and looked very worried. He came towards them and stopped. He seemed to come to a decision though and started to say something as Ned and Jeremiah came up to him, but they were too full of their news to let him finish.

'Has he gone?' demanded Ned.

'What?' said John, thrown by the sudden question?

'Josey, has he gone? We called at the Ship on the way back from market and they said he was going back to London.' Ned paused, unwilling to ask the next question. 'Has he taken Mary with him?'

John had spent the whole time from when his head had cleared from the blow he had received crashing into the cooking pan on the wall until now, trying to decide what to do. Mary had fallen to her knees next to José and begun to howl with grief. She had stayed there for what seemed an age. John had checked the man on the floor for signs of life – there were none, he'd checked too many animals on the farm not to be sure – he was dead. At first he tried to get Mary to move, but she pushed him away. It took a while for her to accept that José was not going to wake up, that he was dead. She lifted up his shoulders and laid his head against her chest. She stroked his hair – there was no sign of blood. Her tears of sorrow for having hit him turned to sobs of grief as at last she accepted that he was dead – her sobs turned to howls as she realised that she had killed him.

Eventually she cried herself to a state of exhaustion. Her anguished tears subsided and her breathing slowed down. Gradually the house became quiet again. The grandfather clock in the hallway ticked away the night and when it struck a quarter past two it was the first time they had heard it all night. The candles had burnt right down, nearly a week's supply in one night. The stove had died down too and the two loaves were ruined, so brown and dry that they were useless for anything except feeding the hens. Mary looked up:

'Oh John, what have I done? He's dead isn't he?'

'Yes love, he's dead, but it was an accident. You didn't mean to kill him did you?' said John, careful to try not to set her off crying again. His big sister, dependable, solid, always there for him, she never cried, she sorted everything out. Mary who had lived through the early deaths of both their parents and still coped was now an exhausted heap of remorse.

'No,' she said bitterly, 'but he attacked you, why did he do that?'

'He was drunk,' said John compromising to save her more grief. 'People do strange things when they are drunk, things they regret, things they don't really mean to do.' Mary began to sob again and John realised that he would have to do something to help his sister. 'Mary we need to do something. I think we should hide the body.'

'No,' cried Mary, 'I want to keep him here, next to me.'

'You can't love, you know that, he's dead, he'll have to be buried. I think we should hide him while we think of what to do.' John knew that it would take both of them to move the body, José was a big man, but he was going to have to do it himself. Mary jumped up, buried her face in her pinafore and rushed out of the room; she had come to understand finally that José was dead, that she had killed him. She ran, with clumsy footsteps, out of the kitchen, up the stairs and along the passageway to her room. John followed and too late, heard her dragging something in front of the door. He lifted the latch but could not open the door. No amount of pleading would persuade her to open the door. Eventually she stopped talking to him and the sobs subsided – he heard the bed creak as she lay on it and the sobs, interspersed with cries of grief gradually stopped as she fell into an exhausted sleep. John returned to the kitchen. It was half past three. He sat at the table and looked at the body, unconsciously hoping it would move, but it didn't. What could he do? He thought of Mary. 'Just start and do something,' she would say, 'if you don't start you'll never get done.'

He trimmed the candles first, he banked up the fire, took the burnt loaves out to the hen house, returned and shut the oven door, the mundane jobs helped him. He put the hay knife back in the loft and tidied up the rest of the kitchen. In doing so he his mind started to work a bit better and he thought of a plan for the body. He fetched the barrow from the yard and managed to get it through the kitchen door. By brute strength he lifted and pushed and pulled the body onto the barrow. The stiffness of death had gone by now so the arms and legs flopped about as he moved each part of the body onto the barrow. Eventually, sweating profusely, John got the body onto the barrow and out of the kitchen. He wheeled it across the yard and into the barn. In the corner was the potato harvest carried there by Irish pickers in October. He shifted a dozen sacks away from the wall and dragged the body behind them. Then he piled the sacks back into place so that nothing could be seen. He had only the light of a half moon and an oil lamp hung on a nail in the barn so he would have to come back and check in the morning. Fortunately it was winter, so the body should not start to smell for a day or two; he might have time to work out what to do – it couldn't stay there for ever.

By the time he had finished it was time to get on with the farm chores. Because he was on his own, Mary still hadn't appeared, the morning was filled with the regular tasks. He had just finished checking that the body was well hidden and was heading back to the kitchen for a bite to eat when his two brothers came into the yard. By now John had made up his mind to tell them exactly what had happened. He started to speak:

'Ned, last night, I had a fight with José and Mary ....,' but he never finished, Ned interrupted him, his plan, and the truth remained buried.

'Has he gone?' demanded Ned.

'What?' said John, thrown by the sudden question?

'Josey, has he gone. We called at the Ship on the way back from market and they said he was going back to London.' Ned paused, unwilling to ask the next question, but did so driven by his fear of the answer. 'Has he taken Mary with him?'

For what seemed an age of time, John didn't know what to do. He stood in front of Ned and Jeremiah, mouth open, head spinning, what should he say now?

'What's up John, you lost a shilling,' said Jeremiah.

'No, no I haven't,' said John coming to a decision in his head, 'what did you say Ned?'

'Is Josey still here? They said at the Ship that he would be gone when we got home. Has he gone? Did he take Mary?' asked Ned again.

John breathed in deeply; there was a way of saving Mary. He would need to speak to her first, but for the first time since last night he began to hope.

'Yes, José has gone, but Mary is still here. She's in her room, she won't come out and she won't let me in. She has barricaded the door. I think she is heart-broken about him.'

Sarah, Eston Nab – Spring 2015

Billy and Sarah had been lost in their own thoughts. Both wondering how Mary had come to be married, but had been buried with her family name. The sun rose into the spring sky and as it reached its highest point Billy looked at his watch, another memento from his time at the steel works.

'Dinner time Sarah.' he said. There was no reaction. He leaned over and put his hand on her shoulder, she stirred and opened her eyes, sheltering them from the sun as she did so.

'I must have gone to sleep Grandda,' she said, stifling a yawn. Both Billy and Peggy had remarked how tired Sarah was when she came to stay. They were concerned about how their daughter's chaotic way of living was affecting their only grandchild, especially at a time when she was working towards exams as well as having to deal with her changing body and emotions; emotions that had begun to make her question her existence and her relationship with her mother. Billy wondered again if she would remember her question from the year before and ask him again. He still had no idea how he would answer.

'No matter love, you just lie there and wake up slowly, its dinner time – time for our sarnies,' said Billy softly. He reached over to the haversack in which they had packed their dinner and opened the flap. He pulled out a small blanket and spread it out on a piece of flat rock besides them. Onto it he put the food they had prepared earlier that day. The sight of the food, simple as it was, stirred Sarah from her day dream – she was hungry. For once she had no questions as they sat either side of the rock eating, in silent harmony, taking in the view. They finished their dinner and lay back on the grass looking up at the sky. An oyster catcher flew over them and Sarah watched it as it disappeared from sight behind the Nab. She returned to her previous thoughts on Mary Webster and turned towards her Grandda:

'If Mary was married to José, why does it say Mary Webster on the gravestone, why didn't she keep her married name? Women couldn't get divorced then could they? Did something happen that made her want to forget her husband?'

Billy thought back to what his Grandma Bella had told him and her warning that what was in the past was often best left in the past. Billy had been to see the parish records and the births, deaths and marriage records at the library. The young lad at the counter – all lads were young now – had been really helpful. They had found Mary's marriage certificate: Wife, Mary Elizabeth Webster, spinster; husband, José Domingo Santa-Cruz, sailor. They had also found Mary's death certificate: Mary Elizabeth Webster, died 14th October 1879, aged 59, cause of death tuberculosis, but no amount of cross checking and the dogged enthusiasm of his library-assistant helper had discovered anything else about Mary's Spanish sailor beyond the marriage certificate. Grandma Bella said there had been all sorts of rumours, the most persistent of which was that he had disappeared one night and gone down south, to London. The winter of eighteen fifty / fifty one was a time of great change and upheaval in Eston with the new mine opening and the new branch line opening from Eston junction so that sort of disappearance would not have been remarkable or noticed given the great influx of new people at the time. Billy considered his answer carefully:

'Well I don't think anyone really knows pet. We know that she got married, but there are no other records of José, no death, no children. We assume he just left her; there was some talk of him disappearing off to London. She must have stayed on at the farm because she's buried in the Eston Cemetery, in the family grave. No one knows why she didn't go with him. We'd have had a different life if she had wouldn't we? What do you think happened?'

Sarah looked down towards the cemetery through the telescope and wondered: what might have happened to José. Ever the dreamer she smiled:

'Perhaps he had to go back to sea to make his fortune – and was killed by pirates.'

Mary & John, Eston – 1850

John was given time to think and time to decide how to explain to his brothers, by the arrival of the Farrier's lad from Guisborough to collect the horses. Ned and Jeremiah spent some time haggling over the price. The lad wasn't too keen to deal with anyone except the Spanish sailor the Farrier had told him to ask for – José's fiery temper was already well known and the lad didn't want to run into him and find that he'd paid the money to the wrong person, but in the end the deal was done. The horses were rounded up and strung together – the lad left after getting a promise from Ned that the money would get to its rightful owner. All three brothers shared a common thought; the removal of the horses made their chances of surviving the winter much more likely, they could use the money to replenish the lost hay.

The lad's visit and his conversation with Ned pushed John further along with his plan to protect Mary's secret. He turned his attention to finding a way to get rid of the body, still hidden in the barn.

While Ned was agreeing a price for the horses Jeremiah had gone up to his sister's bedroom to talk to her. He had tried to get her to come out of her room. Jeremiah was not known for diplomacy; nor was he a great lover of José who had teased him scornfully about his slow speech – Jeremiah had shouted through the door:

'Good job that Dago's gone pet, now we can get back to normal.'

Mary had screamed at him, her voice so piercing and out of control that he could make no sense of anything she said. Jeremiah had retreated. Ned had laughed off the scream to the lad saying that their sister had a great sense of humour and she often screamed at them all.

John needed to speak to Mary before his two brothers managed to and before she spoke to anyone else, but Mary continued to hide in her room and refused to see or speak to any of them.

The next morning the carrier came for his cart. He proved to be a much more difficult buyer than the Farrier's lad and in the end the only way that they could get him to take the cart was to offer to take it up to his new yard – a fenced-off piece of land up by the new rail head. Ned and Jeremiah agreed to take the cart as much anything to escape John's bad temper and Mary's continuing howls of grief. They said that they would call in at the Ship on the way back to ensure that José had gone and to have the drink they hadn't managed on their last visit.

John tried to hide his impatience as they got the cart hitched to the old horse. They would have to help it by turning the spokes of the back wheels whenever there was any sort of a slope, even empty it was too much for a single horse. When they turned the corner and disappeared he went up to Mary's room and called through the door.

'Mary, I don't mind if you don't want to come out but I need to talk to you. Will you come to the door and listen?' he began. There was no answer from inside the room for a while, he held his breath and waited. He was about to repeat his plea when he heard the bed creak and footsteps crossing the floor. He waited a few more minutes:

'Mary can you hear me?' he asked. There was a long silence and then.

'Yes, but I'm not coming out. I'm going to stay here and die,' came the reply.

John was the brother who was closest to Mary and he used his knowledge and understanding to good effect:

'I don't want you to come out I just want you to listen, can you do that for me please Mary?' Another long pause, then:

'Alright, I'll listen,' came the reply.

John sighed with relief and paused again to collect his thoughts.

'Ned and Jeremiah have taken José's cart away,' he began, 'they think that he has gone off to London. The whole village does, José told them at the Ship the other night that was what he was going to do.' There was silence from behind the door so he carried on. 'They called in at the Ship on the way back from Stokesley.'

'Spending my money no doubt, cheeky buggers,' came from behind the door. John smiled, the first time in a long while and let out a long sigh. He hadn't realised he had been holding his breath. He went on with his explanation.

'The landlord said José had sold the horses and the cart and was planning to go off to London, going off on the train from the Junction to Darlington,' he was interrupted.

'But he didn't say anything to me about that. He would have said, he wouldn't have gone without me,' the voice behind the door stopped. 'Would he? No, no my José wouldn't do that to me. Why didn't he say John?'

John didn't answer straight away. He sensed that what he said next would make all the difference to how Mary reacted. He compromised on his original thought. 'Well I didn't know him as well as you, love, so I'm not sure,' he began.

'No, no, not José, we loved each other, we told each other everything, trusted each other. José would have told me if he was planning anything,' said Mary, her voice bright and determined.

John tried to think of a way that he might get Mary to accept what had happened. 'Mary, the Farrier's lad from Guisborough came yesterday,' he paused, 'to fetch away the horses and then today a Carrier came to get the cart. José agreed to sell them in the Ship the other night. Did José tell you he planned to sell them?'

'No,' said Mary, 'but I'm sure he would have done, eventually.' This time the voice wasn't as resolute as it had been.

John decided to push Mary a bit further. 'Mary, why did you hit José with the telescope?' he stopped and waited. There was a long tense silence this time, on both sides of the door. It became so quiet that John could hear the Grandfather clock down in the hallway, it marked a half hour in the silence and still there was no response from behind the door, until:

'He was going to kill you John,' a pause and then a loud sob and a gulp of breath. 'I couldn't let him do that,' another long pause. 'I had to; I promised Mam I'd look after you always, when she died.' The voice tailed off and John heard a noise of scraping as Mary slid down the door and slumped onto the floor, her voice very quiet now. John had to kneel down and put his ear to the bottom of the door to hear her. The crying began to subside:

'He wasn't a nice man was he John,' sobbed Mary.

John knew instinctively that this was the moment that would decide if he and his sister were going to get out of the tragedy they had got into. He decided to wait for Mary to speak. His patience was rewarded.

'He was running away wasn't he? He couldn't cope with living up here.' Mary stopped again and drew a long breath before going on, 'You and your brothers were right. I've been a right lummock haven't I?'

Mary's last remark seemed to lift another great weight off John's shoulders. It was a further sign that Mary was beginning to realise what had happened and to get back a small part of her old self. John just needed her to accept a little more of their predicament – she did:

'John, what are we going to do?'

'I'm not sure love, but we need to do something,' replied John. He took a risk. 'Mary, will you come out now. I need your help to sort this out.' John waited once more, he had no idea how long they had been there. He realised that he was holding his breath again and then, just as he began to notice that his right leg was going to sleep, there was a scrape of furniture behind the door and the latch clicked. Mary came out.

Despite himself John gasped. She looked dreadful. Her normally clean and tidy hair was starey and stuck out like an unruly teasel, her face was blotchy red, her eyes raw from crying. Her clothes were crumpled and there was a tear in her dress. John caught the strong smell of urine; Mary had been so consumed with her grief that she hadn't bothered to get out of bed to use the chamber pot until it had been almost too late, but this was his big sister and he loved her. They went into each other's arms and clung together. For the first time in his life John felt that he was able to give back some of the love, courage and support that Mary had given him, unstinting for the past 21 years. They shuddered with emotion as they stood in the passageway clinging to each other for another strike of the clock before they went down stairs to the kitchen. Mary stood in the doorway, reluctant at first to enter the room, but the room seemed normal. There was no sign of the traumatic events of the night before last. She took hold of John's arm and almost whispered to him:

'Where is he John, where have you put José?'

'He's in the barn, love, behind the potatoes. No one knows, except us. Everyone else thinks that he's gone to London,' he paused again, picking his words with care, 'Mary, we need to move him, to set him to rest somewhere.'

Mary slumped down at the bench by the kitchen table. She lowered her head into her arms and began to cry again. John put his hand onto her shoulder and squeezed it:

'We must love, he can't stay in the barn much longer, someone'll find him.'

Mary raised her head, a desolate look of despair on her face, 'I know John, you're right. It's just,' she stopped, unable to go on.

'Mary, we need to decide. Where can we take him? I've racked my brains and cannot think.' said John after a pause.

They sat for a while in anxious but companionable caring silence. John got up and moved the kettle onto the hob. 'I'm going to make a cup of tea love, do you want one?'

'Yes John, I think I would, I feel really thirsty and dry now I come to think about it,' his sister replied.

Mary drank three mugs of tea and ate a piece of cold meat and a lump of bread. The ordinary actions went further towards bringing her back to normality.

'I know where we can lay him to rest,' she said suddenly. The phrase seemed at odds with what she had done, but she just could not bring herself to say 'bury him'.

John turned back from the stove where he was making up the fire. Outside dusk was setting in. The short

December day was disappearing so they needed to decide soon or they would lose the light and their two brothers would be coming home.

'You know José had that mine working, him and those two daft men from Hull bought into, just past the Nab,' Mary continued.

'Yes,' said John.

'How deep did they go into the outcrop before they got tired and lost interest?' Mary asked.

'I don't know, they didn't have lamps or anything, so it can't have been far,' said John, still not sure what Mary was getting at.

'But deep enough to hide someone I would think,' said Mary slowly. Nothing more was said for a few minutes each realising as they thought about it that this was going to commit them to a lifetime's secrecy. No one other than themselves would ever have to know what they planned to do.

'Won't anyone suspect,' said John at last.

'Why would they,' said Mary. 'Everyone laughed at José when he bought the mining rights to that outcrop,' she added bitterly. 'It's just an outcrop of rock, there's no ironstone anywhere near it, that new mine-superintendent told everyone as would listen when he found out. It's away back off the path to the coast and covered in scrub and brambles.' She stopped and sobbed for a few minutes. 'I tried telling José, but he wouldn't listen, he was ever stubborn; once he'd made his mind up.'

'How can we get him up there?' asked John.

'We'll take the small cart, we can pull it together. If we come back with some kindling from the wood, it'll give us reason for going up there, but we'd best go now before it gets dark,' replied Mary.

They sat in silence again; the clock chimed the quarter and seemed to push them into action.

'Come on then,' said John, 'let's do it.'

After all their planning and precautions, they met no one. They backed the small hand cart into the barn and shifted the sacks of potatoes that John had painstakingly put in front of the body. John had been fearful that his brothers would discover the body when they loaded up two sacks of potatoes for the mine that morning but they hadn't. With Mary to help they lifted the body easily, now limp and unwieldy, making strange unsettling noises and starting to smell a bit when they moved it, but they were used to moving dead carcasses so were not put off their task. The journey to the outcrop was uneventful and undisturbed. They stopped the cart at the corner of the wood and carried the body the few hundred yards to the abandoned mining claim. The drift was about twelve feet into the rock. They laid the body against the wall as far in as they could and using two abandoned shovels and a pick with a broken handle they filled in the hole in the outcrop. They piled the larger rocks and boulders over the spoil that they had shovelled in and once they were finished they stood and looked at the scar in the outcrop, not much of a memorial to José except for the futility of his scheme and the tragedy of his death. The gradual disappearance of the body had upset Mary once more, at one point she sank to her knees and burst into tears, sobbing uncontrollably for what seemed to John to be ages. The sun had gone down behind the Nab long before and the whole cliff face was now in deep shadow. Then suddenly Mary seemed to be incensed by something she saw or remembered and for a while she worked feverishly to throw rocks and boulders into the small but rapidly filling scar on the cliff face. By the time she had become exhausted the claim had been covered over completely. They gathered up all the abandoned tools and signs of human endeavour that the three would be prospectors had left behind and loaded them onto the cart. The soil that they threw over the rocks soon worked its way into the cracks and before long to all but the closest inspection the outcrop returned to being an untouched natural feature that faded into the wood just above it. José Domingo Santa Cruz, born Joseph Tideswell, was laid to rest in an unmarked grave far from the city of his birth and unmissed by all but one person; who's dreams he had shattered for ever.

They covered the tools in the cart with kindling and turned back towards the farm. No-one took any notice of them as they went past the village in the last failing light. There was no movement from the Ship where their two brothers were presumably still drinking. When they got back to the farm John put the cart away and attended to the end of day chores in the farm. When he returned to the kitchen there was a pot of stew on the hob, but no sign of Mary. He went up to her room but the door was barred again and the faint sound of anguished, miserable grief came from inside. He went downstairs again and left his sister in peace. Mary grieved for the rest of the winter; her red-eyed haggard look was accepted by the village and her two elder brothers as the result of that dammed Dago waster taking her in and then abandoning her. With no one to share her pain with she kept it inside and it turned her in on herself shunning all contact with anyone outside the farm.

The branch line to Eston opened in the New Year and the mine expanded. The fledgling community next to the mine head, named after its illustrious neighbour on the other side of the world expanded as more and more new people moved in to the area. What finally brought Mary out of herself was anger. John, unable to cope with his knowledge and Mary's inability or refusal to come round to accepting it forced him away from the farm. He took a job at the mine and went to lodge with a woman in newly built Prospect View. Mary was infuriated, but it jolted her out of her grief. She threw her energy into the farm. She seemed determined to work herself out of the pain of losing a husband and then a brother as well.

Sarah, Eston Nab – Spring 2015

The sun was well past its high point and with the time drifting past three the warmth of the spring day was beginning to fade. Billy began to collect their few bits and pieces and put them into his small back pack. Sarah was still peering up at the sky watching a crocodile cloud drift across an otherwise clear blue expanse above her as she lay on the ground. Her Grandda reached over to pick up the telescope from next to his granddaughter and disturbed her dream.

'Do we have to go Grandda?' she asked.

'Yes pet, we do, your Grandma will be thinking of getting the tea, so we should get back.' Peggy, his wife, was a stickler for time keeping. They would be well advised to get back on time. Sarah echoed his unspoken thought.

'I suppose so; can I just have one more look through the glass Grandda?' Sarah thought it should be called a glass, it sounded like the way an old sailor would have described it. 'We've still got time to get home before Grandma gets back from town,' she said.

Billy grinned, as usual Sarah was right. So despite his natural inclination to get everywhere on time or even earlier if possible he handed the telescope back to Sarah and waited for the inevitable question.

Sarah picked up the telescope again and began to look across the wide estuary. She was looking for the place where the old branch line had been joined to the main line at Eston Junction. Her Grandda had shown her where it was before, but this time she wanted to find it herself. She moved the glass backwards and forwards in the direction she remembered they had looked before. She still wasn't sure where it was and Grandda had his eyes closed. The telescope became heavy in her hands so she put it down, carefully, on the grass by the rock she lay on. She rolled over on her back to look up at the sky. She thought about Mary and how William had decided to leave her his telescope when he died. He must have done so because here it was still in the Webster family, but who had it then.

'So who did Mary give the telescope to if she did not have any children?' she asked her Grandda.

'It went to Jane, who was her niece' he replied, eyes still closed.

'I wonder when Jane got it?' said Sarah, 'Maybe she got it on her eighteenth birthday,'

'More likely her twenty first in those days,' replied Grandda.

'When would that have been Grandda?'

Billy pulled out his small, battered notebook and turned to the back pages. 'Well let's see, Jane was born in 1853. You remember we found that out from the family headstone in Eston cemetery. So she would have been twenty one in 1874.' Grandda paused and then went on: 'I suppose you'll want to know about how Jane got the telescope now.'

'Yes, that would be good,' replied Sarah already off into her own version of events.

Mary & Jane, California – Summer 1874

Jane, eldest daughter of John and Ann Webster, treasured and pampered, spoilt and ruined, was waiting for her Aunt Mary to bring the family telescope. She wanted it for no reason other than that her Aunt Mary had it and because of her father's indulgence she would get it. John Webster's twenty one years of devotion to his eldest daughter had produced a selfish demanding young woman whose demands were taking their toll on him. To keep up with them Aunt Mary's younger brother had taken a second job at the new Chaloner pit on the other side of the Eston Hills. Great things were expected of this new mine. John walked the three and a half miles over the Eston Hills, and back, every working day to be a part of the new mine's ambitious plans to expand mining to feed the seemingly insatiable demand for iron.

It was a chilly, wet, windswept summer's day. Jane did not notice. She did not notice the intermittent splashing of rain on the window or hear the occasional rattle of the window latch in the narrow front parlour when a gust of wind blew up the street. Through the window, grey and white remnants of cloud were being blown ragged across the sky. She lifted her nose slightly and sniffed at the apple scent from the logs burning in the grate. An indulgence she knew, but she deserved it. Absently, she passed her fingers along the stiff lace-cuff of her long sleeved, high-necked white blouse, without acknowledging the crisp, clean feel of the cotton, or the effort her mother had put into making it so smooth. The fire had dried the air in the room and she touched her top lip with her tongue. She ignored the slightly greasy taste of a thinly buttered scone, taken from the plate that lay in front of her on a starched tablecloth, and placed in her mouth with infinite care, in an attempt to mimic what she imagined to be the correct manners of society.

Her Aunt Mary was late. Jane sighed again; she could not abide people being late. The sooner she was where she belonged the better. She was convinced it would not be long before she could satisfy her desire to move to a proper house. A house in Darlington, far away from this grubby, dirty, noisome street of hastily-built leaky cottages that she had the misfortune to have started her life in. Fancy having to live in a village named after an ex colonial territory in North America; Jane prided herself in her knowledge of geography and the places of the world. It was in part some justification, however small, for wanting the telescope now.

Mary hated visiting her niece. She could almost sense the measured condescending look oozing along the street as she turned into California Road. She knew that Jane hated living here. She knew that her niece considered that she should be in a better place by right. Mary wasn't the first to wonder if Jane really was a Webster child, but she reached the end of the street, turned into Prospect View and caught sight of her niece through the cottage window and as usual saw the instant likeness to her brother John. The same high forehead and pinched long nose; the high, raised cheek-bones, and small thin straight mouth above a slightly receding chin. Long fair hair tied up in a fashionable bun, yes, it would be difficult to mistake Jane for anyone else but John's daughter. What had her brother allowed her to become?

Mary reached the front door. All the other cottages had a plain whitewashed step and bare walls – but not this one. On either side of the door was a narrow wooden box from which roses were growing up the walls. Mary had to admit it made a pretty sight; Jane had a good eye for colour and what went well. She shook her head, nothing for it but to knock. It wasn't right coming to the front door, any other cottage or working people's house and she would have been round at the back – up the lane and straight in through the open kitchen door – but not with Jane, 'etiquette' had to be followed; Mary stumbled over the word. Only official people, trouble normally, came to the front door, rent collectors and the like.

There was a distinct wait after she had knocked, fancy having to knock when she was close family, Jane sat just a few feet from the door, daft, annoying; Mary sighed again. She guessed that her sister-in-law, Ann, would be coming to the door eventually – certainly Jane would never come herself. At last the sound of scraping shoes came from behind the door. The latch lifted and the door was pulled open, with painful slowness; a tiny, hunched figure – all in black – half bent over, stood in the doorway.

'Oh it's you Mary; get yourself in its pouring with rain. Is she expecting you?'

'I hope so,' said Mary, 'she asked me to come. I hope it's not a wild goose chase on a day like this, though who knows with Miss Jane.'

She stepped into the cottage. The cottages in the street had been built quickly, with just two rooms downstairs and a loft. The front door was saved for special occasions, christenings or marriages or burials or even rarer, visits by official people – doctors for example. The life of the cottages was through the back door – into the communal kitchen and living space used by the whole family. The bedroom was in the loft – accessible by ladder where children, and adults who could climb, all slept.

Not this particular cottage. John had managed to split the downstairs front parlour into two narrow rooms, partitioned by a thick curtain hung from the ceiling on hooks and a doorway fashioned from bits of old discarded pit props salvaged from the mine entrance. Through this 'doorway' was the kitchen and a living area for everyone else. The front parlour that Mary walked into was Jane's. On the left of the door behind a once respectable but now faded canvas screen was a single bed, disguised as a sofa during the day. On the right, in front of the window, stood a small half-moon table and two chairs; the rest of the space was filled with an odd assortment of rescued furniture; a sideboard – flood damage disguised by stain; a small chest – one leg propped up with a block of wood and in the middle of the room an old carpet – the pattern only just discernible in the dull light from the window or occasional flicker from the fire. This was Jane's apartment. She had read the term in a London newspaper and had adopted it immediately as being French and therefore fashionable. Across the narrow room the doorway to the back room was hidden by a curtain whose pattern stopped where it had been neatly, but suspiciously, cut off, to accommodate the lowness of the door.

Despite being only five feet from her Aunt and deliberately facing away from the front door Jane's shrill piercing voice asked:

'Who is it mother?'

'You know fine well who I am,' said Mary, 'don't play your silly games with me Jane.'

There was a distinct pause. Then, just as Mary was beginning to think that she had got through to Jane, her niece rose, straightened her dress, turned and looked at her Aunt. The practiced, aloof glare came across the space between them and as usual Mary had to brace herself to receive it and not be totally intimidated.

'Well, what do you want?' Mary demanded sharply.

'Come now Aunt Mary, please sit down. Mother, help Aunt Mary with her coat,' said Jane ignoring the sharpness of her Aunt's question with ease.

The thought of poor Ann having to deal with the sodden wool shawl that was her coat made Mary angry for a moment, but then she laughed at Jane's ludicrous antics.

'It's fine Ann. I can manage no bother. You go and rest your feet.' Mary hung her dripping wet shawl on a nail behind the curtain. Then she brushed past Jane to sit down in the chair on the other side of the table. She helped herself to tea and the remaining half a scone. Ann was a good cook, wasted on this stupid girl.

Ann looked lost for a moment and then, bending over, shuffled out through the curtain and disappeared into the back room, grateful to avoid the impending argument between her strange daughter and her determined Sister-in-law. Silence fell in the front room. Mary spooned the heavenly sugar into her cup and noisily stirred the tea until the over-sweet tea was ready to drink. She sat back and waited – old William Snow had taught her patience and she put it to good practice from all those years ago. Her reward came several minutes later when a peeved look came over Jane's face and she flounced into the chair. Next to the empty tea-stained saucer – what use were saucers – was a newspaper. It was a copy of the 'Yorkshire Post and Leeds Intelligencer'. Mary glanced at it quickly and then looked away. Jane noticed the movement and seized the initiative again; she knew that Mary could not read.

'I see from the newspaper that a new eating establishment is to be opened in Harrogate. I am planning an excursion there, to take tea.'

The idea of Jane even thinking of travelling right across Yorkshire just for a cup of tea made Mary laugh and she regained the initiative.

'As I said Jane, what do you want?' she asked again.

'Oh dear Aunt Mary, always so impatient,' Jane sighed and dabbed her mouth with a napkin that she had folded carefully by her plate. 'I think I shall send a note to Emily and travel with her, she has a cousin, whom I have not met, Alexander, perhaps he could be persuaded to accompany us, for our security,' her voice tailed off.

Mary had a moment's pity for the unfortunate Alexander. Jane's efforts to find herself a man, who could take her into the society that she was convinced she belonged to, were famous. On the other hand Alexander could look after himself.

'That's all very well, but what is it that you've asked me out for on this horrible day?' Mary returned the conversation to her original question, but it was no good Jane was warming to her theme and ignored Mary's question again.

'Emily says that this new café' – she pronounced this in her newly practiced French accent and was quite pleased with the result, lost on Aunt Mary of course, but nonetheless quite pleasing – 'is the place to be seen in North Yorkshire at the moment.'

Mary had a moments worry about her brother's ability to provide the money to transport his daughter half across the county and back, but then she gave up and as usual despaired of John. He had dedicated his life to his eldest daughter and by all accounts his life was unlikely to last that long, there was nothing to be done. She had tried many times in the past, but she knew he would die before he admitted that he had ruined his daughter.

'Jane,' she interrupted loudly, 'what is it you want? I've things to do back at the farm even if you don't, so tell me now what this visit is about?'

Jane paused in her imaginings of living the fashionable life of a Darlington Lady and looked across at her Aunt. How could she still live in that hovel of a farm; even these new cottages in California were better than that, not that they were good enough of course, but still they were better than Aunt Mary's tenant farm in Eston. She picked up the newspaper and scanned the front page. She noticed a short article on world news and decided to read it out to her Aunt, no harm in emphasising the difference in their standing in the community.

'I see from the newspaper that the first horse-drawn carriage has just been seen in Bombay, that's in the colonies as you know' – knowing that her Aunt wouldn't know any such thing. 'Which reminds me; I have been notified by Mr and Mrs Harrington, the headmaster and his wife, that my application to teach young ladies, at the new school in the village, has been accepted. I am to start in a few weeks' time.'

'Bombay is in India, on the south west coast, they ship tea to Liverpool from there,' Mary interrupted quietly. Silence ensued for several minutes. Then Jane smiled slightly but firmly:

'Ah yes, you would have heard that from your old sailor, what was his name, Snow wasn't it.' She decided to end the game with her Aunt; it was too easy to bait her like this. 'That reminds me of why I asked you to come and call. Father has said that as I am now of age then I should have the family heirloom, such as it is.'

It was the last comment that annoyed Mary more than the loss of the telescope that William Snow had left her. Just as William Snow had promised it to her, Mary had promised John that he should have the glass so it would stay in the Webster family. She also knew that John had promised his daughter that if she had the opportunity to become a teacher at the school she could have the telescope to help in teaching the children geography and history. Mary sighed, resigned to the inevitable and tired of playing her niece's games but determined to show no sorrow at the news.

'Aye, your father spoke to me about it; I'll bring it over on Sunday. Now if there's nothing else I've jobs to attend to and don't worry I'll see myself out.' Mary rose, fetched her shawl from the hook and left the cottage, resolved never to return and never to see her niece again.

She took the telescope to her brother whilst he was working at his second job, night-watchman at the Trustee mine, on Sunday evening. He looked gaunt and exhausted, eight years younger than Mary but already old. He managed the two jobs by sleeping through most of his night-watchman's shift, but even so he could not keep it up for ever and Mary begged him to look after himself, but John Webster was a determined, stubborn man and had promised his eldest daughter the best he could give her, and this was the only way he knew how.

So on Sunday morning, after milking the farm's two cows, and before she went to see her brother Mary took the telescope and walked for the last time up to Eston Nab. She had decided that she would never go back up after this. She sat on the same rock that she had shared with old William Snow all those years before and looked out over the Tees Valley through the glass for one last time. The changes since the first time that she had witnessed the magic of the telescope were unbelievable. The small village of Middlesbrough had grown so much since she was a girl. The forty people in 1829 – many of who she had known – were now 40,000; she struggled to understand what that meant but the view through the lens showed a large smoky, noisy, bustling town with streets criss-crossing what had been flat pastureland when she was young.

It was not just the size of Middlesbrough that had changed though; Mary moved the telescope across the once empty marshes and pastures of the Tees estuary and picked out settlements and industrial works; foundries, iron smelters, engineering, all manner of manufacturing had spread along the banks of the Tees since that day she and William had sat on Eston Nab. There were nearly a hundred blast furnaces along the river banks and the area had started to be called Ironopolis.

What was a bit easier to connect with was the impact the changes had made in her village. In 1850 good quality ironstone had been discovered in the hills behind the village and the quiet agricultural community had been changed dramatically by the rapid growth of a mining boom. There were now three drift mines in the hills below where she sat. Each one had a tramway incline along which the tubs, each holding at least two tons of hand-hewn ironstone, travelled to the tip-yard. The tip-yard in the centre of the villages of Eston and California was now the hub of the community that had grown so much since she was a child. Teesside was famous now. Everyone in the village still talked about the visit of Mr Gladstone twelve years before.

In 1829 William had felt and heard the sound of an anchor cable running out on a ship anchoring in the Tees four and a half miles away and they had clearly heard the sound of an Oyster Catcher as it flew high above them. Now the air was filled with the loud clamour of voices from the mines below where Mary sat, and the rumbling and crashing from the wagons on the incline. From the tip-yard a railway branch line had been built to carry the wagons of ore down to the ironworks at Eston Junction. It was from there that her niece Jane would catch a train to Middlesbrough and from there use the vast network of new lines that now covered the country and made it possible for Jane to think about visiting Harrogate so easily. Everything had changed; her quiet natural world had gone.

Now, when Mary thought about it, she smelt an all-pervading stench of raw sewage from the open drains behind the overcrowded closely-built streets where a single toilet, no more than a midden, was used by everyone – even Jane, she smiled at that thought. In the distance, down by the river, dark with streaks of polluted industrial waste drifting with the tide up and down the estuary, she could see the blue-black smoke from the iron works; she could feel and hear the vibration of the mine workings beneath her inside the Eston Hills. She could taste the grit in the rain from the quarry along the hill to her left as a shower passed overhead and she had climbed over the incline towards the Nab. She had touched the smooth iron rails that were used to transport the iron ore all over the world.

All these man made senses had overtaken the simple natural beauty of the land that Mary had been born into and which she recalled with sadness. A sadness that was tied to her memory of William Snow, whose gift to her was now to be lost as well. For a last time she swept round the horizon, closed the lens and wrapped the telescope back in the old piece of hessian in which she kept it safe and set off down to the mine-head to give it to her younger brother to pass on to his daughter. Mary wept as she stumbled down the path, her childhood memories lost forever.

Sarah, Eston Nab – Spring 2015

Billy woke Sarah from her day dreaming and said it was high time they left the Nab and returned to Grandma and Grandda's home in Prospect View. He wrapped the telescope in a soft faded yellow cloth and slid it into a length of plastic drain pipe that he had cut and fitted to protect the glass when they went out. The old leather case had finally disintegrated after Billy had inherited it from his Grandma Bella in nineteen sixty four. When the telescope was at home it sat on a wooden stand that Billy had made at woodwork evening classes during one of the many slack overtime free periods at the steel works he had joined as an apprentice with his best friend Joe when they were both sixteen. As Billy packed his haversack he glanced over towards the coast where the Redcar blast furnace was leaving a smoky trail in the sky. It had had its share of adventures, changing hands, being nationalised, de-nationalised, re-nationalised, being moth-balled by its previous owners, an Indian multi-national company – the Tata Corporation who had sold it to SSI three years before.

There were plenty of rumours about the future of the site and possible closing, but for now Joe's eldest son had a job there – not for long now he was joining the army. Billy suspected it would be a better prospect than the blast furnace. Selfishly, Billy had been relieved that he had retired from the works before it had been moth-balled. He and Peggy had escaped the effects of the sixteen hundred lay-offs; the impact on their families, and all the businesses and sub-contractors that supported one of Teesside's largest employers. Billy viewed the latest crisis with the fatalistic realism of the people of Teesside. Opponents of the country would call it apathy, specifically the English disease, but in truth the ability to deal with whatever came along had stood the country, the Tees Valley, and in particular the Webster family in good stead over the years since industrialisation had come to the area. He finished packing and strapped up the haversack before putting it over his right shoulder. He hoped the furnace would stay open, for everyone's sake, but he was fatalistic about the outcome.

They followed the path along the edge of the Eston Hills until it branched off down towards the fast-disappearing remains of the original drift mines, inclines and banks. The old works and the other mine workings were long gone. Billy could remember it. He clearly remembered when the mine had closed at Eston; he was eight years old. He recalled the quiet subdued period afterwards while people had to get used to new jobs, new scenery, new neighbours and the end of an era that had started just ninety nine years before, not even a century of steel and stone for Eston.

Step five – Sally

Spring, selfish daydreams
Fumes, queues, text, noise, shops, youth, choice
Material things

Sarah, Dorman Museum – Summer 2015

Sarah and her Grandda were sitting in Café Bahia near the corner of Albert Park having their dinner. They had been looking round the Dorman museum. They had come to find out what it must have been like to be living on Teesside when Tommy died. Sarah knew that her Grandda had been born during the war – he would have been just a year old when Tommy was killed.

'I don't want you to die ever, Grandda,' she said.

'When I was young neither did I lass,' replied Billy, not sure where her thoughts were going.

'So would you mind dying now Grandda?' asked Sarah.

Grandda paused and thought for a while. As usual an unthinking comment had got him into heavy discussion with his granddaughter.

'That's a big question; everyone has to die, sometime,' he began.

'Yes, Grandda, I know that, but not today, you're not allowed to die today,' Sarah interrupted.

'Alright Lass, I'll keep that in mind.'

They sat in silence. Sarah was eating a doughnut; sugar covered her fingers and stuck to the corners of her mouth. Billy was struggling with another haiku, this one about his own life. Sarah finished her treat and thought about the sort of food they had seen in the exhibition – food that people had eaten in the nineteen forties and fifties. She wondered what it must have been like, living on rations, never knowing what you might be get to eat the next day. She thought of some of the times with her Mam when there was not much to eat. It wasn't like rationing, just what happened when her Mam lost her latest job. Although her Mam always seemed to be able to get another job they never lasted. Would that be how she would grow up, drifting from job to job. Why had her Mam ended up like that? What had her childhood been like? Her Mam would never talk about it. Perhaps she could get her Grandda to tell her.

'Grandda?' Sarah began. She wanted to get him to talk about her Mam, but wasn't sure how. He was quite happy to talk about the older Websters, the ones that were dead, but when she tried to ask him about their own family he would say it was not interesting and change the subject.

'What love?' Billy recognised the voice and knew another question was on its way. This time his Granddaughter trapped him and he began to tell her about himself.

'What was life like when you first started work at the steelworks,' she asked?

Billy thought for a while, wondering what to say.

Sarah sat in silence. She was holding her breath. Would he tell her anything about himself? It was several minutes before he began to speak and she glanced over to see if he was alright. Grandda's eyes were a bit misty and he seemed to be looking through her into the far distance. When Sarah looked closer she saw a small tear in the corner of his left eye. She was about to ask why, when Grandda began to talk.

Billy & Joe, Steel Works – Winter 1964

Billy and Joe went through secondary school and out the other end of the shining new public education system with only one of the three available options in their sights. In fact when they left they had nothing in their sights, except girls, and even then their sights were blurred by the images in Joe's elder brother Pete's magazines. Spurred on by the glossy pictures, they were much preoccupied by the legendary furry haven at the top of Elsie Tomkinson's skirt, and whilst they had each persuaded the other that they had already visited, in reality, neither had gotten further than a clumsy grope climbing up the stairs of the Saturday night bus. Elsie, who it should be noted, had been to Scarborough; northern haven of sin and sex, had laughed at their attempts and at the top of the stairs had turned, lifted the hem of her dress and revealed to each one a bewildering mass of cotton frills which left both young, spotty adolescents no wiser on how to reach the warm moist haven that the magazine described in graphic detail.

Leaving school they turned up at Dorman Long's Lakenby works where they completed their apprenticeships and began work for real.

* * *

It was still dark when Billy got up for the early shift, five o'clock on a bleak cold February morning. Unlike Joe, who rolled out of bed ten minutes before he had to leave home to catch the bus, Billy needed time to wake up, time to – Peggy never understood what he was doing – to get his head into work. He washed his face in the hand basin and dried it on the towel on the nail behind the door. In the kitchen he sat with a mug of builder's tea, thick, brown, three sugar trenchers sweet and a doorstep of bread and marg. He couldn't face breakfast so early in the morning – that could wait until the morning break. He filled his flask with hot tea and put it, together with his metal bait box, into the heavy canvas shoulder bag. Bag over shoulder and cap in hand from another nail behind the kitchen door Billy stepped out into the back lane and set off down towards the corner to cross the road and wait for Joe and the bus, whichever came first. To be fair, Joe very rarely missed the bus, but he was never early either. As Billy waited he rolled his first cigarette. He took the tobacco tin from his pocket; it was a nineteen thirties Players medium navy cut tin that had belonged to his Grandda Tommy. Billy held the tin in the palm of his left hand. From the open tin he took out a packet of Rizla cigarette papers and took one from the pack. He held it between the thumb and first finger of his left hand. He teased some tobacco from a half plug in the tin and dropped it into the palm of his right hand. He shut the tin and put it back into his pocket. Billy placed the paper onto the palm of his left hand and spread the tobacco across the paper. With one side of the paper anchored by his left thumb he rolled the paper around the tobacco, lifted the tube to his mouth, licked along the paper's edge and sealed the cigarette. As Billy lit the cigarette with a Swan Vesta match taken from the same pocket as the tin, Joe came round the corner and their bus appeared in the opposite direction. They sat half way back on the top deck wreathed in early morning smoke, another day at work another shift towards retirement.

* * *

The two bodies leaned forward, each one with the weight on the ball of the right foot. The left wrists bore the weight of the shovels as the right hands guided them toward the heat of the open furnace door. An intense orange white heat that grew as the crushed ore on the shovels moved towards it.

The two bodies completed the rhythmic movement. As the shovels reached the mouth of the furnace the right hands twisted the handles of the shovels anti-clockwise. The left hands loosened their grip and the right knees tensed. The shovels stopped in mid-air and the crushed ore flew in through the furnace door to be enveloped in heat and light and to disappear, consumed by the fire.

The two right-balled feet pushed back, the bodies twisted to the left and the arms came back. The knees bent, the shovels were lowered and driven into the shrinking pile of ore. The arms pushed and the knees moved in behind the wrists, left behind left and right behind right, the weight of the bodies pushed the shovel blades into the ore. The movement stopped – the bodies balanced on both feet. The muscles tightened and the tendons pulled, the knees straightened and the shovels were full. Full enough to feed the furnace, trained enough not to strain the backs. The bodies turned and the movement began again. Billy and Joe were at work, each with their own thoughts, Peggy or pigeons. The days passed in companionship and the sweating heat of Lakenby Ironworks.

Billy & Peggy, Prospect View, Eston – Spring 1978

Sally Webster was born eight years after her parents married. By then they had each come to terms with the idea of never having any children. Billy refused to go and see any doctors about their inability to produce a child. He buried the 'little problem' in his work and his writing. Peggy was not so successful in coming to terms with the unspoken village stigma and she took into herself the idea that it was her that was incapable of having any children – there must be something she was doing wrong. And then, just as they felt they had come to terms with their childless marriage, Peggy conceived.

As far as Peggy could work out Sally came into their lives on Saltburn Beach, right at the southern end of the beach under the cliffs, late one evening in September of nineteen seventy five. Peggy wanted to know why, after all their years of trying she had finally become pregnant. She smiled at the word. Her mother would never use such a word. A happy event was the best that she would get from her Mam. The doctor dismissed her questions about how it had happened. It did not matter he said, the main thing was she was expecting. Peggy smiled again, another misnomer – she was expecting things every day, why couldn't people just come out with it – she was pregnant.

She carried the baby right through the winter and into May with no particular worries. They did out a corner of the bedroom as a nursery; a cot from one relation, bedding from another, clothes from her parents, a pram – January sales – from his. Then at the end of March Peggy developed some pain and was in and out of hospital all through April until the last day of the month when the doctor wouldn't let her home again. In a blur of gas and pain Peggy Webster gave birth to a girl. Mother and baby both clung to life for three weeks until first the baby, they'd called her Sally, and then finally Peggy began to get stronger. The baby did well after that, but the cost to Peggy was high. The birth had been followed by a serious operation and it was a distraught Peggy that had eventually been able to get Billy to understand, through a series of heart stopping sobs and gasps, that Sally would be their only child. They clung to the little girl with obsessive love and determination. Sally Webster wasn't born with the right character to cope with all the attention and her parents were to pay the price of their devotion for the rest of their lives. Peggy always said that Billy spoiled his daughter most and if pressed he had to agree.

Sarah, Stewart Park – Summer 2015

They were sitting in Nana Tom's café, near Stewart Park having tea and a bun, Grandda's favourite. Sarah had been silent for a while and Billy wondered what she was thinking about. He was about to ask her when she asked him a question instead; a question that he had known would come at some time.

'Grandda,' even then she stopped before she asked.

'Yes, pet,' Billy was trying to finish the last five syllables of a Haiku – he wasn't concentrating on his granddaughter so her question caught him unprepared. From the time they had started to trace the family history, and especially since she had begun to get him to talk about his own life, he had known that they would get to one of the most painful memories he had – she asked it now. It went through his guard and got an honest and raw response, a response that left them silent for a long time as each followed their thoughts back to the nineteen eighties when his parents had died.

'What happened to your Mam and Da? It said on the gravestone that they died on the same day. How did that happen?' came Sarah's question.

'They were killed in an accident,' he paused and then continued, the painful part, 'it was your Mam who found them,' he added; his voice tailed off.

Unwilling to look at each other they both looked out of the window. A woman walked past with a pushchair, one of those three-wheeled enormous things that could carry more than Peggy believed a young mother would ever need. Sarah spoke first:

'Mam must have very young then, was she very upset?'

The woman and her chariot disappeared into the park.

'Aye lass she was. Same age as you are, and yes, she was very upset, I sometimes think she's never recovered from it,' said Billy and then caught up with his thoughts and knew that he was going down a route he had hoped he would be able to avoid, but then he would never be ready to explain the loss. He thought back to her question of a year ago – will I grow up like me Mam? Perhaps what happened to his parents would help explain why Sarah's Mam was like she was and if so, this time, if at all possible, he and Peggy could try and help Sarah not do the same.

Sally, Eston High Street – Spring 1989

Sally left her Grandparents at the bus stop in Eston at five twenty seven on Friday fourteenth April nineteen eighty nine. She turned once and waved to them. Grandma saw her and waved back. Sally walked on over the brow of the hill and waited to cross the road. A van drove by as a dog ran into the road. The van driver, reacting on instinct, swerved to avoid it, skidded and went over the brow of the hill out of control. The van's brakes made a harsh metallic noise that went right into Sally's head so she couldn't think. The tyres on the locked wheels were skidding across the tarmac, they heated up and the friction caused them to squeal and then both sounds stopped – there was a dull thud, something hard hitting something soft.

For a second there was an eerie silence and Sally could see so clearly that everything slowed down. Her heart fluttered as it changed speed in response to the demand for blood from the rest of her body. She recovered and feet unfrozen she ran back up the slope and over the brow of the hill towards the bus stop. The van was on its side, there was no sign of her grandparents or the bus stop except, as she looked more closely, for a foot coming out from under the front of the van. It had no shoe, but it did have Grandda's sock on it.

Sally went down onto her knees besides the foot. She felt nothing in her mind – her life stood still. It was not until the next day, as they sat watching the television;

protests had begun in Tiananmen Square, China following the death of Hu Yaobang, that Sally began to cry.

At first Sally's Mam and Da thought that she was coping with the tragedy well. They did their best to keep her away from reminders of the accident – the verdict that the inquest recorded. Sally didn't go to the funeral, she seemed so upset at the time they thought it best that she didn't. Instead she went to stay with her Aunt. She did so again when the inquest was being held. Peggy, her mother seemed more affected by it all. The injustice of the verdict, no one was blamed, it was an accident, a terrible accident; death by misadventure was recorded. Sally's Mam sat through the proceedings, her face with no expression, no reaction, her mind right inside itself – seething inside. She longed to hit out at the Coroner, the police and in particular, the owners of the dog – unscathed by its adventure – and the driver of the van. Without intending to she took out her suppressed anger on those who would accept it, her family; by so doing she drove her daughter away from the one place that she might have had a chance to learn to deal with her grief.

Outwardly Sally did cope well, but the circumstances that she found herself in served to make it difficult for her. She changed schools. She missed the first half of her first term when she should have been making friends and getting used to the bigger school. By the time she began to go regularly, after half term, her parents were preoccupied with the inquest and had little demonstrable time for her problems at school.

Sally's first absence was an accident. It was the first morning of the inquest and her uniform wasn't ready. By the time it was found in the washing pile and ironed by her distracted, fraught, tearful Mam, Sally knew she would have missed the bus so she set off to walk down Church Lane and then through the cemetery. It was at the entrance to the cemetery that she met Vee. Sally never found out her real name, but she was the first person to listen to her since the accident. Vee's way of helping and coping with her own life was not what Sally needed but it was, she decided, what she wanted.

Sarah, Stewart Park – Summer 2015

After Billy had finished talking about the death of his parents there was a deep silence across the table between him and his granddaughter. Billy didn't think that this was the right place for the depth of conversation they were having, but it had started and he knew his granddaughter well. He wasn't going to be able to stop her inquisitiveness now without a lot more painful questions. As usual the next question was not what he expected, but it was painful, nonetheless.

'But Mam had you and Grandma didn't she, that must have helped her mustn't it?' Sarah asked.

Her Grandda didn't answer straight away. Sarah watched as he disappeared into his memories and as she waited she drifted into her own about how her Mam might have coped with losing her grandparents when she was so young. Billy wondered how much his unpredictable (no she was very predictable), scatty, indecisive daughter had told Sarah about her own childhood and how her life changed after her grandparents had died. He recalled his wife's warning that Sarah should be told soon. If not by Sally herself then certainly Billy should. How else would she be able to learn from her mother's mistakes? Billy winced inside; he didn't like to think of his daughter making mistakes and not too far below his conscious thoughts he shared the blame for the way her life had turned out. He recalled the next low point in Sally's life and hoped fervently that Sarah would never experience the same in her life.

Sally, Magistrates Court, Teesside – Spring 1990

Billy wasn't sure how he came to find out. He knew that the letter and summons had appeared on a Tuesday morning. It was on the anniversary of his parents' death. The official looking envelope was addressed to Mr. W. Webster, parent or guardian of Miss S J Webster, Prospect View, Eston, Cleveland. He opened it. The words Magistrates' court, the official-looking letterhead registered in one part of his brain but the name Sally Jane Webster did not. His mind split the two apart and refused to recognise any connection between the summons and his daughter. Clearly there was a mistake. There could be no way that Sally would ever get herself into enough trouble to attract the attention of the police let alone reach a magistrates court. No, it was a mistake. He put the letter back into its brown envelope and stood it up behind the telescope on the sideboard in the parlour, next to the clock. He went off to work; the whole family left the house for work and school as they did every weekday morning during school term.

The clock in the parlour ticked all day, it chimed the hours just as it had done in the old farmhouse outside Eston and now in the small house in California. It was a forgiving piece. William Webster, Tommy's Da had mended it in eighteen eighty eight when part of the mechanism had broken. He had taken it by cart to the clock menders in Guisborough – the repair would only be visible to someone who knew what to look for. A less-careful inspection would reveal where Billy had adjusted the pendulum with one of Joe's metal pigeon-leg rings. He had added the ring to slow it down – now it only gained about five minutes a week. It was a Sunday evening ritual for Billy to set it right for the start of the week.

They sat at the kitchen table. It was supper time. As usual, when Sally was in the house, every door was open so if you listened you could hear the sound of the clock in the parlour coming through to the back room.

Billy had just finished telling them about his latest poem when he remembered the letter. His wife and daughter humoured his writing, they had been laughing at his poem about a juggler and his coloured blocks with letters on each side. For once the room had a light companionable feeling that a family would give it when nothing in particular was worrying them all.

'You'll never guess what came through the post this morning,' said Billy when the laughter had stopped, 'a summons, from the Magistrates Court, for our Sally. How daft is that. Not very nice though, making that kind of a mistake, you'd think that they'd check before they sent them out wouldn't you. It could really upset someone who was a bit sensitive.'

The clock struck the quarter to. The same childhood rhyme went through Billy's mind and he had just got to the line about 'two screws are loose', when he caught up with the change in the atmosphere in the room. At the other end of the table his wife was glaring at her daughter. The clock finished its chiming and the faint reverberation was replaced by the quiet ticking as it journeyed on to the next hour.

'Well girl, are you going to tell him or must I,' said Peggy.

'Tell me what,' asked Billy, the beginnings of concern starting in his mind.

'It's nothing Da, just a silly mistake,' said his daughter. Her tone was altogether too bright.

'What's a mistake?' Billy asked.

'Terrorising an old man and stealing his winnings was a mistake was it,' said Sally's Mam.

All of two pounds thought Sally to herself as she listened to the 'how did we ever get to this,' tone creep into her mother's voice – a tone that she hated.

Billy got up and walked into the parlour. He picked up the letter from behind the telescope. As he did so the two parts of his brain that had been united in their determination to be unconnected clashed together. He came back into the kitchen. He sat down at the table. He re-opened the letter. He re-read it. This time the message was clear. His daughter, his twelve year old daughter, was summoned to appear at the Magistrate's Court – next Thursday, at ten o'clock.

* * *

The three young girls, very young now, in their plain school uniforms, no make-up, hair tied back in pony tails, stood together in the dock. They had been sworn in and the charges read to them. The words crashed about in Billy's head. They had met with the solicitor earlier; a bespectacled young man with a round face and an earnest expression who had advised them of the possible outcomes. He had stressed the need for Sally to accept the gravity – he had laid great stress on the word gravity, at odds with his otherwise high-pitched voice – of what was about to happen. Billy had held his daughter's hand and smiled at her, willing her to take heed. Peggy had prayed silently and kept her hands together, fingers crossed – she had no allusions about her daughter's ability or willingness to follow any sort of plan or advice.

The case proceeded, papers were read, questions asked and before Billy had time to absorb what had happened the Magistrates had adjourned to consider their verdict. The three girls stood close together. They looked nervous, defiant, vulnerable, and bored in turn as they waited for something to happen. Whilst they did so the Magistrate's clerk, that's who Billy imagined the be-suited man at the left of the bench was, appeared to be continuing with some other court business as he waited. Two people who had not appeared for their summons were bound over to appear again. A request for bail was accepted, another denied and then the Magistrates reappeared. As they were coming in to the room a man, perhaps as little as five foot in height came into the court with a large bundle of papers. He approached the bench carefully and stretched up to hand the papers to the clerk as the Magistrates moved into their seats, as he did so his trousers rode up above his ankles – he was wearing short black socks with suspenders. The chief Magistrate – Billy assumed the one in the middle was the chief – a lady from Nunthorpe, looked up as she prepared to take her seat. In her mind she was balancing the charge against the background of the three girls as she considered the options at her disposal for sentencing. Two of the girls she had already decided on, but not Sally, until she looked up. Sally had seen the man and his suspenders, suspenders that settled her fate – she giggled, and a severe reprimand became probation. Sally moved from being a young person with experience of what the law could do to a recognised law breaker. She was on a plateau half way up a mountain. Sally would spend the rest of her life flirting with the descent into real crime. Billy and Peggy looked at each other in despair.

Sarah, Stewart Park – Summer 2015

Sarah waited patiently as she watched her Grandda deal with his memories. At one point she thought about interrupting him, but loving instinct stopped her. As if in response to her thought Billy winced inside; he didn't like to think of his daughter making mistakes; he shared the blame for the way her life had turned out. Sally was on her own; unlike him she had no loving, dependable partner to share the responsibilities of bringing up a daughter. That led him to a question that he had tried to ask his daughter several times over the last fourteen years with no success. Who was Sarah's father? He glanced across at his granddaughter. She was looking out of the window, watching a small dog chewing a discarded pizza box. Hopefully she hadn't tuned into his thoughts this time – she often did.

The question of her father was not one that Billy wanted to face from Sarah, but sooner or later, sooner now that Sarah was nearly fifteen and asking about her family, she would ask and Sally was the only person who could answer. Always assuming she knew was Peggy's retort when they had last talked about it. His thought took him back to the year that Sarah was born – another chaotic event in Sally's life.

Sally, Middlesbrough – December 1999

It was New Year's Eve; the streets full of people. Sally Webster was clubbing. She and her four girl friends were dancing, enjoying themselves and the atmosphere, false or otherwise, was of anticipation for a new year, a chance for a change, a new start. Sally was often planning new starts, but at that moment she wasn't thinking about the future, she was thinking about her next drink and who she could get to buy it. They'd met up with three lads from Cargo Fleet on the way to the Empire and it was one of them that Sally had her eye on for a drink. Sally needed a pee and a cigarette – she put her head close to Marnie's ear and told her where she was going. After her pee she went out through the open fire-escape door into the street behind the club for a smoke.

Across the street were two predatory eyes, eyebrows drawn tight across the face, pale watery blue irises set in close-muscle rigid concentration – set into a head that didn't move. The eyes looked across the narrow blocked-off street end, past a tree that was struggling to bring colour and nature to the centre of the town. A tree in a grey-black, block-built, half-pyramid shaped enclosure, home to two cans, three plastic bags, a dozen cigarette butts and a pink and yellow size four sock – left foot.

The eyes had been attracted to a chest, pushed out beyond a half fastened jacket. As the chest moved the left breast brushed backwards and forwards against the edge of the jacket. The eyes looked for a nipple – there was none to see, but the line of a bra traced across a red tee shirt and the muscles in the eyes tightened again. Blood pumped faster into the mind behind the eyes and the mind undid the jacket and lifted the tee shirt.

The chest, its sixth sense alerted, appealed to the hand at the end of the leather jacket, a jacket that was without its matching black leather bag. The hand went up to the open jacket and drew it across the breast, hiding it from view. The owner of the chest, despite being an experienced clubber denied her eyes their instincts. She didn't look up, she turned back towards the club and went back through the wide open fire doors – the eyes followed her in.

Neither girl was able to say with any accuracy when they had left the club. They knew that they had got a taxi to the village and had walked together to the end of the road. Marnie had been less drunk than Sally, she had done more dancing and had got sore feet. Her new shoes had given her blisters on her heels and on the little toe of her left foot. They had shared a last cigarette before separating for the last few hundred yards walk home.

The eyes had kept watch across the dance floor as the girl tried to find someone, some man to dance with. Her friend appeared to be set up with someone, but the one that the eyes had followed in from the street was less successful – she compensated by drinking more than her friend. On the table, where they sat with three other women – all in their twenties he was sure, were several untouched drinks waiting for the dancer to catch up with the drinker. The eyes were not concerned with the dancer; it was the drinker that they were focussed on. The girl was not the last to leave. If she had been the eyes would have left before her, leaving her safe in the anonymity of an unnoticed departure, but she didn't. One of the girls went to the phone. The eyes walked past to hear her calling taxis; they checked the time and made a call as well.

The drinker and the dancer got into the third of the taxis that came. The eyes crossed the street, got into their taxi, and followed. Where were they headed for – it was important to know the layout. Linthorpe? No. Marton? No. Ormesby? No, must be Eston, nowhere else in that direction, surely. Yes. The taxi carrying the girls stopped in the high street. They haggled with each other over who would pay, half-heartedly as far as the eyes could see from further down the street. The dancer handed over the fare and set off up the slope past the shops, the dancer supporting the drinker. The other taxi, still off-hire, drove past them, turned into a private car park and stopped – the passenger and the driver sat and waited.

The two girls went past the entrance to the parking area and disappeared along the street. Two doors opened and closed, two pairs of feet began to follow the girls, keeping far enough back to be unnoticed – there was an unusual lull in activity, a window of unnatural oblivion in the otherwise busy first hours of the New Year. The two girls stopped at a junction in the road.

'You going to be alright getting home Sal?' asked Marnie.

'Don't be daft, Marn, you sound like me Mam. I've been up this street more times than I want to remember – I'll be fine,' said Sally. She hiccupped in the cold early-morning dampness and giggled. They parted.

Sally would have been fine, if her back gate had been half open as it had been for the last half year waiting for her Da to repair the catch, but Billy had had an hour before they went to the club and so he had fixed the catch and, although not locked, the gate was shut – it threw Sally. She struggled to work out how to open it. The door was locked for some reason:

'Bloody stupid idea that, on New Year's Eve.' she said to herself.

She opened her bag to look for a key. She found it and in trying to get it to fit the lock managed to drop the key on the floor. Sally bent down to pick it up as the feet reached her. As she stood up a hand gripped her shoulder and turned her so she was pinned against the back yard wall. Two fingers were pressed against her mouth and a voice hissed:

'Want some help darling; let me give you a hand.'

Later, much later, Sally was to recall the irony of the night, the stupid anguished, hearty breaking irony of the night. She had spent the first three quarters of New Year's Eve and into the early hours of the first day of the New Year trying to find a man to have sex with. She had dreamed about what it would be like and made up her mind that it would be a magic; it was the New Year and she wanted sex. A man that she could choose to let take her somewhere, anywhere and make love to on the first day of the year. What happened? Some man, she did sometimes think it had been two men, but was never sure, had chosen her, without her permission. There had been no signs of a struggle, no sign of restraint or resistance – just sex that she had wanted, but not chosen – she would chew at the memory for the rest of her life. It affected her relationships and left her frustrated and unfulfilled as she battled with her desire and her lost dreams.

* * *

When Marnie had finally persuaded her to go to the police and report it – she'd noticed how many men were involved, deep down she knew there was nothing to repair the scars. They recorded the incident, those men, and promised to look into it. Sally still recalled the comment of the man behind the counter – she'd almost decided to lash out at him, but Marnie had held onto her arm.

'So as far as you know you've not had anything stolen?' he'd said, pen poised over his book.

The police's promise was the sort of promise that Sally gave to anyone that she wanted something from. With no witnesses, no evidence, no injury – well no outward injury, and a two-day delay there was no action of any kind from anyone except from Sally herself. Eight weeks later, much later than her normal regular cycle would stretch to; Sally had to admit she might be pregnant. She never did find out who Sarah's father was.

The rape was an undiminished sore just under the surface of Sally's life. She coped with it by becoming even more chaotic and disorganised in her life. The part that was most painful and confusing was that it signalled the only time in her life after her Grandparents death that Sally got on well with her mother. The birth of Sarah brought them together for a period of two years when both of them focussed on the joy that Sarah brought. Surprisingly, Sally was a good mother, unconventional granted, but she was able to develop and continue a caring and successful relationship with Sarah. Her relationship with her mother didn't last. They fell out over child minders. Despite being a loving mother Sally was bored at home all day, she wanted to go to work; Peggy didn't want her to. They argued, at first mildly and then bitterly, until Sally ended the two year honeymoon with a throw-away comment. A comment that her mother never came to terms with:

'Mam, you've never wanted anything to do with me ever. I had to get raped to get you to take any notice of me.'

If they had been able to talk in depth about their feelings, instead of just the practical needs of motherhood they might have been reconciled, but Peggy was practical first and Sally was not. Peggy tolerated her daughter for Sarah's sake – but that was all.

Sarah, Eston Nab – Autumn 2015

They were back up on Eston Nab. Sally had dropped Sarah at the end of California Road on her way to work. Sarah was surprised that her Mam had managed to stick to her enforced work at the community centre. Her Mam hated it, but she was persevering. Perhaps it was being with Iqbal. Sarah liked him. He had lots of interesting things to say and talked to Sarah as an adult. Her Mam didn't seem to have much trouble starting any job; her trouble seemed to be keeping them.

It was one of those autumn days when once the sun was up in the sky it would be warm. Peggy had been busy cleaning and had chased them out of the house with warm clothes and hot soup in a flask to climb the hills behind the house. When they set off it had been early enough in the day for them to need hats and gloves, but as they had climbed the path through the overgrown mine workings they had stopped to take them off and pack them into Sarah's back pack, she had finally persuaded Grandda to let her help carry things. They had found their usual picnic spot and spread out a small plastic-backed picnic mat – a red and yellow tartan patterned rug, bought by Peggy for Billy's Christmas present. Nestled into the gully between two sets of rocks the sun was high enough to make them feel warm, sheltered from a cold breeze.

Sarah had the telescope on her knees and was wondering what to look at. Billy noticed her fidgeting and twitching her hands around the brass eyeglass.

'Why don't you see if you can pick out where your Mam is working?' he said. Billy knew about Sally's latest visit to the magistrate's court and the resulting community-service order, had she told Sarah the truth, probably not. He began to despair again. What would happen to Sarah? Like their granddaughter Billy and Peggy had taken to Iqbal and had hoped he would be a good influence on Sally. It had looked as if he would be until she had landed in court again. Billy didn't think the lad would stay around after Sally's latest misdemeanour. He sighed and reached for his pen and pad. One reason they had come up to the Nab was to look down at the Redcar blast furnace that was about to close, possibly for ever. Billy had declined Joe's request to attend some of the protest meetings. Billy felt in his heart that this time there would be no reprieve so it would not be honest to go along and protest when he did not believe it would make any difference this time. Besides, he had retired and this was a time for a new generation, not some silly old fool with mistaken memories. From up here on the Nab they had a good view of the smoke from the furnace, both soon to disappear.

'Alright Grandda, I'll look for Mam, she has to drive down Normanby Road to the community centre, I'll start there,' Sarah said. She raised the telescope to her eye and peered through it towards Eston and then towards the place that her mother had been ordered to work her hundred hours of community service. The view through the lens was blurry, but she went through the motions to please her Grandda.

Sally & Marnie, Middlesbrough
– Autumn 2015

It was only a question of time before the right supervisor was on the same shift as Sally and she picked the wrong customer to work her scam on. As usual Sally considered it to be someone else's fault and her bad luck that she was caught. The store had a strict process and policy to get its staff to adhere to the company rules of employment so this time Sally found herself summonsed to appear at Middlesbrough Magistrates court – she didn't tell Sarah what had happened. She adopted her usual approach to such events, see what happened and deal with it when it did. She had dropped her daughter at Prospect View as if she was going to her early shift and returned to her house. She had spent time getting herself ready in sensible, plain clothes. The single mother with a dependent daughter at a vulnerable stage in her life and gave a commendable performance for the court. Watching Sally would prompt an objective view that she could be introduced to acting given enough effort and commitment – perhaps that's where Sarah got her imagination from.

Sally's sentence, she considered it to be a mean punishment and worse than she deserved had been a fine, which she would struggle to pay, but the worst bit in her eyes was a hundred hours community service – twenty days. She was to report to the Beechflat Community project to help with whatever jobs they wanted doing. It was a centre where people with learning difficulties were helped to get some form of qualification – scary people in Sally's opinion.

After her first morning she had met up with Marnie in town to do some shopping.

'The place gives me the creeps Marnie. I'm not going back there,' she said as they sat sharing a chicken parmo and drinking cola.

'Don't blame you Sal, those sorts of places should look after themselves – not expect ordinary people to get involved. You coming to the club tonight?' said Marnie.

'Probably. I've agreed to take Iqqy to another pub this evening. He wants me to show him where the Ship Inn is in the old part of the town. Apparently it's the oldest pub in Boro so he says. I hope he doesn't try and go in, it's a bit rough down there,' said Sally, in between mouthfuls of deep-fried chicken topped with bechamel sauce and cheese.

'Why not, do him good to see all parts of the town. How're you two getting on by the way. Have you found out if he's brown all over yet?' asked Marnie.

Sally didn't answer straight away. She wasn't sure what she wanted to say. She had known Marnie most of her life and the two of them had compared the men they had had, or not had, throughout that time, but for some reason, Iqqy was different. He didn't like her calling him Iqqy, but Sally used stupid names and throw away comments to deal with anything that might become serious in her life. Most of the time it resulted in the butt of her nervous, self-defence mechanism dropping her before anything serious did happen. It was a technique she had learned after her grandparents had been killed, from the girl called Vee and it suited her character, but Iqbal hadn't been put off and he hadn't left – neither of them knew quite why that was.

'No,' she said, her voice defensive, despite her efforts to sound unconcerned.

'Sorry,' said Marnie, drawing out the word into two long syllables to show her frustration with her friend. Very often the two of them had swapped the men in their lives and compared them when the man had left both, either in disgust or through their lack of commitment or serious interest, but not this time. Sally was proving to be defensive, almost protective of the tall, slim, angular young man that they had met in the pub in Ladgate Lane.

'I think you're falling for him, Sal. What does Sarah think of him? Have you shown him to your Mam and Da yet,' she asked.

'Leave it Marn. I don't know what I think. He's interesting. Serious though. Mad keen on his college course,' said Sally.

'He must be half your age Sal. What about his family? You met any of them yet?' asked Marnie.

'No,' said Sally, not liking the way the conversation was going. Marnie was asking all the questions that Sally normally had no trouble in avoiding or ignoring – they usually went away – when the man went away, but this time he wouldn't and Sally was forced to admit that she was pleased that he hadn't.

'Well I'm going to the club tonight – maybe I'll see you there. You got any money by the way?' Marnie asked this last question with no expectation of a positive response and was amazed by the answer.

'Yes, I've got fifteen quid. I promised Sarah and Iqqy that we'd go to Saltburn on Sunday,' said Sally.

'Bloody hell, Sal! What's this lad got on you? Next thing we know you'll be making him Sunday dinner,' said Marnie.

Sally laughed, 'Not while me Mam's still alive I won't,' she said without thinking.

'So he has been to meet them?' said Marnie.

Peggy Webster's Sunday dinners were renowned and if Iqqy whatever his name had been allowed into Prospect View for Sunday dinner things were getting serious.

'You told Sarah you've lost your job yet?' asked Marnie.

'Leave it Marnie,' came the short reply.

'You haven't have you?'

The two women parted without speaking. Their friendship would survive the difference. It wasn't the first time and wouldn't be the last.

Sarah, Eston Nab – Autumn 2015

Hope, unselfish dreams
Untouched imagination
Whatever will be

Sarah and her Grandda lay back on the grass and looked up into the sky. They had been watching an Oyster Catcher fly across the sky; it had come up from the coast. It was the wrong time of year for it to be nesting; perhaps the chaos of the demonstrations near the doomed blast-furnace had disturbed it. Their picnic was half eaten and the remains lay on the rug between them. The telescope was balanced across Sarah's knees. She picked it up again and looked once more along the escarpment through the lens. She was hoping to see her Mam. Once again there was no sign of her.

Sally had finally told Sarah about losing her job; she'd gone off that morning to complete her second week at the Beechflat Project in Middlesbrough. According to her Mam she was really enjoying herself. It was a bit strange at first, but now she was having a good laugh she'd said. When she had dropped Sarah at the end of Prospect View Sally had promised her daughter faithfully that when she had finished her half day she would come up to meet them on the Nab and spend time with Sarah and tell them about her week.

Sarah looked again, west along the Eston Hills towards the path that came up from the village below; the path that came up through the houses, over the Parkway and then up through the trees. This was the third time that she had looked and her Grandfather could feel the disappointment building in the girl's body. The first time she had looked she had picked out two people in the distance walking along, holding hands and Sarah, always the romantic optimist had wanted it to be her Mam and Iqbal, but it wasn't. The couple had come up to them, stopped and looked across the estuary for a while and then moved on. Billy Webster sighed and wondered if his daughter would ever get her life into any sort of order. He doubted it.

'Grandda!' said Sarah suddenly, look, there's someone's head just above the bushes coming up the path from the village.' She looked again, several times, until her Grandda noticed a small tear forming in the corner of her eye and feared the worst, it would not be Sally, but then he was interrupted by an excited scream:

'It's Mam, she coming,' cried Sarah, 'everything is going to be alright?'

Billy registered the comment and wondered at it. Sarah seemed to be putting great faith in her mother's promise to make a go of her enforced time at the community project. He hoped, fervently, that she would stick it out and not disappoint her daughter again.

Sarah looked again, it was definitely her Mam. She had turned along the path on the top of the escarpment and was walking along towards them, tottering along, more used to Corporation road than the Eston hills. Sarah could not wait. She put the telescope down by her Grandda and jumped up. She took off along the path running as fast as she could towards her Mam.

* * *

Sally had struggled up the path through the bracken, gorse and shrubby bushes of the upper slopes of the north facing Eston Hills. Walking in the countryside had never been a favourite with Sally – one of the few things she agreed on with her mother. It was her Da that had introduced Sarah to walking and now the two of them would often go tramping about on the hills above where Sally was climbing, stumbling along in a pair of trainers she hadn't worn for longer than she could remember – they were rubbing her heels. She couldn't get it into her head, no shops, no people, no sensible flat pavements, no buzz of traffic, nothing. Over the back of the Nab it was so quiet it had worried Sally the one and only time she had gone with them, to appease her Da and satisfy a birthday wish of her daughter. She hadn't done it again.

She paused at a bend in the path. A piece of rock, rounded by the weather and the passage of countless feet, stuck out, making a step about two feet high. Sally sat down on it and lit a cigarette.

'First of the day,' she thought proudly, 'No, second, or was it three. Not many anyway,' she consoled herself with the compromise. She reached into her bag for her mobile – new slim style, pink and grey, cheap, pay as you go deal. She texted Marnie with an absent half-thought-out message. The cigarette was half done when her phone rang – Madonna.

'Hiya Sal.' It was Marnie.

'Yeah.'

'Where are you?' her friend asked.

'You'll never guess,' Sally answered.

'Shops?' The first place Marnie would always look for Sally.

'No.'

'Bed?' Marnie started to go through the list of Sally's favourite places.

Sally laughed, 'Not today Marn, I'm out and about today.'

'Out and about where?' asked Marnie, bored with the game now.

'I'm up on the Nab,' said Sally.

'Bloody hell Sal, what did you say?' asked Marnie, sure she had heard wrong.

'I'm up on the Nab,' Sally repeated, pleased with the reaction from her friend.

'You gone soft in the head or something?' demanded Marnie

'No, nothing like that. I've come up to meet Sarah. She's up on the Nab with her Grandda. You know what they're like, always wandering about up here. What are you doing?'

'I'm going into town. Do you want to come? I could pick you up after you've seen Sarah,' said Marnie.

Sally paused before replying – she could get that new top she'd seen in TK Maxx.

'You still there Sal?' asked Marnie.

'Yeah, I'm here Marn, I'd love to come,' she paused again, 'but I've promised Sarah and I've some things to sort out.' She stopped. Just then she needed Marnie to say OK and leave her alone, but she knew Marnie wouldn't. Marnie had no kids, no partner, nothing, no commitments – she was lucky; Sally was right Marnie would not take no for an answer.

'I could come to the top of the street, wait by the footbridge – you won't be long will you. Tell you what, I'll be there in half an hour, give you time to see Sarah and be back down to the bridge. I've got to go, I've reached the lights, see ya!'

The phone went dead, Marnie had gone. Sally now had another choice to make on top of the three others she had already been given that morning. Her cigarette had burnt out on the rock beside her; she put her phone back into her bag and walked on up the path.

* * *

Billy had watched his granddaughter go. Sally appeared to have stopped at the top of the path up from the village, for a smoke and a rest probably. He sighed at the thought of his daughter's lifestyle. Her only real saving grace was her care and devotion – in her own way – to Sarah. A well-used window of regret opened and he peered through it, at his daughter when she was a child. He recalled his happiness and unrestrained joy when Sally was born and when she and her mother had both survived. His own and Peggy's unstinting care and precious attention to her when they had realised that she would be their only child and he wondered again how they had messed up her life so much. For some reason, the memories triggered a tune in his head and he began to hum it. Spanish? No Italian. Yes, that's right – something about growing up and having children of their own. The tune wound its way into his head and wouldn't go away. He watched as the two of them met.

Sally was still sitting down. Sarah appeared to be dancing round her – he could see her waving her hands around as she did. Gradually Sarah stopped her dancing and came to a stop in front of her Mam. It was too far away for Billy to hear, but he thought they were arguing. He saw Sarah hug herself and sink to her knees. Sally stood up and bent down over her daughter. Sarah appeared to pull away from her Mam. Billy heard some muffled shouting and they faced each other, anger clear in their stances. Billy began to wonder if he should go along and intervene, but he decided in a moment of insight that this was a crucial moment in the relationship between mother and daughter and despite the pain of not interfering he waited.

To distract himself he picked up the telescope and peered down towards Redcar, to the blast furnace, where history was repeating itself. Steel-making was leaving the Tees. A blurred view of demonstrators held his attention for several minutes. With absent concentration he tried to see if he could pick out Joe and his family in the crowd. He smiled; the glass was too old and scratched to make that possible. He took it from his eye and looked at it, recalling the many events in the Webster family history that it had witnessed. If only it could talk, but then perhaps it was best that it couldn't. He thought of the last year and he and Sarah's discoveries about the family's fortunes. Had anything they had found out helped Sarah in her search for an answer to her question. The thought brought him back to the Nab. He shut the telescope and returned it to its cloth wrapping. He turned to look along the path and breathed a sigh of relief.

His scatty loveable daughter and his magical granddaughter had started to walk towards him, hand in hand at first and then arm in arm. He wondered how his daughter had got on with her second week at the centre – Sarah would have heard by now why she was there – just as well, they needed to work things out for themselves.

Billy's heart wanted good news and his head prepared for the worst. As he waited he peered across the valley towards the river. A river that had seen generations of Websters live and survive through well over one hundred and eighty years of upheaval and change; from farmers to miners, to teachers, to carers, to steelmakers, to shop assistants and now to what. What would happen to his Granddaughter? Would she grow up like her Mother? He turned again to look along the path. Sally and Sarah

Webster were wrapped in each other's arms now as they walked along. Never mind just Sarah, what would happen to them both? He sat down to wait, he would hear soon enough. As he sat there the song had changed to a poem and was going round and round in his head, until he got out his notebook and began to write some of the elusive words down.

Last Steps in Steel and Stone

History walks away from us
In timeless steps
Repeating ways
To teach us all to pause

Long years across
Touch family lines and marriage ties
That live within the time they have
No future knowledge clouds them

This covered land
Beneath the brick and stone and iron
Is tarred and scarred and flattened yet
No sense of what's to come

Young hope, no scars
Young life, no doubt
What will be then?
What has been now?

Don't plan to seek, or seek to plan
Predict or look to question yet
To live in hope
On steel on stone for

Yesterday never returns